Majority State Ownership of Oil and Mining Sectors in Africa

Majority State Ownership of Oil and Mining Sectors in Africa: The Resource Curse Undermined shows that countries in sub-Saharan Africa with majority state ownership of their major oil or mineral export sectors suffered from more severe versions of the natural resource curse than other similar countries.

Examining natural resource–exporting nations in sub-Saharan Africa between 1966 and 2000, Quinn shows that, on average, states with majority state ownership of these sectors featured lower or negative growth, lower incomes, declining alternative export sectors, more debt, lower levels of investment, lower levels of political and civil rights, and more domestic conflict than other similar countries. These results remained fairly consistent across both cross-country data and in paired case studies. One surprise finding is that these countries either had depreciating currencies or did not feature high levels of currency appreciation, on average, which is inconsistent with resource curse literature predictions. Rather, most countries with majority state ownership had high levels of currency overvaluation, which operated in a similar manner as currency appreciation.

This work should appeal to students and faculty interested in the political economy of development, the natural resource curse, and African development, as well as to politicians, policymakers, and NGOs working in these areas. The strong recommendation of the book is that governments should own 50% or less of these sectors.

John James Quinn (Ph.D., UCLA) is Professor of Political Science at Truman State University, where he writes about issues concerning African development and democratization using the lenses of international relations, comparative politics, and international political economy. His African experiences include being a Peace Corp volunteer in the Democratic Republic of the Congo (formerly Zaire) as well as being a visiting professor at the University of Ghana-Legon. His primary research interest links majority state ownership of significant economic sectors in Africa to subsequent political, economic, and social outcomes. He has also written on the diffusion of the Rwandan genocide and Mobutu's ouster, the determinants of French ODA to Africa (during and after the Cold War), the links between democracy and development in Africa, causes of corruption cross-nationally, African foreign policies, and the types of political parties that emerged in Africa following the recent multi-party elections. He is the author of prior two books: *The Road Oft Traveled: Development Polices and Majority State Ownership of Industry in Africa* and *Global Geopolitical Power and African Political and Economic Institutions.*

Routledge Studies on the Political Economy of Africa

1. **The Political Economy of Energy in Sub-Saharan Africa**
   Edited by Lucky E. Asuelime and Andrew E. Okem

2. **The Political Economy of Land and Agrarian Development in Ethiopia**
   The Arssi Region since 1941
   Ketebo Abdiyo Ensene

3. **The Political Economy of Livelihoods in Contemporary Zimbabwe**
   Edited by Kirk Helliker, Manase Kudzai Chiweshe and Sandra Bhatasara

4. **The Politics of Economic Reform in Ghana**
   Edited by Richard Aidoo

5. **The Political Economy of Government Subsidised Housing in South Africa**
   Edited by Sithembiso Lindelihle Myeni and Andrew Emmanuel Okem

6. **Oil and Development in Ghana**
   Beyond the Resource Curse
   Edited by Nathan Andrews and Pius Siakwah

7. **Political Settlements and Agricultural Transformation in Africa**
   Evidence for Inclusive Growth
   Edited by Martin Atela and Abdul Raufu Mustapha

8. **The Future of Zimbabwe's Agrarian Sector**
   Land Issues in a Time of Political Transition
   Edited by Grasian Mkodzongi

9. **Majority State Ownership of Oil and Mining Sectors in Africa**
   The Resource Curse Undermined
   John James Quinn

For more information about this series, please visit: www.routledge.com/Routledge-Studies-on-the-Political-Economy-of-Africa/book-series/RSAPE

Majority State Ownership of Oil and Mining Sectors in Africa

The Resource Curse Undermined

John James Quinn

Routledge
Taylor & Francis Group
LONDON AND NEW YORK

First published 2025
by Routledge
4 Park Square, Milton Park, Abingdon, Oxon OX14 4RN

and by Routledge
605 Third Avenue, New York, NY 10158

Routledge is an imprint of the Taylor & Francis Group, an informa business

British Library Cataloguing-in-Publication Data
A catalogue record for this book is available from the British Library

ISBN: 978-1-138-39033-1 (hbk)
ISBN: 978-1-032-85254-6 (pbk)
ISBN: 978-0-429-42339-0 (ebk)

DOI: 10.4324/9780429423390

Typeset in Times New Roman
by Newgen Publishing UK

For my parents, Dennis P. Quinn and Joan C. Quinn.

Contents

Tables

Acknowledgments

This work began as a conference paper, and much time and effort was spent trying to place it in a journal as an article. The piece, given its methodology, was difficult to place in journals given priorities and length. To follow the methodology of the puzzle I was working on, as well as to incorporate more background about the challenges of development for these types of countries, a book was the best outcome. Nonetheless, I would like to thank various anonymous reviewers who saw earlier versions (Chapters 1 and 2) that had been submitted to journals. Also, briefly Ryan Conway joined me as a coauthor for a few conferences on an early version of the work; so I want to thank him for participating and contributing to some of the literature review. I also want to thank people at the various conferences who gave invaluable feedback. I also want to thank the editors and assistant editors at Routledge for their work on this manuscript. I appreciate their patience with the delays associated with COVID and other personal delays. In particular, I want to thank Leanne Hinves for contacting me about publishing with Routledge and working on the project through contract. Also, I want to thank the anonymous reviewer for Routledge for their comments. Within Routledge, others have helped steering me and the manuscript through the process, including Helena Hurd, Katerina Lade, Matt Shobbrook, Henry Strang, Leela Vathenen, as well as Jyotsna Gurung, Suriya Rajasekar, and others in later stages as well as in copy-editing. I also want to thank my sister Maura for proofing nearly all the chapters. Terry Olson, Dennis P. Quinn, and Even Holway also proofread the work and offered useful comments. I also want to thank my family for their forbearance during much of the book's drafting. Finally, any errors in argument, spelling, typos, and omissions are mine.

Abbreviations/Acronyms

AFDL	Alliance des forces démocratique pour la liberation du Congo-Zaire/Alliance of Democratic Forces for the Liberation of Congo-Zaire
AG	Action Group
AMFI	American Mineral Fields International
BCL	Bamangwato Concessions Limited (later just BCL)
bcm	billion cubic meters
BDC	Botswana Development Corporation
BDP	Botswana Democratic Party
BDVC	Botswana Diamond Valuing Company
BRI	Belt and Road Initiative
BRIC	Brazil, Russia, India, China
CA	countervailing actions
CAR	Central African Republic
CDB	China Development Bank
CEMAC	Communauté Économique et Monétaire de l'Afrique Centrale/Central African Economic and Monetary Community
CEOs	chief executive officers
CFA	Communauté Financière Africaine/African Financial Community
CNMC	Chinese Nonferrous Metals Corporation
CNNC	China National Nuclear Corporation
CNOOC	China National Offshore Oil Corporation
CNPC	China National Petroleum Corporation
COGEMA	Campagnie générale des mateires nucleares/General Nuclear Materials Company
COGER	Compagnie Gabonaise de Raffinage/Gabonese Refining Company
COMINAK	Compagnie minière d'Akokan/Mineral Company of Akokan
CREC	China Railway Engineering Corporation
Debswana	Debswana Diamond Company (Proprietary) Limited (formerly De Beers Botswana Mining Company)

Debt Service X Ratio	Debt Service to Export Ratio
DRC	Democratic Republic of the Congo
DTC	Diamond Trading Company
EIA (USEIA)	Energy Information Administration (US Energy Information Administration)
EITI	Extractive Industries Transparency Initiative
Eximbank	Export-Import Bank
FDI	foreign direct investment
FNLA	Frente Nacional de Libertação de Angola/National Front for the Liberation of Angola
FOCAC	Forum on China-Africa Cooperation
G8	The Group of Eight Industrialized Nations
G20	The Group of Twenty (of the World's Major Economies)
GATT	General Agreement on Tariffs and Trade
GDF Inv-cap	gross domestic fixed investment per capita
GDF Inv% GDP	gross domestic fixed investment as a percentage of GDP
GDFI	gross domestic fixed investment
GDP	gross domestic product
Gécamines	[Société] Générale des Carrières et de Mines/General Partnership of Quarries and Mines
GNI	gross national income
GNPC	Ghana National Petroleum Corporation
GOC	Gabon Oil Company
HIPCs	Heavily Indebted Poor Countries
IFI	International Financial Institution
IMF	International Monetary Fund
IOCs	International Oil Companies
ISI	Import Substitution Industrialization
KOF	Konjunkturforschungsstelle/Economic Cycle Research Institute
KORES	Korea Resources Corporation
LNG	liquefied natural gas
Mb/d	thousand barrels a day
Mbtu	thousand British thermal units
MDRI	Multilateral Debt Relief Initiative
MNC	multinational corporation
MPLA	Movimento Popular de Libertação de Angola/Popular Movement for the Liberation of Angola
MPR	Mouvement Populaire de la Révolution/Popular Movement of the Revolution
MSO	majority state ownership/majority state owned
MSO-1	MSO of oil or mineral sectors

MSO-2	all MSO-1 countries plus countries with MSO of most capital-intensive industries but without MSO of an existing oil or mineral sector
MT	megatons
NCNC	National Council of Nigerian Citizens (formerly National Council of Nigeria and the Cameroons)
NGO	nongovernmental organization
NICs	newly industrializing countries
NNOC	Nigerian National Oil Corporation
NNPC	Nigerian National Petroleum Corporation
NOCs	National Oil Companies
NPC	Northern People's Congress
OAU	Organization of African Unity
ODA	Official Development Assistance
OECD	Organization for Economic Cooperation and Development
ONAREM	Office nationale des resources minières du Niger/National Office of Mineral Resources of Niger
OOF	other official flows
OPEC	Organization of Petroleum-Exporting Countries
PETRANGOL	Fina Petróleos de Angola/Petroleum Refinery of Angola
PSAs	production-sharing arrangements
Real GDP/cap	real GDP per capita
RFI	resource for infrastructure (agreement)
SADC	Southern Africa Development Community (formerly Southern African Development Coordination Conference)
SINOPEC	China Petroleum & Chemical Corporation
SNH	Société Nationale des Hydrocarbures/National Hydrocarbons Corporation
SOGARA	Société Raffinage du Gabon/Gabonese Refining Company
Somaïr	Société des mines de l'Air/Air Mining Company
SONANGOL	Sociedad Nacional de Combustíveis de Angola/National Oil Company in Angola
SOPAMIN	Société de Patrimoine des Mines du Niger/Mines Heritage Society of Niger
TAZARA	Tanzania-Zambia Railway
TBPD	thousand barrels per day
tcf	trillion cubic feet
UMHK	Union Minière du Haut-Katanga/Mining Union of Upper Katanga
UN	United Nations
UNIP	United National Independence Party
UNITA	União Nacional para a Independência Total de Angola/National Union for the Total Independence of Angola
VN	la Voie Nationale/The National Route

WAGP	West African Gas Pipeline
WTO	World Trade Organization (had been GATT)
WWII	World War II
ZCCM	Zambia Consolidated Copper Mines
ZCCM-IH	ZCCM Investments Holdings Plc (formerly ZCCM)
ZXJOY	Beijing Zhongxing Joy Investment Co., Ltd.

1 The Resource Curse and Majority State Ownership of Oil- or Mineral-Exporting Sectors in Sub-Saharan Africa

> It is commonly observed that a sudden wealth, like a prize drawn in a lottery or a large bequest to a poor family, does not permanently enrich. They have served no apprenticeship to wealth, and with the rapid wealth come rapid claims which they do not know how to deny, and the treasure is quickly dissipated.
>
> —Ralph Waldo Emerson

> The fault, dear Brutus, is not in our stars,
> but in ourselves …
>
> —William Shakespeare, Julius Caesar Act I, Scene II, 140–141

Striking it rich with a discovery of gold, silver, diamonds, or oil is a common historic motif. Many an explorer or miner spent years, or a lifetime, hoping for such a find. In the age of exploration, many nations sent out explorers to find gold or other precious metals. Thus, a country discovering natural resources under its own soil, such as gold, silver, copper, diamonds, or oil, should have considered this find as an unqualified blessing. At first glance, one would likely expect that countries with significant quantities of petroleum, natural gas, minerals, or other natural resources would have just discovered an important source of future investment funds to help pave their nation's path to economic prosperity. The existence of natural mineral or petroleum resources should also be associated with increased inflows of foreign direct investment (FDI). Wealth flowing from obtaining mineral or oil resources can provide a stream of investible revenue, later leading to economic growth.

In the wake of WWII, one key ingredient identified by many economists for development to ensue in the third world was adequate levels of capital or investment.[1] Access to investible funds would help developing nations achieve the big leaps forward necessary to be on a positive developmental trajectory. An increase in capital was considered the necessary component for growth in the neoclassical, the Lewis, and the Harrod-Domar growth models. An endowment of mineral or oil might alleviate constraints on credit and bolster economic expansion.[2] Thus, the presence of natural mineral or petroleum resources should provide an advantage

DOI: 10.4324/9780429423390-1

for developing countries aiming to "modernize." In fact, the idea that countries should try to develop or modernize as quickly as possible became among the most important overarching goals for the many newly independent nations in the wake of the worldwide decolonization movement following WWII.[3]

Access to sufficient investment for industrialization was seen as the most significant challenge for developing countries striving for rapid industrialization. Most developing nations were thought to be unlikely to save sufficient levels of investment to move the needle on development. In fact, many suggested that a vicious negative cycle could emerge whereby poverty begat poverty. Nurkse held that poor, small market countries would never be able to amass enough investment to escape.[4] Leibenstein suggested this was made worse by the Malthusian issue of population growth increasing more rapidly than economic growth.[5] Beyond a lack of capital, a lack of access to technology was viewed as an additional obstacle. W. W. Rostow, for example, held that many developing countries lacked enough technology or scientific expertise to achieve sustainable growth.[6]

Finding oil or other natural resources therefore should have been an immediate blessing for developing countries because it could easily lead to access to badly needed investment funding. The discovery of such resources would also increase countries' abilities to draw in the technology necessary to exploit them.[7] It could have also helped eliminate the problems associated with the dual gap analysis, which holds that foreign currency was required to obtain inputs to spur development.[8] An increase in the exports of natural resources theoretically would likely lead to the provision of significant sources of sustainable foreign currency, allowing for a diminishment of bottlenecks associated with industrialization in the developing world.[9]

Importantly, mining or oil endowment of significant size can provide the needed ingredients for many aspects of industrialization. Iron ore, copper, oil, coal, and aluminum were part of the industrialization of earlier societies. Significant supplies of oil and natural gas could provide cheap sources of energy for industrialization. Countries can gain clear benefits from a well-structured and managed mineral or oil sector: it can provide foreign exchange earnings; it can produce revenue through taxes and royalties; it can help jump start development in poorer areas; and it can improve the skills of nationals through learning by doing. In short, and it could become the basis of economic development.[10]

The Natural Resource Curse

Beginning with the research of Sachs and Warner, many development scholars noticed an unexpected, and empirically based, phenomenon: many developing nations with an abundance of natural resource exports experienced worse economic performance than otherwise similar countries.[11] This clearly counterintuitive finding helped launch a body of literature referred to as "the resource curse."[12] The surprising results showed that countries with abundant natural resources, which made up a significant portion of the countries' exports, grew more slowly than did other similar countries.[13] This finding was even stronger looking only at countries dependent on mineral or oil exports, and especially oil for some.[14]

Despite considerable divergent approaches in methodology, a consensus emerged among scholars: countries with significant oil- or mineral-exporting sectors grew more slowly than did countries without these natural resources.[15] Despite this early strong consensus, Ross suggested that the early literature on the mineral resource curse lacked large-N empirical studies confirming these results.[16] Later work would fill this gap, especially for oil.[17] Mining countries were also shown to have suffered from lower growth levels too.[18] Countries with greater than 50% dependence mineral exports of mining had an average of *negative* 2.3% growth level from 1990 to 1999.[19]

The second major negative economic outcome associated with the resource curse follows from the first: countries with natural resources have lower per capita incomes over time.[20] Thus, significant increases in wealth could occur in the short run. However, this was associated with later lower growth which would keep levels of wealth low, despite the initial spike. A high level of dependence upon natural resource exportation has been linked to other measures of poverty. Importantly, several other measures of human welfare – including the UN Human Poverty and Human Development Indices – have been employed as factors dependent upon the change in the abundance of natural resource wealth.[21]

A third common outcome associated with the mineral or oil resource curse is high levels of debt.[22] Since governments can come to rely upon higher incomes when commodity prices for resources are high, future mineral export wealth is a form of collateral against which many countries easily borrow money during price downturns. Given that mineral or oil resource production tends to be price inelastic, while international prices fluctuate greatly, governments are likely to just keep producing once production has begun. These growth spurts (when prices are high) and growth collapses (when prices are low) require either stabilization funds or lending to finance normal expenditures during downturns. Unless governments limit spending or save surpluses during booms, countries can become heavily indebted trying to stabilize spending during downturns. In contrast, richer countries (or companies) can stockpile their output and wait for higher prices to reap higher returns. Unfortunately, once higher prices return, it often is more politically expedient to redistribute money than to pay back these loans. Politicians are not always long-term thinkers, and a sudden windfall can be spent without raising taxes on the politically powerful (depending on who owns the minerals). These windfalls may also be spent on projects that promote prestige, increase social welfare, increase redistribution spending, and keep poor policy regimes in place – ignoring the need to adopt "tough" growth-oriented policies.[23] The overall result of these tendencies is higher levels of debt.

A fourth major resource curse outcome is that mineral- or oil-rich countries tend to also over concentrate investment into their natural resource export sector, which has the effect of "putting all their eggs into one basket."[24] This means that these countries tend not to industrialize as much or to invest as much in other export sectors, which in much of the developing world, and especially sub-Saharan

Africa, is agriculture.[25] The overreliance of a developing economy on the export of one or two primary sectors can itself be a source of low growth, especially when the world market prices for those commodities decline or if they experience significant volatility. This is despite having a source of investible income which could conceivably lead to a spurt in industrial investment and later output. The deepening of investment in the major oil or mineral export sector is especially problematic for development if it diverts investment away from other sectors with higher potential returns.[26]

These outcomes are also associated with what is called the "Dutch disease."[27] As the mineral or oil sector booms (and busts), several things happen. During periods of expansion of natural resources, especially when prices are high, the country's currency appreciates, and this makes other exports less competitive in foreign markets. Over time, this effect leads to a shrinking of other export sectors.[28] Associated currency appreciation can affect even import competing sectors as the prices for domestic labor and capital rise across the economy.[29] Thus, the costs of imports decline relative to increases in domestic prices, paired with lower prices due to currency appreciation. This can result in the loss of domestic market share without commensurate protection.[30] These effects may be particularly pernicious if the declining sectors (exporting or import competing) have more positive economic and social externalities (e.g., learning by doing) than the natural resource sector.[31]

By contrast, if the new oil or mineral resource becomes long-lived with a stable revenue stream, the shift in comparative advantage toward this new sector would be less problematic for development. If, however, the prices associated with this rising export sector feature significant price volatility, the "new normal" will create instability for government funding and revenues. This situation imperils government financial stability as well as potential growth trajectories, even if these sectors reflect the country's new long-term comparative advantage.[32] The avoidance of such dilemmas usually requires medium to long-term planning, which often necessitates stronger political institutions. Importantly, the poorest and least developed mineral- or oil-exporting countries, such as in sub-Saharan Africa, are less likely to have political institutions capable of maintaining fiscal discipline through such mechanisms as rainy-day funds or long-term price contracts.

A fifth commonly cited consequence of natural resource endowments is that they can create or exacerbate conditions that lead to domestic conflict.[33] According to Collier and Hoeffler, the extent of primary commodity exports has a significant, but nonlinear impact on the likelihood of civil war – when they constitute about 33% of GDP, the likelihood of war is at its greatest.[34] Others also suggest that the relationship might be curvilinear: with increasing chances of civil war up to some inflection point, after which the chances of civil war begin to decrease.[35]

Many authors have found that resource abundance in countries where the resource was concentrated in one or a few geographic areas provide readily accessible sources of financing for civil wars, rebel coup attempts, competition among warlords, and, generally, looting and violence.[36] Other elements of geography matter as well: Are the resources located offshore, onshore, or near the capital?[37]

Such contingencies would matter for potential rebel leaders: are the resources located away from the government's ability to control them? Are these resources located where the rebels can control them? Lujala et al. write that "abundant natural resources provide a pool in which rebels can acquire a stake to finance their welfare."[38] A few natural resources have been particularly linked to increased intrastate conflict (i.e., oil, gas, and diamonds).[39] Some scholars have suggested the ability of nonstate actors to loot these resources make such states more prone to civil conflict.[40] Moreover, these resources could also be linked to external conflict through a "diffusion" effect.[41]

A sixth common empirical and theoretical finding linked with mining and, especially, oil in developing countries is higher levels of corruption.[42] Countries with significant mineral (fuels and ores) exporting also have increased rent seeking opportunities and corruption.[43] This is especially true during periods of great windfalls in countries with relatively weak institutions and without democratic institutions.[44] This is, in turn, linked to lower economic growth.[45] In the case of Africa, Heilbrunn argues that an increase in corruption is natural for primarily agricultural states that find oil.[46] These countries were unlikely to have featured strong institutions for taxation and finance at the time of discovery. The shift to becoming a rentier state and the class formation building on these new rents follow.[47] By contrast, Ross suggests that there is no prima facie evidence for increased corruption and decrease of government quality, but an increase in secrecy arises, which can be perceived as more corruption in petrol states.[48] This can lead to rent seeking, which many see as per se corruption.

Finally, one of the most potentially important findings concerns the propensity for mineral- or oil-rich countries to feature authoritarian or nondemocratic political systems. Although a number of developed resource-rich countries feature democratic institutions, the empirical record illustrates that most developing resource-rich countries have been authoritarian.[49] Auty explained this high prevalence of authoritarian regimes in terms of the effect that the resource curse has in retarding political change, slowing any movement toward democratization.[50] Ross suggests that this is worse for oil countries than mineral countries, but mineral exporters are worse than non-oil, non-mining nations.[51] Herb suggests that abundant resources diminishes the need for increased taxation, which often results in less pressure for political representation as part of the deal.[52] In addition, these sectors can create more resources for patronage with which to co-opt potential opposition members as well as purchase more social peace.[53] This statistical link between natural resource wealth and political regime type has strong empirical support,[54] even though some suggest that differences in measurement impact findings.[55]

A few scholars have suggested that the mineral resource curse is a time-bound phenomenon. Jones Luong and Weinthal suggest that this was mostly apparent during the 1960s and through the 1990s.[56] Ross also suggests that it was most prevalent during the Cold War period.[57] He suggests that most of the negative effects were seen starting in the 1960s and 1970s after countries began seizing control of their oil economies and while prices were high. Some have also suggested that by only including countries with high levels of resource exports on a relative level may lead to selection bias of the sample and/or false inferences. Countries which successfully maintain mineral or oil exports as well as exports from other sectors would not be included for study in many samples, as they are chosen for inclusion given their resource dependence.[58]

Challenges for Oil or Mining Sectors in Developing Nations

Beyond a discussion of the traditional resource curse outcomes, careful thinkers must be aware that oil and mining extraction and exporting pose particular problems, especially for institutionally weak and developing nations, like those found in sub-Saharan Africa.[59] Many relevant factors of mining or oil exploration shape the nature of its international linkages and can affect the rate and structure of development in a country, complicating conclusions about resource curse variables.

First, mining and oil sectors tend to be capital- and technology-intensive industries. These aspects (along with others to be discussed below) often lead the sector to be highly concentrated and vertically integrated even in developed countries.[60] The capital- and technology-intensive nature of much of mining and oil results in high fixed costs of entry and requires depth of technical knowledge. Moreover, the processing of minerals and oil are also highly capital-intensive (and technology-intensive), which helps explain why few developing nations export refined materials. Few African nations have any comparative advantage in most aspects of mining, gas, or oil exploitation – aside from having the resource under their soil. Even at the international level, the barriers to entry formed by the capital, technological, and energy needs of mining have resulted in mineral extraction being dominated by a few large firms located in industrialized countries.[61] The one exception vis-à-vis comparative advantage for developing nations is artisan mining.[62]

Second, even determining the magnitude or even location of many mineral or petroleum resources requires highly skilled, capital and technologically intensive procedures unavailable for most developing African nations.[63] Because of this, the World Bank began a project to help developing countries and mining companies find and map these resources.[64] In the past, mining or oil companies had more information of the quality and quantity of the resources for which they were bidding than did host governments. Kamarck argued many years ago that the cost of exploration for mining or oil reserves is a small percentage of the budget of a large corporation, such as Exxon-Mobile; however, these costs would be a large part of an African government's budget.[65] The longer the return to profits, the more investors care about potential instability in the areas of investment. Thus, the time between the discovery of a mineral and the large-scale mining of it "is usually measured in decades" and not years.[66] Conversely, the returns in profit for investment into petroleum exploitation usually come much faster than those for minerals.

Third, mining, oil, and gas sectors usually require skilled management, access to foreign markets, and skilled and semi-skilled labor – at least in higher level positions.[67] This is especially true for the later stages in refining the ores. Most ores are mixed with other elements. As such, these compounds must be separated using chemicals and/or heat, or both, to release the concentrated form of the metal or mineral of interest. The petroleum industry is similarly quite capital and technologically intensive, even if it tends not to be very labor intensive.[68] This is especially true for petroleum refining.

Fourth, properly understood, minerals and oil represent nonrenewable resources: once the resource is exhausted, the sector is no longer viable – though the time to depletion ranges greatly by nation and commodity.[69] Therefore, the leadership of mineral- or oil/gas-exporting countries has an implied fiduciary responsibility to make medium to long-term investments that can eventually replace a declining mineral-exporting sector and earn the country hard currency. The closer to exhaustion the sector is, the greater the responsibility is. Unfortunately, when such countries suffer from the Dutch disease, it reduces the likely success of the diversification of the economy despite the eventual depletion of the natural resource. Such dilemmas are harder for developing and weak states to manage compared to more advanced states. Moreover, a country that uses its rents from mining or oil primarily for patronage or other forms of current consumption – instead of investing in developmental projects –can be viewed as living off capital and squandering these resources and not merely maintaining a standard of incomes.[70] However, not all diversification works well, especially investment against a nation's comparative advantage. For example, even when countries in Africa did invest in manufacturing, the investment had often been in capital-intensive import substitution industrialization (ISI) or government sponsored industry and done in ways that have not prospered.[71]

Fifth, and with some overlap of the previous point, profits from oil and mining sectors can easily become viewed by most citizens as belonging to the nation as whole. Such resources are often viewed as being part of the patrimony of the nation.[72] High profits from these sectors can create intensified calls for the sharing of profits, for more social services, and for more jobs in the "people's" sector.[73] It can also result in calls for subsidized prices for domestically consumed output associated with these sectors, though this is more common for gasoline or kerosene. These claims on profits on the part of society are likely even higher when prices are booming (see next point). Sharing the short-term surpluses or profits of a nonrenewable resource is at odds with the longer-term fiduciary obligations on state leaders managing these dilemmas.

Sixth, supply from oil, gas, and mining sectors tend to be relatively inelastic.[74] A sharp increase in demand can lead to a sharper increase in price, which in turn leads to very large windfalls for governments and companies given the slow increase in production available in the short term. Similarly, sharp decreases in demand can lead to dramatic drops in price for these commodities, especially for minerals which are less demand inelastic than petroleum. Few incentives for slowing marginal production exist. This can lead to dramatic decreases in revenues for both governments and companies, adding momentum to the boom/bust nature of these markets.[75] This tendency can be even stronger in developing nations, which have few financial reserves to draw upon, or few other strong exporting sectors, during economic downturns. Indebted developing nations have even less ability to reduce their levels of exports during supply gluts: few can stockpile their resources waiting for better prices while having to service their debts and maintain governmental financial obligations.

Seventh, few mining sectors have been successful in creating cartels that could better manage long-term prices to handle this problem. The only partial exception is for gem quality diamonds and oil (for periods of time).[76] Ironically, if a cartel successfully raises average prices above longer-term market prices, it creates incentives to draw new producers into this sector or for consumers to look for substitutes. For example, OPEC countries accounted for about two-thirds of non-communist oil supplies in 1973, but this fell to less than one-third by 1986 when OPEC prices collapsed.[77] This resulted from both increases in conservation as well as new suppliers emerging in the wake of the higher prices. Nevertheless, most commodity cartels have failed to increase prices in the longer term. OPEC did come close to succeeding in keeping prices high for several decades, and it clearly continues to exist and exert pressures on price.[78] Diamonds are the likely only exception.

Eighth, transportation costs are quite high in sub-Saharan Africa, and this clearly can impact the development of a mining or oil sector. This is even truer for most mining sectors.[79] Pipelines and offshore production are a possible solution for relatively cheap transportation of oil and gas, though these costs mount the further they are found from shore or a main port. This solution, however, is not a possibility for minerals. In fact, governments of developing nations with significant mining exports learn that they must establish administrative nodes or wings for the transportation of mining output.[80] Besides gold and diamonds, most minerals have a low value to weight ratio, as the examples of coal, iron ore, and copper illustrate. This often means that affordable long-distance transport by ship or rail is required. Transport by truck can be efficient for shorter distances.

Unfortunately for most countries in sub-Saharan Africa, few navigable rivers or natural harbors exist, and many countries are landlocked. Most countries in tropical Africa lack significant or modern highway or rail systems, the building and maintenance of which can be quite expensive, especially in forested areas.[81] By way of example, Gabon discovered iron ore in a forested area far from the coast and has tried to build a railway capable of transporting ore to its ocean port.[82] The discovered deposits are thought to contain more than 500 million tons of iron ore.[83] A proposed railway to this area has been under consideration since 1960, but a link to this area has yet to be completed. In 2007, Gabon awarded a contract to a Chinese company to build a railway and exploit the ore; however, the project faced opposition from civil society and was later abandoned.[84] By contrast, when oil is close to shore, it can be carried away by tanker, but it also has to be conveyed to either a refinery or a port. However, oil from the mainland would still have to be brought, but often by pipeline – which still requires significantly high, upfront costs.

Ninth, mining, oil, and natural gas sectors can become enclaves within the larger economy, though mining may have more demand for labor.[85] As such, mineral, oil, and natural gas export sectors are often better integrated with foreign markets than the local economy. For example, developing economies have a limited demand for these materials, especially for heavy minerals. Also, given the capital-intensive nature of these sectors, few backward or forward linkages are likely to develop in these capital scarce nations.[86] Additionally, many foreign firms are reluctant to share technology which would limit their later ability to make profits.[87]

Tenth, many oil- or mineral-exporting countries are quite dependent upon just one commodity, which, as mentioned above, tends to fluctuate in price in world markets, far beyond the control of the home government.[88] Price collapses can rock the stability of government spending and planning, especially as so many poor countries tend to continue to produce for market even under conditions of low prices, given the price inelastic nature of production. Commodity dependence is often also held to lead to poor governance as well as low growth.

Finally, both mining and oil are associated with significant negative environmental externalities which are difficult for developing nations to manage. As major footprint industries, they have significant impacts on the local ecosystems and socio-political environments.[89] This is especially so if the mineral, gas, or oil deposits are found in protected or densely populated areas.[90] Mining requires moving earth from below to above ground, resulting in the possible pollution of both ground and surface water. For example, slag heaps storing waste brought from below ground can be spread by rainfall because it penetrates the heaps and carries potential contaminants into rivers, ground water, or agricultural fields. Some ores can also start to oxidize and become quite acidic, again impacting local water and soil. Toxic heavy metals are abundant in deeper soil and can be introduced into the local agriculture and water ecosystems through mining.[91] The more radioactive or poisonous the materials dredged up are, the more of an issue this is. Oil extraction is associated with spillage, and the venting or flaring of methane greatly increases greenhouse gases. The cost and technology to capture natural gas can be beyond the grasp of many developing nations.

The general premise of the resource curse literature is that all countries are impacted by their discovery and exploitation, though it is generally worse in poor and developing nations. Given the relatively low levels of capital, technological depth, and skilled workforces in sub-Saharan Africa, these developmental challenges are likely to impact all such countries, even if some variance is evident. Nonetheless, this work argues that the variance will be mostly associated with one structural variable: majority state ownership (MSO) of the mineral- or oil-exporting sector.

Majority State Ownership vs. Resource Curse

One potentially understudied variable, which is very often associated with natural resources in the developing world, is the MSO of these major export sectors. In fact, many of the negative outcomes attributed to the resource curse have been shown to be associated with the MSO of significant economic sectors in sub-Saharan Africa. Compelling reasons exist, therefore, to posit that many, if not most, of the negative outcomes associated with the resource curse are significantly linked to this form of ownership. The political and economic incentives associated with MSO make resource curse outcomes stronger, especially in developing nations during the Cold

War period. This book argues, tests, and then illustrates that many of the negative outcomes associated with the mineral or oil resource curse were made worse, or made more severe, in countries with greater than 50% government ownership (MSO) of its major mineral- or oil-exporting sectors. This is tested in countries from sub-Saharan Africa during the Cold War and up to 2000.

Other authors have identified MSO of economic sectors in developing nations as having negative consequences for rapid development.[92] The World Bank and other scholars have argued that state ownership led to inefficient outcomes, but most such commentary often came from sector-by-sector or company-by-company comparisons in contrast to a country level measurement.[93] Ross, however, did speculate that several of the emergent explanations for the resource curse lend some focus to "state-centered" explanations which include the role of parastatals.[94]

Others have also come to look at some of the consequences of ownership of oil and negative outcomes.[95] This argument is that MSO has implications for the political economy of the broader society as well as the sector itself. Strong initial logic and evidence can be marshaled to show that MSO of these important sectors makes the resource curse more likely. In sub-Saharan Africa, research has shown that countries that featured MSO of either (or both) a major oil or mining export sector or of most of the nation's capital-intensive industries during the Cold War period had more inward-oriented development policies.[96] Inward-oriented development policies that have held lead to lower levels of growth.[97] The inward-oriented policies that have been shown to be linked MSO in sub-Saharan Africa are these: (1) higher rates of currency overvaluation, (2) higher rates of agricultural taxation, (3) lower levels of agricultural exports, and (4) higher rates of protection through tariffs and nontariff barriers (NTBs). MSO was also linked to lower value added in manufacturing, higher rates of inflation, higher levels of debt relative to exports, and generally lower levels of per capita investment. Importantly, these policy outcomes were also demonstrated to be linked with lower incomes in the region. The results are quite similar to policies predicted by the resource curse literature.

Other outcomes often attributed to the resource curse have also covaried with MSO in sub-Saharan Africa. For example, MSO of most capital-intensive industries or of a significant mining or oil-exporting sector was linked to fewer multiparty systems in the region, thus undermining the likelihood of more democracy. In a cross-national, cross-regional study, countries with MSO of either a natural resource or of most manufacturing featured higher levels of corruption/lower levels of bureaucratic efficiency – each of which have negative developmental impacts by lowering investment, which leads to lowered growth.[98] Also, Ross had suggested MSO of resources lower levels of transparency, which could easily be linked to corruption, though he does not test for this.[99] And many hold lower levels of transparency and accountability to be counterproductive for development and growth.

On a sectoral level, a significant body of literature has shown that particular sectors or companies under MSO were less economically efficient. For example, the World Bank has long argued (and shown) that majority or full state ownership of productive enterprises is inefficient and wasteful.[100] Scholars at the World Bank have suggested that state ownership of mining may be one of the things that makes mining problematic.[101] Sandbrook demonstrated that 100% state-owned sectors in African countries were the least efficiently run, followed by majority state-owned sectors, and then less than 50% state-owned companies.[102] Tangri also argued that state-owned enterprises, generally, underperformed economically due to "inappropriate pricing policies, poor investment decisions, substantial overstaffing, and chronic management problems."[103] Finally, Ross speculated that state ownership could be a partial or potential explanation for developmental difficulties.[104] Ross later argues and gives theoretical reasons why state ownership of oil makes resource curse outcomes worse, though he does not test this proposition directly.[105] Other scholars have also argued that state ownership can impact development of oil states in Eastern Europe.[106]

Interestingly, and perhaps ironically, the original Sachs and Warner paper on the resource curse included a measure which captures some direct and indirect economic effects (as well as causes) associated with MSO in their variable, openness (SOPEN).[107] This measure included some variables which helped lead to MSO (the adoption of socialism or state-led industrialization), as well as some variables that are held to emerge with MSO (high currency overvaluation/illicit market premiums, high tariffs, currency rationing/exchange restrictions).[108] Their measure of openness, which included these listed other variables shown to be associated with MSO or its measure, was found to be negatively and significantly associated with growth – which is perhaps the greatest negative outcome associated with the resource curse.

African Neo-patrimonialism, Majority State Ownership, and Weak Institutions

MSO of a country's most important economic sectors can affect development trajectories in several important ways, especially in weak state environments such as in sub-Saharan Africa. The effects of MSO will be both direct and indirect, and they will be found both within the particular sectors owned by the state as well as in the larger political economy.

Within African studies circles, it has been widely acknowledged that rents and patronage have been the glue for most one-party and no-party (military) regimes for most of the independence period. Whether or not scholars use the term neo-patrimonial, patrimonial, patronage networks, weakly institutionalized systems, or rent seeking, patronage has been a main feature of most African political systems following independence.[109] Such regimes are defined as where "the chief executive maintains authority through personal patronage, rather than through ideology or rule of law."[110] One of the defining features of neopatrimonialism is that significant levels of resources are distributed outside of formal legal-rational bureaucratic means. These types of regimes are also highly personalist and can change and bend with the holders of power.[111] Nearly all sub-Saharan African countries are seen as featuring some degree of neopatrimonialism.[112]

Since neo-patrimonial regimes are defined as ones in which the distinctions between public resources and private resources are conflated or collapsed, allowing politicians to manage state-owned sectors increases their opportunities to distribute resources associated with these sectors. Thus, MSO of natural resources increases neopatrimonialism on its face.[113] MSO of such high rent-creating sectors as mineral- or oil-exporting sectors removes barriers between the economic and political spheres since the political elite control and manage both.[114] Shafer argues specifically that state ownership eliminates the "political insulation" that provides privately owned companies some shelter from political demands.[115]

Within this environment of MSO, political elites are more likely to enact policies aimed at increasing rents from these sectors to be distributed through patronage networks – rather than maximizing long-term economic returns. The idea that political elites establish policies that maximize short-term political goals in lieu of long-term economic ones is widely held among political economists.[116] Moreover, this is a common background view for those who write on neopatrimonialism or the "normal" workings of the African state.[117] As such, it follows that where an major oil- or mineral-exporting nation in Africa has MSO of this sector, then it will be run with a view to maximize political support in the short run rather than maximizing economic returns in the longer run. Therefore, decisions concerning whom to hire, how to invest "profits," and how much to reinvest are likely to be via a shorter-term political calculus rather than via a medium- to long-term economic calculus. This is consistent with a rational actor model.[118]

The principal–agent model can be used to illustrate the dynamics involved with MSO of these resources in patronage-based systems.[119] Unlike the owners of privately owned companies, CEOs, managers, and other leaders within the MSO sector cannot keep "profits" generated by them. As managers or MSO sectors, they would only be entitled to salaries – any other taking of resources could be seen as corrupt. And, also, unlike privately owned companies, they would not be issued stock which would allow them to share in the profits of the company. Nor are there rich and powerful owners who convene from time to time to assess the performance of the managers with an eye to personal economic gains.

Especially in societies with strong neo-patrimonial traits, the leaders and managers of these companies would owe allegiance to the political elite who placed them in these positions of power. Likewise, they would view the political elite as "the principals" that they must please, much more than they would see "the people" as their principals to please. What the political elite wants to maximize is rents to be distributed as patronage to their political party, followers, and their close associates (as well as for personal enrichment).

In theory, with state-owned sectors, the "principals" in this dynamic are "the people," and the agents are the political elite who should manage the sectors on behalf of the people. However, the collective action costs of imposing strict discipline upon the agents, who are the political elite of the country, or the managers appointed to run economic sectors, are quite high for a variety of reasons. No group can be more dispersed and harder to organize than "the people," and no group could have higher collective action costs.[120] Because the agents are political elites or those appointed by political elites, and because the political elites hold a disproportionate share of both political and economic power in these societies, the ability for the citizens to hold them to account is very limited. These collective action costs are necessarily even higher when one factors in the effects of authoritarian systems – a common government type in much of sub-Saharan Africa.[121] Even with the partial liberalization of the region, most are rated as not free or only partly free.[122] Aroni has argued that state ownership in developing countries effectively eliminates control by principals, where agents pursue their own self-interests.[123]

Given the logic of the principal–agent relationship and moving into a neopatrimonial context, we should not expect to see strong institutions at either the political or sectoral level in countries with MSO of their largest economic sectors. Creating (or maintaining) strong institutions to increase efficiency, eliminate waste, and increase profits are clearly not in the short-term interests of patronage-based governing elites.[124] Strong and autonomous institutions could clearly limit the political elites' access to the coffers of these companies.[125] Thus, institutions are likely to become more extractive or coercive under these conditions.[126] The personal incentive that was missing from the Soviet model for increasing productivity is also missing for the curbing of corruption or the increasing economic efficiency in MSO sectors. Countries with MSO of natural resources would *not* likely allow many fragments of political or economic accountability.[127] And in countries with MSO of other major sectors of the economy, we will likely see similar outcomes. This logic can even be extended to other aspects of operations undertaken by MSO sectors, such as pollution control, minimum wage laws, worker safety laws and so forth.[128] Poor policy, inefficiency, and corruption will likely reign because no powerful groups have the personal self-interest to reform the system.

When political elites become the agents of the people (on behalf of their management of the state-owned mineral or oil sector), instead of taking upon themselves the attendant fiduciary obligations to manage the sector on the behalf of the country as a whole, they have incentives to use these sectors to help fund and manage their political control of the government or to fund their personal enrichment. These policies may be politically expedient, but they are not beneficial in the long term for the country involved.

This situation makes institutional reform for increased accountability under state ownership or any movement away from state ownership of patronage politics quite difficult. With patronage politics at the heart of so many regimes in the region, the holders of power would have strong self-interest against reforming practices which would make it more difficult to hire workers or raid coffers. As a result, a status quo ruling elite is quite likely to strongly oppose reforms, and they are even likely to advocate the removal of institutional checks that might hinder them from using these sectors for patronage or personal reasons.[129]

Moreover, few powerful individuals within these societies would have the personal self-interest to either monitor or curb corruption or increase efficiency in MSO sectors or industries. Alam argues that there are three main potential responses or "countervailing actions (CA)" to corruptly managed sectors within the principal– agent paradigm.[130] People facing corrupt systems can reduce their dependence upon corrupt officials (*evasion* CA) of the system itself, or they can challenge the corrupt officials or inefficient practices of the system (*direct* CA).

Finally, they can use other forms of corruption to undermine or circumvent the officials (*illicit* CA) and the system.

Following this logic, workers or managers in these sectors are quite unlikely to engage in direct CA within the ruling party or within majority state-owned sectors. The lack of incentive to challenge corruption likely leads to even weaker institutionalization of these sectors as well as the bureaucracies that oversee them. If so, most people will primarily use evasion or illicit CA – as opposed to direct CA. This would result in these institutions remaining inefficient or even becoming more corrupt. This analysis expects this to be the case for MSO mineral- or oil-exporting countries in sub-Saharan Africa.

Thus, even if a group within society rises to reform the systems, the agents running the MSO institutions can easily maintain themselves in power: with a simple majority vote on the corporate board of the local affiliate, politicians can gain access to the cash flow of the most lucrative sector of the domestic economy. Given their interests in raiding the resources they are presumptive stewards over, clear structural incentives exist for them to intentionally reduce the institutionalization of the sectors to help them gain access to these resources.

Therefore, when the state takes over the most significant economic sectors in the economy, within a context of weak institutions, this should deepen a culture of neo-patrimonial corruption, which could spread to other parts of society. For example, an MSO oil or mineral export sector could easily finance and subsidize many other inefficient state-owned firms and politically motivated white elephants, at least in the short term.[131] Despite the economic inefficiency of such projects, these would generate good political returns, in the forms of higher employment through the state. Regardless of the short-term political returns, MSO of so many economic sectors usually leads to lower growth as MSO enterprises tend to become giant consumers of domestic credit without creating strong returns.[132] Thus, these countries are likely to experience lower levels of growth as investment levels are insufficient to stimulate the economy.[133]

Although a privately owned and taxed oil or mineral sector could provide ample revenue to fund a patronage-based society, an MSO exporting sector could provide even more: the political elites' access to both economic and political power should increase dramatically in the short term. For example, the ruling party or elites can control the hiring and firing of many more employees, how profits are reinvested or expatriated, how accounting procedures are established, how many people are hired and what their salaries are, and who controls the cash flow. Evidence indicates that the rate of non-agricultural wage earners employed by the state in MSO countries was over 70%, whereas it was just over 37% for non-MSO countries.[134] This latter number is still quite high in cross-regional comparisons.

In addition, government-run economic sectors would likely face less scrutiny from other government agencies within these types of nations. The practice of elites distributing rents and resources from the state-owned sector likely creates disincentives to create institutions of restraint or other institutions of economic accountability.[135] It is highly unlikely that the very people who are benefiting from the flow of resources and distribution of jobs would seek to regulate (effectively) this practice. This lack of accountability would likely expand into most government-run agencies: where the high stakes sectors are poorly regulated, the lower stakes ones are not likely to be better regulated.

Consequently, if these political elites have easy access to revenue flows from the mineral or oil sector, then they do not need to (and are unlikely to want to) create strong institutions or bureaucracies associated with promoting other aspects of their economy.[136] In fact, they have incentives to create extractive institutions for their own benefit or that of the ruling elites.[137] Since the transfer of rents from the significantly large natural resource sectors ought to be sufficient for patronage politics, they need not allow a private sector to emerge that could one day support a political opposition. There is less need for alternative revenue producing sectors if the export sector is wealthy enough. This political explanation could partially help explain the neglect of traditional economic sectors, beyond any "Dutch disease" effect. Such countries would likely have (or are defined by) quite high levels of corruption – both of which are highly corrosive to the independence of institutions.[138] MSO of the main economic sectors in nations creates incentives to undermine the institutional capacity of these sectors. Given scholarship arguing that strong and growth producing institutions are key to development, this is no small thing.[139]

MSO and Inward-Oriented Economic Policies

Inward-oriented policies were associated with MSO in this region given the incentives of the political economy of the time. During most of the Cold War, African leaders had quite a bit of autonomy over economic, fiscal, and monetary policy and could count on support from either the US or the Soviet Union to keep them afloat during hard times.[140] These policies (i.e., higher rates of currency overvaluation, higher levels of agricultural export taxation, high levels of debt, lower levels of investment, and higher levels of inflation) were inward-oriented as well as mechanisms to support patronage systems. They increased or produced rents and perquisites that were dispensed to supporters.[141] For example, currency overvaluation with currency rationing (which necessarily accompanies overvaluation) allows elites to distribute import licenses and (now) scarce currency to politically important groups while not changing the absolute dollar amount received for exports.[142] This means that the currency peg of the currency against some other currency (often the dollar) no longer retains its value, which reflects a depreciating currency (i.e., the actual value of the currency is worth less on parallel markets relative to official exchange rates). Should the currency appreciate, with a peg, then one would see currency undervaluation.

The overstaffing of government bureaucracies, state-owned industries, state-owned mining sectors, or state-owned oil sectors allow political elites to provide jobs to their followers. These MSO sectors could also count on significant subsidies from the state since there are few short-term costs borne for implementing them. In addition, when political elites undertake large debts, this can ease short-term political difficulties associated with such policies; it leaves the issue of making the policies sustainable to future managers or politicians (or generations). High agricultural taxation rates can fund the patronage machine in a relatively politically costless way as it diverts funds from the politically weak to the politically powerful.[143] Finally, funds shifted away from investment requirements can maintain political power in the short term, though this can come at the cost of long-term development. So too can resources be shifted into social services and away from growth promoting investments.[144]

Second, other policies, such as higher rates of inflation, higher levels of debt, and lower rates of investment, are consistent with the interests of political elites with publicly held property rights. State managers do not own assets per se and cannot bequeath either profits or their management rights to their heirs. Under these conditions, the political elite become agents who manage these assets on behalf of the owners, who are now "the people," and these agents have different interests than the principals.[145] State managers have less interest in the long-term preservation or viability of the sectors they run than would managers/owners of an asset (i.e., a bourgeois class). In fact, if state managers were to keep surpluses resulting from efficient management, it would be considered corrupt since these gains are not profits, but the assets of the owners. As such, they cannot benefit legally from the sale of company assets and are therefore personally less concerned with the corrosive effects of inflation, oversized debts, or under-investment, especially in the long term. Only through large salaries can they legally or ethically take any of the surpluses they created. In addition, countries that are net creditors as well as owners of industries may prefer higher rates of domestic inflation and overvaluation. Inflation reduces the relative value of their debts and their real expenditures on labor as well as subsidizes any imported inputs necessary for producing their goods. ISI industrial growth can occur under conditions of high inflation and are therefore less threatened by changes in the rates of inflation. Furthermore, as state managers often act simultaneously as political elites, or are beholden to the latter, these policies bring significant political benefits, as previously mentioned.

Third, neither the economic nor the political costs of adopting these policies are usually borne directly by those making them. In fact, these burdens tend to be shouldered by politically weak groups – ones that are not easily represented. Since most agricultural production in sub-Saharan Africa comes from small holders and farmers who typically have problems organizing, the agricultural sector is usually heavily taxed.[146] The few countries with large and powerful landholders follow two patterns. On the one hand, where there is MSO, we expect policies to remain inward-oriented, but large and powerful farmers have often been given side-payments or will gain access to the benefits of these policies, such as cheaper imports.[147] On the other hand, where there is less than MSO of the economy, policies are likely to be more directly favorable to agriculture as a whole, such as lower rates of overvaluation and agricultural taxation.[148] Finally, debt is paid for by future generations (who cannot protest) and the benefits accrue to the current generation (who can). This seems to be in place even in wealthier, more accountable polities.

We would not expect more currency appreciation in MSO countries; in fact, we expect the opposite. Countries in sub-Saharan Africa with MSO of either most capital-intensive industries or large mining or oil-exporting countries had currency *overvaluation*, which entails a currency depreciation relative to the official exchange rate of the country.[149] However, real appreciation of different currencies might tell a different story as it includes more prices from non-tradable sectors. The resource curse literature describes high levels of currency appreciation for both categories of countries. Importantly, the effects of currency overvaluation can result in the same outcomes as currency appreciation associated with the resource curse – and these results are nearly identical to resource curse outcomes.

An overvalued currency increases incentives to move out of exporting markets and into domestic only markets, as currency overvaluation is an implicit tax on exports and a subsidy for imports.[150] It also reduces the money gained by exporters when their earnings are translated back into domestic currency. In fact, one of the knocks on inward-oriented policies as outlined by the Berg Report was the impact of currency overvaluation on exports, imports, and even corruption.[151] As a result, it also increased pressures for tariffs and resulted in the rationing of now scarce foreign currency.

In sub-Saharan Africa, countries with MSO of either mining or oil sectors OR the most capital-intensive industries were shown to have higher levels of currency overvaluation than did other similar African nations.[152] This was also evident in the subset of only MSO mining countries. Currency depreciation is measured by comparing parallel markets valuing a declining currency compared to the official fixed exchange rate. It is often measured as a ratio of official values divided by parallel market values.

Lack of Diversification of the Economy

Many scholars have argued that rentierism often leads to countries with less diversified economies, since the ruling elites are more interested in the redistribution of rents and rent seeking than in the creation of other productive economic sectors. Rentier states are ones that "derive most of their revenues from external rents. Rents are paid by foreign actors, accrue directly to the state, and only a small fraction of the population is engaged in the generation of this rent, while the rest nevertheless might benefit from the distribution and use of it."[153] Four criteria are found in a rentier economy: "(1) the economy must be one where rent situations predominate, *where more than 40 percent of national income is derived from oil revenue*. (2) The origin of rent must be 'external' to the economy, that is, *from foreign sources* … (3) *Only the few receive rent* in a rentier economy … (4) *Government must be the principal recipient* of the rent."[154] Countries with high levels of natural resources are clearly candidate countries to be mostly rentier systems.[155] Thus, this description (especially with point number 4) seems to suggest that a developing nation with a significant mineral- or oil-exporting sector and which is majority state-owned would be considered to be rentier almost by definition. And, interestingly, most Middle Eastern states, from which the study was made, did feature MSO of its oil or industries. Nonetheless, given the definition of rentierism just outlined, it is expected for rentierism to be deepened or created by MSO.

Given the prior discussion of the effects of inward-oriented development policies upon the ability to maintain rival export sectors, we expect countries that had MSO, and therefore more inward-oriented policies, to have experienced more decline in rival sectors. Moreover, given the arguments about incentives to take on too many employees, to take on too much debt, and with the expectation that the political elite will have a shorter time horizon than a private business class or group, we expect that such countries will have less diversified economies. In addition, with the state taking the role of entrepreneurs for most industry, banking, and oil or industrial sectors, such countries will have a less vibrant entrepreneurial class. Potential entrepreneurs would be more likely drawn into the protected sectors given the higher returns. Thus, it is expected that inefficiencies, overstaffing, and currency overvaluation are the clear culprits in what could be seen as Dutch disease, especially as overvaluation is – in effect – a tax on exports at the very time other export sectors need to be strengthened to reduce dependence upon the one.

Plan of Book

The book hopes to show that significant mineral- or oil-exporting countries in sub-Saharan Africa, in which the government owned more than 50% of such sectors, exhibited more severe symptoms of what was called the resource curse. In this work, the resource curse hypothesis is not directly tested. What is tested, rather, is the proposition that developing countries with significant mineral or oil exports will experience more severe resource curse problems in countries featuring MSO of these sectors. This proposition is tested in sub-Saharan Africa during the Cold War period and through 2000. This gives it a semblance of most similar design as well as a crucial case test by only including countries which already are resource dependent by percentage of exports, but by also introducing a variable which has not been claimed as a cause by most of this literature.[156] This should eliminate, to a great degree the confounding effect of commodity dependence, as all of the countries included in this study should have this condition. Moreover, by stopping the study in 2000, most of this analysis takes place before massive increases in aid, trade, and FDI associated with China joining the WTO.[157] We will first look at aggregates of variables often associated with the resource curse by MSO and non-MSO countries. Then we will disaggregate the analysis of MSO/non-MSO by oil and mining, which is the work of Chapter 2.

Chapter 3 will explore these variables on a more case by case basis for countries which are major oil exporters, again distinguished by MSO and non-MSO countries. A discussion about oil and its developmental challenges is also included. We will also include some variables which seem aligned with inward-oriented policies, and which seemed clearly important to development writ large. The MSO countries are Angola and Nigeria, while the non-MSO countries are Cameroon and Gabon.

Chapter 4 will also explore the variables of interest on a case study basis for countries which are major mineral exporters, again distinguishing effects by MSO and non-MSO countries. A discussion about mining and its developmental challenges is also included. The MSO countries are Zaire/DRC and Zambia, while the non-MSO countries are Botswana and Niger.

Chapter 5 includes an analysis of significant changes in the years after 2000 for the region and the country case studies. It will focus on mineral or oil exporters in Africa generally, as well as look for current trends in ownership and economic development. Finally, the last chapter will conclude with the major findings of the book as well as their implications.

Choice of Cases/Time Period

The region of sub-Saharan Africa and the time prior to 2000 is chosen for several reasons. First, this region has many of the poorest people in the world and knowledge of how mining or oil impacts development can be quite useful in helping it develop. Second, many countries in this region had significant mining- or oil-exporting sectors, though significant variance in the level of ownership was also apparent. Third, the region matches the author's areas of knowledge and relative expertise. Fourth, by only looking at the period of the Cold War and just beyond, many of the effects of the international climate are held relatively constant. In addition, Ross suggested that the late Cold War period was when the resource curse effects were strongest, thus we control for this.[158] Also, given recent World Bank publications showing that many mining countries experience negative growth through 2000, it makes sense to test this during what is considered the strongest part of the resource curse phenomena.[159] Finally, by using countries only from a single region, more control for many of the region's commonalities is exerted as in a most similar design: most countries have had similar levels of development in the 1960s, most have featured low levels of human capital, most have dealt with issues of nation building, most countries have featured one-party or military rule during the Cold War period, most had been colonized, and most were weak vis-à-vis the international system and community.[160]

Notes

1 Meier (1984, 16).
2 For a summary of such arguments, see Gilberthorpe and Papyakis (2015, 383).
3 See, for example, Young (1986), Sutton (1990, 33–56), Rapley (2007).
4 Nurkse (1953).
5 Leibenstein (1957); see also Killick (1978, 13).
6 Rostow (1960).
7 Some were less than sanguine about the developmental opportunities of natural resources and many scholars feared that positive externalities would be minimal and quite likely be limited to enclaves. See Gilberthorpe and Papyrakis (2015).
8 Stevens and Dietsche (2008, 57).
9 For bottlenecks associated with ISI, see Hirschman (1968).
10 Bosson and Varon (1977, 7).
11 Sachs and Warner (1995, 1997).
12 For early works, see Auty (2001a, 2001b) Sachs and Warner (1995, 1997).

13 Auty (2001a), Kolstad and Wiig (2009), Ross (1999, 2012, 2016), Sachs and Warner (1997, 1995), Stevens (2003), van der Ploeg (2011).
14 Auty (2001a, 2001b)Sachs and Warner (1995, Gelb (1988), Karl (1997) olstad and Wiig (2009), Ross (1999), 1997), Stevens (2003).
15 Stevens (2003, 7). Importantly, not all scholars agree that a resource curse can be found empirically. Davis (1995) found no relationship between minerals or oil and key economic measures. Also, Lederman and Maloney (2007) used Sachs and Warner's (1995) data and suggested that no strong evidence proved that resource abundance was associated with negative growth. For an overview of positive, negative, and mixed findings linking mining with growth, see World Bank (2002, appendix E). Also, Stephens and Dietsche (2008) and Rosser (2006).
16 Ross (1999).
17 See, for example, Wantchekon (1999), Jensen and Wantchekon (2004), Auty (2001a), and Ross (2001).
18 For stagnation in mining countries in sub-Saharan Africa, see Wheeler (1984).
19 World Bank (2002).
20 Bulte, Damania, and Deacon (2005), Sachs and Warner (1997), World Bank (2002), van der Ploeg (2011).
21 Bulte, Damania, and Deacon (2005), Deacon (2003), van der Ploeg (2011).
22 Manzano and Rigobon (2001); van der Ploeg (2011). Also, this manuscript considers countries with more than 30% of exports to be significant exporters. See Chapter 2 for operationalization.
23 Ross (1999), van der Ploeg (2006).
24 Karl (1997), Ross (1999), Stevens (2003), van der Ploeg (2011).
25 de Ferranti et al. (2002), Stevens (2003). Importantly, we should remember that, in the original version of the resource curse literature, agriculture was included as an alternative declining export sector.
26 van der Ploeg (2011).
27 Davis (1995), de Ferranti et al. (2002), Di John (2011), Ross (2016).
28 Ross (2012), van der Ploeg (2006).
29 Ross (2012).
30 Ibid.
31 Ross (2012), van der Ploeg (2006).
32 van der Ploeg (2006).
33 Murshed (2004), De Soysa and Neumayer (2007), Ross (2016), Wegenast (2016), Wegenast and Schneider (2017).
34 Collier and Hoeffler (2004, 574).
35 Ross (2012).
36 Stevens (2003), Collier and Hoeffler (2004). See also Reno (1999).
37 Ross (2012), Lujala (2010). See also Herbst (2000).
38 Lujala et al. (2005, 3).
39 See Fearon and Laitin (2003), Hegre and Sambanis (2006), Lujala (2010), Ross (2004a, 2004b).
40 Le Billon (2001, 2012), also Lujala (2010).
41 Lobell and Mauceri (2004).
42 Ades and Di Telia (1999); for an overview of literature, see Susan (1999), van der Ploeg (2011).
43 Leite and Weidmann (2001), see also Mbaku (1994, 1999).

44 van der Ploeg (2011).
45 Mauro (1995); also Poirson (1998).
46 Heilbrunn (2014, 149).
47 For a discussion of class formation in Africa, see Sklar (1979).
48 Ross (2012).
49 Auty (2001a), Herb (2005), Jensen and Wantchekon (2004), Ross (2012), Stevens (2003), Wantchekon (1999), van der Ploug (2006).
50 Auty (2001a, 2001b).
51 Ross (1999, 2001, 2012).
52 Herb (2005); see also Quinn (1999, 1993).
53 Stevens and Dietsche (2008), Ross (2001).
54 Ross (2001), Jensen and Wantchekon (2004), Rosser (2006).
55 Herb (2005).
56 Jones Luong and Weinthal (2010).
57 Ross (2012).
58 Ross (2012) suggests measuring the production of mineral or oil exports to resolve this issue, instead of exports. However, adding time (through time series or longitudinal case studies) could help solve this issue as well – one could trace increases or decreases in alternative exports following resource discovery. This is done somewhat in the case studies in later chapters.
59 Much of discussion from Sklar and Bergen (1988); also Karl (1997), Bosson and Varon (1977).
60 For mining, see Cobbe (1979, 20); for oil, see Ross (2012).
61 Cobbe (1979, 20), Bosson and Varon (1977, 40).
62 Africa likely has a comparative advantage in such mining, and it is estimated that over 3.7 million people are engaged in this sector in Africa. Mining is a mix of low technology, high labor, and, of course, the existence of minerals accessible through these means. Moreover, about 18% of Africa's gold and the vast majority of gemstones – aside from diamonds – are brought to market through artisan and small-scale mining (ASM). This book will emphasize large-scale capital-intensive mining. For more on this, see African Union (2009, esp. 26–30).
63 Bosson and Varon (1977).
64 Roelf (2014).
65 Kamarck (1982).
66 Kamarck (1982, 155).
67 Cobbe (1979), Bosson and Varon (1977), World Bank (2002).
68 Ross (2012, 45).
69 Cobbe (1979), Karl (1997).
70 Cobbe (1979).
71 Mikesell (1997, 194); Quinn (2002) suggests that this is even more likely where MSO of mining and/or most capital-intensive industry is involved.
72 World Bank (2002, 10), Radetzki (1985).
73 Mikesell (1997, 195–196); Ross (2001b) makes a similar point about politicians raiding stockpiles of case from timber, though most of these were in fact majority state-owned (parastatals) firms that were raided.
74 Cobbe (1979), Karl (1997), Ross (2001).
75 Karl (1997), Ross (2001).
76 For diamond stability and background to cartel, see Spar (2006).

77 Stanislaw and Tergin (1993, 83).
78 For a discussion of cartels, OPEC, and the rising new international economic order, see Lairson and Skidmore (2003, 285–295); see also Spero and Hart (1997, esp. chapter 9).
79 Moriarty and Beed (1989); also see Herbst (2000).
80 Bosson and Varon (1977, 15).
81 For discussions of geography on development, see Kamarck (1982), Bloom et al. (1988); also Herbst (2000); for a detailed discussion of mining and transportation, see Moore (2006) as well as Speltz (2006).
82 Kamarck (1982).
83 Lawon (2007).
84 Lawon (2007); for civil society actions, see National Committee of the Netherlands (n.d.).
85 For an illustration of the potential of enclave economies having positive externalities, see Auty (2007).
86 Bosson and Varon (1977, 7–8).
87 Bosson and Varon (1977, 19).
88 For developmental aspects of commodity dependence, see Collier (2003).
89 Term from World Bank (2002, 10).
90 See, for example, Edwards et al. (2014).
91 Yabe, Ishizuka, and Umemura (2010).
92 World Bank (1981, 1989, 1995), Sandbrook (1993), Shafer (1983), and Tangri (1999).
93 Ibid.; by contrast, Grosh (1991) argued that state-owned sectors could be as efficient as privately owned ones, at least in Kenya, though she does not categorize countries in the same way.
94 Ross (1999).
95 Although Khanna (2017) suggests that ownership when countries have weak institutions, such as in sub-Saharan Africa, state ownership makes things worse. As the political economy of MSO undermines institutions, they are not independent from each other. See also Luong Jones and Weinthal (2010), Kennedy (2008), and Ross (2012).
96 Unless stated otherwise, evidence and data in this section come from Quinn (2016, 2008, 2002, 1999, 1993).
97 Bates (1981), Easterly and Levine (1997), Lipton (1976), Lofchie (1989, 1994), World Bank (1989), Young (1982).
98 Quinn (2008). This piece used Mauro's variable (1995) of bureaucratic efficiency and corruption as the dependent variable, which Mauro had found to lower levels of private investment, which in turn lowered economic growth.
99 Ross (2012).
100 World Bank (1981, 1989, 1995).
101 World Bank (2002, 2).
102 Sandbrook (1993).
103 Tangri (1999, 24).
104 Ross (1999).
105 Ross (2012).
106 Kennedy (2008), Weinthal and Jones-Luong (2006).
107 Sachs and Warner (1995).
108 Quinn (2002).
109 Bates (1994), Bratton and van de Walle (1997), Callaghy (1984), Clapham (1996), Englebert (2000), Joseph (1999), Quinn (1999, 2002), Sandbrook (1993), Tangri (1999), Young (2000).

110 Bratton and van de Walle (1997, 458).
111 See, for example, Le Vine (1980) and Jackson and Rosberg (1982).
112 With perhaps the single exception of Botswana. See, for example, Pitcher, Moran, and Johnston (2009).
113 For an overview (and critique) of the use of the term neo-patrimonial, see ibid. The definition used here is closer to that used by Bratton and van de Walle (1997).
114 Quinn (1999, 2002, 2008).
115 Shafer (1983, 96).
116 Bates (1981), Geddes (2003), Quinn (1993, 2002), Tangri (1999), van de Walle (2001).
117 Chabal (1999).
118 For rational choice assumptions, see Geddes (1995). For the application of rational choice to African political economy, see Bates (1994); for rational choice neoinstitutiontalism, see Hall and Taylor (1996).
119 For another discussion of the principal–agent dynamic, see North (1981); for its use with state-owned enterprises, see Jones Luong and Weinthal (2010); for principal–agent paradigm linked to corruption, see Alam (1989), Quinn (2008).
120 Olson (1965).
121 For fragments of democracy and accountability, see Sklar (1987).
122 For partial economic and political liberalization of the region following the end of the Cold War, see Quinn (2016).
123 Aroni (1982).
124 For similar arguments, see Weinthal and Jones Luong (2006), also Clapham (1996).
125 Ross (2001).
126 Acemoglu and Robinson (2012).
127 For fragments of economic accountability, see Quinn (2000). For fragments of political accountability, see Sklar (1987).
128 The World Bank (1995) has held that state-owned companies pollute more than others.
129 Bienen and Herbst (1996), Haggard and Kaufman (1989), Quinn (2002, 2000, 1993), Tangri (1999), van de Walle (2001).
130 Alam (2002, 820).
131 Torvik (2009).
132 Nellis (1986), Tangri (1999).
133 World Bank (1981).
134 In sub-Saharan African countries between 1966 and 1986. See Quinn (1993, 2002).
135 For institutions of restraint, see Collier (1999). For economic accountability, see Quinn (2000, 2002).
136 See Quinn (2002, 2008), Tangri (1999), and Weinthal and Luong Jones (2006).
137 As discussed above, strong (and nonpredatory) institutions are held to be key to development and economic growth. See, for example, Acemoglu and Robinson (2012), North and Weingast (1989).
138 Ibid.
139 Acemoglu and Robinson (2012), North and Weingast (1989), Hall and Jones (1999). For debates on definitions of institutions, see Greif (2006), Greif and Kingston (2011), and Voigt (2013).
140 Quinn (2016).
141 See, for example, Krueger (1974), Levi (1988), and Bates (1981).
142 Lofchie (1994).
143 Bates (1981), Lipton (1976).
144 Shafer (1983).

145 Probably the first major exploration of this idea is found in Berle (1959). For a more contemporary analysis of the owner–agent problem see North (1990).
146 See Bates (1981), Lofchie (1989), and Lipton (1976). See also Widner (1993), also Quinn (1993).
147 See especially Bates (1981).
148 Quinn (2002).
149 Ibid.
150 See Bates (1981); also Lofchie (1989).
151 World Bank (1989).
152 Quinn (2002).
153 Beblawi (1987).
154 Yates (2015), citing the work of Beblawi (1987).
155 Herb (2005).
156 For definition and power of a "crucial case" study, see Eckstein (1975).
157 Though some rise was evident post-1989, the rise was even greater post-2000. The rise of China is addressed in Chapter 5.
158 Similar or stronger results were found stopping at 1989.
159 World Bank (2002).
160 Clapham (1996), Harbeson and Rothchild (2013).

References

Acemoglu, Daron and James A. Robinson. 2012. *Why Nations Fail: The Origins of Power, Prosperity, and Poverty*. New York: Currency Books.

Ades, Alberto and Rafael Di Telia. 1999. "Rents, Competition, and Corruption." *American Economic Review* 89(4): 982–993.

African Union. 2009. *Africa Mining Vision*. Addis Ababa: African Union.

Alam, M. S. 1989. "Anatomy of Corruption: An Approach to the Political Economy of Underdevelopment." *American Journal of Economics and Sociology* 48(4): 441–471.

Alam, M. S. 2002. "A Theory of Limits on Corruption and Some Applications." In A. J. Heidenheimer and M. Johnson, eds., *Political Corruption: Concepts and Contests*. New Brunswick: Transaction Books, 819–834.

Aroni, Yair. 1982. "State-Owned Enterprise: An Agent without a Principal." In Leroy P. Jones, ed., *Public Enterprises in Less-Developed Countries*. Cambridge: Cambridge University Press, 67–76.

Auty, Richard M. (ed.). 2001a. *Resource Abundance and Economic Development*. Oxford: Oxford University Press.

Auty, Richard M. 2001b. "The Political Economy of Resource-Driven Growth." *European Economic Review* 45: 839–846.

Auty, Richard M. 2007. "Natural Resources, Capital Accumulation, and the Resource Curse." *Ecological Economics* 61(4): 627–634.

Bates, Robert H. 1981. *Market and States in Tropical Africa: The Political Basis of Agricultural Policies*. Los Angeles: University of California Press.

Bates, Robert H. 1994. "The Impulse to Reform in Africa." In Jenifer Widner, ed., *Economic Change and Political Liberalization in Sub-Saharan Africa*. Baltimore: Johns Hopkins University Press, 13–28.

Beblawi, Hazem. 1987. "The Rentier State in the Arab World." In Giacomo Luciani, ed., *The Arab State*. London: Routledge, 85–98.

Berle, Jr., Adolf A. 1959. *Power without Property*. New York: Harcourt, Brace.
Bienen, Henry and Jeffrey Herbst. 1996. "The Relationship between Political and Economic Reform in Africa." *Comparative Politics* 29(1): 23–42.
Bloom, David E. and Jeffrey D. Sachs. 1988. "Geography, Demography, and Economic Growth in Africa." *Brookings Papers on Economic Activity* 2: 207–295.
Bosson, Rex and Bension Varon. 1977. *The Mining Industry and the Developing Countries*. Oxford: Oxford University Press.
Bratton, Michael and Nicholas Van de Walle. 1997. *Democratic Experiments in Africa: Regime Transitions in Comparative Perspective*. Cambridge: Cambridge University Press.
Bulte, Erwin H., Richard Damania, and Robert T. Deacon. 2005. "Resource Intensity, Institutions, and Development." *World Development* 33(7): 1029–1044.
Callaghy, Thomas M. 1984. *The State-Society Struggle: Zaire in Comparative Perspective*. New York: Columbia University Press.
Chabal, Patrick. 1999. *Africa Works: Disorder as Political Instrument*. Oxford: James Currey.
Clapham, Christopher. 1996. *Africa and the International System: The Politics of State Survival*. Cambridge: Cambridge University Press.
Cobbe, James H. 1979. *Governments and Mining Companies in Developing Countries*. Boulder: Westview Press.
Collier, Paul. 1999. "Learning from Failure: The International Financial Institutions as Agencies of Restraint in Africa." In Andreas Schedler et al., eds., *The Self-Restraining State: Power and Accountability in New Democracies*, Boulder: Lynne Rienner, 313–330.
Collier, Paul. 2003. "Primary Commodity Dependence and Africa's Future." *Annual World Bank Conference on Development Economics*: 139–162.
Collier, Paul and Anke Hoeffler. 2004. "Greed and Grievance in Civil War." *Oxford Economic Papers* 56(4): 563–595.
Davis, Graham A. 1995. "Learning to Love the Dutch Disease: Evidence from the Mineral Economies." *World Development* 23(10): 1765–1779.
De Ferranti, David, Guillermo E. Perry, Daniel Lederman, and William E. Maloney. 2002. *From Natural Resources to the Knowledge Economy: Trade and Job Quality*. Washington, DC: World Bank.
De Soysa, Indra and Eric Neumayer. 2007. "Resource Wealth and the Risk of Civil War Onset: Results from a New Dataset of Natural Resource Rents, 1970–1999." *Conflict Management and Peace Science* 24(3): 201–218.
Deacon, Robert T. 2003. "Dictatorship, Democracy, and the Provision of Public Goods." Working Paper 20-23. Santa Barbara: Department of Economics, University of California.
Di John, Jonathan. 2011. "Is There Really a Resource Curse: A Critical Survey of Theory and Evidence." *Global Governance* 17(2): 167–184.
Easterly, William and Ross Levine. 1997. "Africa's Growth Tragedy: Policies and Ethnic Divisions." *Quarterly Journal of Economics* 112(4): 1203–1250.
Eckstein, H. 1975. "Case Studies and Theory in Political Science." In F. Greenstein and N. Polsby, eds., *Handbook of Political Science*, vol. 7. Reading: Addison-Wesley, 79–138.
Edwards, David P., Sean Sloan, Lingfei Weng, Paul Dirks, Jeffrey Sayer, and William F. Laurance. 2014. "Mining and the African environment." *Conservation Letters* 7(3): 302–311.
Englebert, Pierre. 2000. *State Legitimacy and Development in Africa*. Boulder: Lynne Rienner.
Fearon, James D. and David D. Laitin. 2003. "Ethnicity, Insurgency, and Civil War." *American Political Science Review* 97(1): 75–90.

Geddes, Barbara. 1995. "Uses and Limitations of Rational Choice." In Peter Smith, ed., *Latin America in Comparative Perspective: New Approaches to Methods and Analysis*. Boulder: Westview Press, 81–108.
Geddes, Barbara. 2003. *Paradigms and Sand Castles: Theory Building and Research Design in Comparative Politics*. Ann Arbor: University of Michigan Press.
Gelb, Alan and associates. 1988. *Oil Windfalls: Blessing or Curse?* Oxford: Oxford University Press.
Gilberthorpe, Emma and Elissaios Papyrakis. 2015. "The Extractive Industries and Development." *Extractive Industries and Society* 2: 381–390.
Greif, Anver. 2006. *Institutions and the Path to the Modern Economy: Lessons from Medieval Trade*. Cambridge: Cambridge University Press.
Greif, Anver and Christopher Kingston. 2011. "Institutions: Rules or Equilibria?" In Norman Schofield and Gonzalo Caballero, eds., *Political Economy of Institutions, Democracy and Voting*. Berlin: Springer, 13–43.
Grosh, Barbara. 1991. *Public Enterprise in Kenya: What Works, What Doesn't, and Why*. Boulder: Lynne Rienner.
Haggard, Stephan and Robert R. Kaufman. 1989. "Economic Adjustment in New Democracies." In Joan M. Nelson et al., eds., *Fragile Coalitions: The Politics of Economic Adjustment*. New Brunswick: Transaction Books, 57–78.
Hall, Peter A. and Rosemary C. R. Taylor. 1996. "Political Science and the Three New Institutionalisms." *Political Studies* 44(5): 936–957.
Hall, Robert E. and Charles I. Jones. 1999. "Why Do Some Countries Produce So Much More Output Per Worker Than Others?" *Quarterly Journal of Economics* 114: 83–116.
Harbeson, John W. and Donald Rothchild, eds. 2013. *Africa in World Politics*. Boulder: Westview Press.
Hegre, Håvard and Nicholas Sambanis. 2006. "Sensitivity Analysis of Empirical Results on Civil War Onset." *Journal of Conflict Resolution* 50(4): 508–535.
Heilbrunn, John R. 2014. *Oil, Democracy, and Development in Africa*. Cambridge: Cambridge University Press.
Herb, Michael. 2005. "No Representation without Taxation? Rents, Development, and Democracy." *Comparative Politics* 37(3): 297–317.
Herbst, Jeffrey. 2000. *States and Power in Africa: Comparative Lessons in Authority and Control*. Princeton: Princeton University Press.
Hirschman, Albert O. 1968. "The Political Economy of Import-Substituting Industrialization in Latin America." *Quarterly Journal of Economics* 82(1): 1–32.
Jackson, Robert H. and Carl Gustav Rosberg. 1982. *Personal Rule in Black Africa: Prince, Autocrat, Prophet, Tyrant*. Los Angeles: University of California Press.
Jensen, Nathan and Leonard Wantchekon. 2004. "Resource Wealth and Political Regimes in Africa." *Comparative Political Studies* 37(7): 816–841.
Jones Luong, Pauline, and Erika Weinthal. 2010. *Oil Is Not a Curse: Ownership Structure and Institutions in Soviet Successor States*. Cambridge: Cambridge University Press.
Joseph, Richard A. 1999. "The Reconfiguration of Power in Late Twentieth-Century Africa." In Richard Joseph, ed., *State, Conflict, and Democracy in Africa*. Boulder: Lynne Rienner, 57–82.
Kamarck, Andrew M. 1982. "The Resources of Tropical Africa." *Daedalus* 1982: 149–163.
Karl, Terry Lynn. 1997. *The Paradox of Plenty*. Los Angeles: University of California Press.
Kennedy, Ryan. 2008. *Lifting the Curse: Distribution and Power in Petro-States*. PhD dissertation, Ohio State University.

Khanna, Arpita Asha. 2017. "Revisiting the Oil Curse: Does Ownership Matter?" *World Development* 99: 214–229.
Killick, Tony. 1978. *Development Economics in Actions: A Study of Economic Policies in Ghana.* London: Heinemann.
Kolstad, Ivar and Arne Wiig. 2009. "It's the Rents, Stupid! The Political Economy of the Resource Curse." *Energy Policy* 37(12): 5317–5325.
Krueger, Anne O. 1974. "The Political Economy of the Rent-Seeking Society." *American Economic Review* 60(3): 291–303.
Lairson, Thomas D. and David Skidmore. 2003. *International Political Economy: The Struggle for Power and Wealth*, 3rd ed. Toronto: Wadsworth.
Lawon, Antoine. 2007. "Gabonese Hope for Windfall as Chinese Develop Iron Ore Deposit." *New York Times*, February 26. www.nytimes.com/2007/02/26/business/worldbusiness/26iht-gabon.4723217.html.
Le Billon, Philippe. 2001. "The Political Ecology of War: Natural Resources and Armed Conflicts." *Political Geography* 20(5): 561–584.
Le Billon, Philippe. 2012. *Wars of Plunder: Conflicts, Profits, and the Politics of Resources.* New York: Columbia University Press.
Le Vine, Victor T. 1980. "African Patrimonial Regimes in Comparative Perspective." *Journal of Modern African Studies* 18(4): 657–673.
Lederman, Daniel and William Maloney. 2007. "Trade Structure and Growth." In Daniel Lederman and William Maloney, eds., *Natural Resources: Neither Curse Nor Destiny.* Washington, DC: World Bank, 15–40.
Leibenstein, Harvey. 1957. *Economic Backwardness and Economic Growth.* New York: Wiley.
Leite, Carlos A. and Jens Weidmann. 2001. "Does Mother Nature Corrupt? Natural Resources, Corruption, and Economic Growth." IMF Working Paper No. 99/85, February 14. https://papers.ssrn.com/sol3/papers.cfm?abstract_id=259928.
Levi, Margaret. 1988. *Of Rule and Revenue*. Berkeley: University of California Press.
Lipton, Michael. 1976. *Why Poor People Stay Poor: Urban Bias in World Development.* Cambridge, MA: Harvard University Press.
Lobell, Steven E. and Philip Mauceri, eds. 2004. *The Internationalization of Ethnic Conflict: Explaining Diffusion and Escalation.* New York: Palgrave Macmillan.
Lofchie, Michael F. 1989. *The Policy Factor: Agricultural Performance in Kenya and Tanzania.* Boulder: Lynne Rienner.
Lofchie, Michael F. 1994. "The New Political Economy of Africa." In David E. Apter and Carl G. Rosberg, eds., *Political Development and the New Realism in Sub-Saharan Africa*. Charlottesville: University Press of Virginia, 145–183.
Lujala, Päivi. 2010. "The Spoils of Nature: Armed Civil Conflict and Rebel Access to Natural Resource." *Journal of Peace Research* 47(1): 15–28.
Lujala, Päivi, Nils Petter Gleditsch, and Elisabeth Gilmore. 2005. "A Diamond Curse? Civil War and a Lootable Resource." *Journal of Conflict Resolution* 49(4): 538–562.
Luong, Pauline Jones and Erika Weinthal. 2010. *Oil Is Not a Curse: Ownership Structure and Institutions in Soviet Successor States*. Cambridge: Cambridge University Press.
Manzano, Osmel and Roberto Rigobon. 2001. "Resource Curse or Debt Overhang?" NBER Working Paper 8390, July.
Mauro, Paolo. 1995. "Corruption and Growth." *Quarterly Journal of Economics* 110(3): 681–712.
Mbaku, John. 1994. "Bureaucratic Corruption and Reform in Africa." *Journal of Social, Political and Economic Studies* 19(2): 149–175.

Mbaku, John. 1999. "Bureaucratic Corruption and Africa: The Futility of Cleanup." *Cato Journal* 16(2): 99–118.

Meier, Gerald M. and Dudley Seers, eds. 1984. *Pioneers in Development.* Washington, DC: Oxford University Press.

Mikesell, Raymond F. 1997. "Explaining the Resource Curse, with Special Reference to Mineral-Exporting Countries." *Resources Policy* 23(4): 191–199.

Moore, Paul. 2006. "Road Transportation and Industrial Mineral." In Jessica Elzea Kogel, Nikhil C. Trivedi, James M. Barker, and Stanley T. Krukowski, eds., *Industrial Minerals & Rocks: Commodities, Markets, and Uses.* Littleton: Society for Mining, Metallurgy, and Exploration, 95–98.

Moriarty, Patrick and Clive S. Beed. 1989. "Transport in Tropical Africa." *Journal of Modern African Studies* 27(1): 125–132.

Murshed, S. Mansoob. 2004. "When Does Natural Resource Abundance Lead to a Resource Curse?" Environmental Economics Programme Discussion Paper 04-01, 1–25.

National Committee of the Netherlands. n.d. "Belinga Iron Ore Mine, Gabon. Taking Civil Society Input Seriously." https://leave-it-in-the-ground.org/wp-content/uploads/2018/11/Exemplary-Cases-of-Good-Chinese-Investor-Responsibility_Case-5-Belinga.pdf.

Nellis, John. 1986. "Public Enterprise in Sub-Saharan Africa." Discussion Paper No. 1. Washington, DC: World Bank.

North, Douglass C. 1981. *Structure and Change in Economic History.* New York: W. W. Norton.

North, Douglass C. 1990. *Institutions, Institutional Change and Economic Performance.* Cambridge: Cambridge University Press.

North, Douglass C. and Barry R. Weingast. 1989. "Constitutions and Commitment: Evolution of Institutions Governing Public Choice in Seventeenth Century England." *Journal of Economic History* 49: 803–832.

Nurkse, Ragnar. 1953. *Problems of Capital Formation in Underdeveloped Countries.* Oxford: Blackwell.

Olson, Mancur. 1965. *Logic of Collective Action: Public Goods and the Theory of Groups.* Cambridge: Harvard University Press.

Pitcher, Anne Mary H. Moran and Michael Johnston. 2009. "Rethinking Patrimonialism and Neopatrimonialism in Africa." *African Studies Review* 52(1): 125–156.

Poirson, Hélène. 1998. *Economic Security, Private Investment, and Growth in Developing Countries.* Washington, DC: International Monetary Fund.

Quinn, John J. 1993. "The Impact of State Ownership of Resources on Economic and Political Development in sub-Saharan Africa." *Ufahamu* 21(1&2): 60–79.

Quinn, John J. 1999. "The Managerial Bourgeoisie: Capital Accumulation, Development and Democracy." In David G. Becker and Richard L. Sklar, eds., *Postimperialism and World Politics.* Westport: Praeger, 219–252.

Quinn, John J. 2000. "Economic Accountability: Are Constraints on Economic Decision Making a Blessing or a Curse?" *Scandinavian Journal of Development Alternatives and Area Studies* 19(4): 131–169.

Quinn, John James. 2002. *The Road Oft Traveled: Development Policies and Majority State Ownership of Industry in Africa.* Westport: Praeger.

Quinn, John James. 2008. "The Effects of Majority State Ownership of Significant Economic Sectors on Corruption: A Cross-Regional Comparison." *International Interactions* 34(1): 81–128.

Quinn, John James. 2016. *Global Geopolitical Power and African Political and Economic Institutions: When Elephants Fight.* Lanham: Lexington Books.

Radetzki, Marian. 1985. *State Mineral Enterprises: An Investigation into Their Impact on International Mineral Markets*. Washington, DC: Resources for the Future.

Rapley, John. 2007. *Understanding Development: Theory and Practice in the Third World*, 3rd ed. Boulder: Lynne Rienner.

Reno, William. 1999. *Warlord Politics and African States*. Boulder: Lynne Rienner.

Roelf, Wendell. 2014. "World Bank Eyes $1 Billion African Resource Mapping Fund in July." *Reuters*, February 5. www.reuters.com/article/2014/02/05/us-africa-mining-mapping-idUSBREA140LT20140205/

Rose-Ackerman, Susan. 1999. *Corruption and Government: Causes, Consequences, and Reform*. Cambridge: Cambridge University Press.

Ross, Michael L. 1999. "The Political Economy of the Resource Curse." *World Politics* 51(2): 297–322.

Ross, Michael L. 2001. "Does Oil Hinder Democracy?" *World Politics* 53(3): 325–361.

Ross, Michael L. 2004a. "What Do We Know about Natural Resources and Civil War?" *Journal of Peace Research* 41(3): 337–356.

Ross Michael L. 2004b. "How Do Natural Resources Influence Civil War? Evidence from Thirteen Cases." *International Organization* 58(1): 35–67.

Ross, Michael L. 2006. "A Closer Look at Oil, Diamonds, and Civil War." *Annual Review of Political Science* 9: 265–300.

Ross, Michael L. 2012. *The Oil Curse: How Petroleum Wealth Shapes the Development of Nations*. Princeton: Princeton University Press.

Ross, Michael L. 2016. "The Politics of the Resource Curse: A Review." In Carol Lancaster and Nicolas van de Walle, eds., *The Oxford Handbook of the Politics of Development*. Oxford: Oxford University Press, 200–223.

Rosser, Andrew. 2006. "The Political Economy of the Resource Curse: A Literature Survey." Institute of Development Studies Working Paper 268.

Rostow, W. W. 1960. *The Stages of Economic Growth*. Cambridge: Cambridge University Press.

Sachs, Jeffrey D. and Andrew M. Warner. 1995. "Natural Resource Abundance and Economic Growth." NBER Working Paper No. W5398, December. http://ssrn.com/abstract=225459.

Sachs, Jeffrey D. and Andrew M. Warner. 1997. "Fundamental Sources of Long-Run Growth." *American Economic Review* 87(2): 184–188.

Sandbrook, Richard. 1993. *The Politics of Africa's Economic Recovery*. Cambridge: Cambridge University Press.

Shafer, D. Michael. 1983. "Capturing the Mineral Multinationals: Advantage or Disadvantage." *International Organization* 37(1): 93–119.

Sklar, Richard L. 1979. "The Nature of Class Domination." *Journal of Modern African Studies* 17(4): 531–552.

Sklar, Richard L. 1987. "Developmental Democracy." *Comparative Studies in Society and History* 29(4): 686–714.

Sklar, Richard and Geoffrey Bergen. 1988. "Mineral Industries and Development in Sub-Saharan Africa." *Soviet-U.S. Cooperation for Africa Conference*, Airlie, Virginia, November 10–12.

Spar, Debora L. 2006. "Markets: Continuity and Change in the International Diamond Market." *Journal of Economic Perspectives* 20(3): 195–208.

Speltz, Charles. 2006. "Rail Transportation of Industrial Mineral." In Jessica Elzea Kogel, Nikhil C. Trivedi, James M. Barker, and Stanley T. Krukowski, eds., *Industrial Minerals & Rocks: Commodities, Markets, and Uses*. Littleton: Society for Mining, Metallurgy, and Exploration, 79–94.

Spero, Joan E. and Jeffrey A. Hart. 1997. *The Politics of International Relations*, 5th ed. New York: St. Martin's Press.

Stanislaw, Joseph and Daniel Tergin. 1993. "Oil: Reopening the Door." *Foreign Affairs* 72(4): 81–93.

Stevens, Paul. 2003. "Resource Impact: Curse or Blessing? A Literature Survey." *Journal of Energy Literature* 9(1): 1–42.

Stevens, Paul and Evelyn Dietsche. 2008. "Resource Curse: An Analysis of Causes, Experiences, and Possible Ways Forward." *Energy Policy* 36(1): 56–65.

Sutton, Francis X. 1990. "Development Ideology: Its Emergence and Decline." In Francis X. Sutton, ed., *A World to Make: Development in Perspective*. New Brunswick: Transaction Publishers, 33–56.

Tangri, Roger. 1999. *The Politics of Patronage in Africa: Parastatals, Privatization, and Private Enterprise*. Trenton: Africa World Press.

Torvik, Ragnar. 2009. "Why Do Some Resource-Abundant Countries Succeed while Others Do Not?" *Oxford Review of Economic Policy* 25(2): 241–256.

van de Walle, Nicolas. 2001. *African Economies and the Politics of Permanent Crisis: 1979–1999*. Cambridge: Cambridge University Press.

van der Ploeg, Frederick. 2006. "Challenges and Opportunities for Resource Rich Economies." Centre for Economic Policy Research No. 5688.

van der Ploeg, Frederick. 2011. "Natural Resources: Curse or Blessing?" *Journal of Economic Literature* 49(2): 366–420. www.jstor.org/stable/23071620.

Voigt, Stefan. 2013. "How (Not) to Measure Institutions." *Journal of Institutional Economics* 9(1): 1–26.

Wallerstein, Immanuel. 1967. *The Modern World System*. New York: Academic Press.

Wantchekon, Leonard. 1999. "Why Do Resource Abundant Countries Have Authoritarian Governments?" Yale University Leitner Center Working Paper 99-12.

Wegenast, Tim. 2016. "Oil, Natural Gas, and Intrastate Conflict: Does Ownership Matter?" *International Interactions* 42(1): 31–55.

Wegenast, Tim and Gerald Schneider. 2017. "Ownership Matters: Natural Resources Property Rights and Social Conflict in Sub-Saharan Africa." *Political Geography* 61: 110–122.

Weinthal, Erika and Pauline Jones Luong. 2006. "Combating the Resource Curse: An Alternative Solution to Managing Mineral Wealth." *Perspectives on Politics* 4: 35–53.

Wheeler, David. 1984. "Sources of Stagnation in Sub-Saharan Africa." *World Development* 12(1): 1–23.

Widner, Jennifer A. 1993. "The Origins of Agricultural Policy in Ivory Coast 1960–86." In Ashutosh Varshney, ed., *Beyond Urban Bias*. Portland: Frank Cass, 25–59.

World Bank. 1981. *Accelerated Development in Sub-Saharan Africa: An Agenda for Action*. Washington, DC: World Bank.

World Bank. 1989. *World Development Report 1989*. Oxford: Oxford University Press.

World Bank. 1995. *Bureaucrats in Business: The Economics and Politics of Government Ownership*. New York: Oxford University Press.

World Bank. 2002. *Treasure or Trouble? Mining in Developing Countries*. Washington, DC: World Bank and International Financial Corporation.

Yabe, John, Mayuni Ishizuka, and Takashi Umemura. 2010. "Current Levels of Heavy Metal Pollution in Africa." *Journal of Veterinary Medical Science* 72(10): 1257–1263.

Yates, Doublas A. 2015. "The Rise and Fall of Oil-Rentier States in Africa." In *New Approaches to the Governance of Natural Resources*. London: Palgrave Macmillan, 45–64.

Young, Crawford. 1982. *Ideology and Development in Africa*. New Haven: Yale University Press.
Young, Crawford. 1986. "The Ideas of Progress in the Third World." In Gabriel Almond, ed., *Progress and Its Discontents*. Los Angeles: University of California Press, 83–105.
Young, Crawford. 2000. "The Heritage of Colonialism." In John W. Harbeson and Donald Rothchild, eds., *Africa in World Politics: The African State System in Flux*, 3rd ed. Boulder: Westview Press, 23–42.

2 Oil or Mineral Exporting, Majority State Ownership, and Resource Curse Outcomes

A Preliminary Cross-Sectional Statistical Analysis

In order to test the impact of MSO on African mineral or oil economies, countries in the region that were significant mineral or oil exporters for 10 years or more from 1966 to 2000 are included. Using only countries from sub-Saharan Africa gives us some control over many of the traditional explanations for poor economic performance and low levels of democracy in the region: being in Africa, dependency, a history of colonization, low levels of literacy, low levels of development, low levels of institutional and state capacity, ethnolinguistic fractionalization, late industrialization, and, of course, mineral or oil exporting. This is not merely a bivariate test per se, since so many regional-level variables are held constant in this most similar design.[1] In this design, not all of the alternative or rival variables are held constant, but this is a first step to establish general covariation within the study. This chapter is looking for a cluster of events associated with the structure of ownership, so the effects of MSO on particular variables are tested both directly and indirectly.[2] However, this investigation only examines these questions on a subset of sub-Saharan African countries: those with significant oil- or mineral-exporting sectors. Thus, we only include countries which had large percentages of exports of fuels or minerals. Therefore, the resource curse outcomes are examined only within countries most likely to have suffered from it, as per the literature.

The study starts collecting data for each country between 1966 until 2000. Countries were included only after independence and after they were considered to be a major mineral or oil exporter.[3] If the country was a major oil or mineral exporter prior to nationalization, these years were included as non-MSO. These prior years capture much of the long-term developmental patterns in the subcontinent before major changes following the end of the Cold War ensued.[4] Also, this analysis does not include the countries with relatively newly discovered oil or mining, such as Ghana, or newly created countries, like South Sudan. By using a most similar design to test a mid-level theory, this helps untangle other potentially confounding variables. Each variable is averaged by type of major exporting sector, oil or mineral, and by type of ownership – MSO and non-MSO.

The presence of the majority state ownership (MSO) of a major oil- or mineral-exporting sector represents the main independent variable. The dependent variables are comprised of the negative outcomes (political, social,

DOI: 10.4324/9780429423390-2

and economic) that are usually associated with the resource curse. The competing measures of potential resource curse outcomes include the following: (1) levels of growth, (2) levels of incomes, (3) levels of currency appreciation (real), (4) levels of debt, (5) levels of diversification of the economy, (6) frequency of civil conflict, and (7) levels of freedoms. Unfortunately, no systematic time-series data on corruption is available for these countries and for these years, so it will be excluded from the analysis.[5]

Two other variables are added to extend the analysis of resource curse outcomes beyond the ones listed just above: currency overvaluation and investment. Currency overvaluation is included for several reasons. First, it is an indirect measure of currency appreciation, as it is the opposite of what is expected by the Dutch Disease. It is hard to measure appreciation in countries with fixed official exchange rates if the country defends its peg, though we do include a measure of real exchange rates. The measure of currency overvaluation compares official rates relative to parallel market rates: if there is currency appreciation, we should see currency undervaluation; if there is depreciation relative to the peg, then we should see currency overvaluation. Second, currency overvaluation was shown to be a distinct aspect of many developing nations' developmental policies, and it was also closely associated with MSO.[6] Like currency appreciation, currency overvaluation creates disincentives for exporters because it acts like a tax on exporters and a subsidy for importers. Interestingly, Sachs and Warner, who helped launch the resource curse literature, included currency overvaluation as a major component of inward-oriented trade policies.[7] Investment is also included as MSO was to have been a cure for the exploitation of foreign ownership which drained profits or surplus value resources out of these nations, measures of levels of domestic investment are also included. Investment is considered to be a key variable for predicting later levels of growth.[8]

Importantly, given past studies of MSO, it has to be measured twice given our sample: First, we include countries as MSO-1 when the state had MSO of the mineral- or oil-exporting sector itself.[9] This is the main thrust of this analysis. However, given the findings that the MSO of most industrial sectors in countries without significant mineral- or oil-exporting sectors could lead to similar economic policies, we also include countries if they had MSO of most capital-intensive industries or a natural resource sector. As such, MSO-2 is a dummy variable that includes all MSO-1 countries as well as one with MSO of most capital-intensive industries and which had a less than majority state-owned major mineral- or oil-exporting sector.[10] Guinea and the Republic of Congo are examples of countries included in MSO-2.[11] Doing this allows us to control for any indirect effects of policy outcomes affected by political elites who controlled significant and most modern sectors of the economy outside of mining or oil which have been shown to lead to inward-oriented policies in the past.[12]

The data for these variables come from a variety of sources. The variables for growth, income, and population come from Penn World Tables 9.1.[13] All the other variables, gross domestic fixed investment (GDFI) per capita, GDFI as a percentage of GDP, Value added-Ag per cap, Value added-Man per cap, debt service to export ratio (ex post) come from the 2002 World Bank Africa Database CDROM.[14] All these variables are weighted by population, except for debt as a percentage of GDP.[15] The diversification of the economy is captured with two variables: "Value added in Agriculture" and "Value Added in Manufacturing." These also come from the World Bank.[16] Both are converted into per capita values to weight them. Currency overvaluation is the ratio of unofficial exchange rates to official exchange rates (2002 World Bank African Database). Real currency appreciation/depreciation is measured by percent change of real exchange rates.[17] Levels of debt as percentage of GNI comes from the World Bank.[18] Years that countries experienced a civil war was coded with a one, and this data comes from the Correlates of War database, intrastate war.[19] The average level of political and civil rights comes from Freedom House. These numbers range from one, completely free, to seven, completely not free.

Countries Included

Sub-Saharan countries that had an average of 30% or more of merchandise exports for ten years or more of mineral or petroleum exports are included. Those countries whose percentage of exports from mineral or fuels fell below 15% for more than 3 years were then dropped (from those years onwards). So, for example, a country like Rwanda would be classified as a major mineral exporter from 1966 to 1974.[20] Countries that had high levels of such exports, but which were smuggled from elsewhere or were reexported were excluded due to difficulties of measurement. All sub-Saharan African countries from 1966 to 2000 are included unless they were still under colonial rule. In that case, such countries are included from their first year of independence (post-1966). The following countries are therefore included: Angola, Botswana, Cameroon, Congo (Brazzaville), Congo-DRC, Gabon, Guinea, Lesotho, Liberia, Mali, Mauritania, Niger, Nigeria, Rwanda, Sierra Leone, Togo, and Zambia.

The year 2000 is used as a benchmark since Ross (2012) and others have suggested that part of the resource curse idea was mostly limited to the years of the Cold War and its immediate aftermath. Also, privatization began more in earnest by many countries after 2000.[21] This way we test the idea during a time of when many felt the resource curse was in full bloom.

The basic test employed is a t-test examining differences in means for countries with and without MSO of these sectors, and it is estimated for all countries for all years.[22] Then just oil-exporting countries are examined, and then just mineral-exporting countries. The second measure of MSO-2 is also examined for 1966–2000 for all countries, then just mining, and then just oil. So the variables to be tested with t-tests are (1) growth, (2) per capita incomes, (3) levels of debt (measured by both debt service as a percentage of exports and as the percentage of debt to GNI), (4) levels of fixed investment (in per capita terms and weighted by GDP, (5) value added in agriculture per capita, (6) value added in manufacturing per capita, (7) levels of currency overvaluation (as ratio of parallel markets over

Table 2.1 Indicators for MSO and non-MSO countries: Both oil and mining, 1966–2000

	MSO-1	*Non-MSO-1*	*MSO-2*	*Non-MSO-2*
Growth	–1.8073***	1.435***	–0.85***	1.5***
Real GDP/cap	$1,756***	$2,991***	$2,128***	$2,989***
Value added-Ag per cap	$86.61***	$156.84***	$87.02***	$178.09***
Value added-Man per cap	$32.93***	$74.67***	$38.12***	$82.95***
Currency ratio Unof/Of	5.89-E10***	1.48-E7***	4.31-E10***	3.58***
Real Currency Appreciation	1.09%	–0.74%	0.31%	–0.33%
GDF Inv-cap	$78.73***	$428.13***	$147.84***	$485.15***
GDF Inv % GDP	17.86%***	24.36***	19.86***	24.09***
Debt/GDP	108.02%***	85.98%***	121.81%***	62.97%***
Debt Service to Export Ratio	18.46%***	12.77%***	18.53%***	10.82%***
Political/Civil Rights	5.65***	5.27***	5.75***	5.00***
Intrastate War	0.164***	0.0685***	0.1519***	0.051***

MSO-1: MSO of principal mineral- or oil-exporting sector. MSO-2: All MSO-1 countries plus those oil or mineral countries with MSO of only most capital-intensive industries. *Significant at 90% or higher; **significant at 95% or higher; ***significant at 99% or higher.

Table of differences in a few resource curse outcomes by ownership. Combined mineral and oil cases.

official markets), (8) levels of real currency appreciation, (9) levels of political and civil rights, and (10) average percentage number of years in civil war.

Findings

We can see in this match on Table 2.1 that with mining and oil combined every variable but one linked to the resource curse was worse for the countries with MSO-1.[23] They were also statistically significant. The countries with MSO of their mining or oil sectors experienced negative average growth; they had lower GDPs per capita; they had lower value added in either their agricultural or manufacturing sectors; they had higher levels of currency overvaluation; they had lower levels of investment (however measured); and they had higher levels of debt and debt service. Moreover, they experienced more intrastate conflict in addition to having lower levels of political and civil rights.

These results were similar when all countries with either form of MSO were combined (MSO-2). Here too, we see that countries in the MSO-2 category had negative (and lower) growth, lower incomes, lower value added in either their agricultural or manufacturing sectors, lower levels of investments, and higher levels of debt than non-MSO-2 countries. They also experienced lower levels of political and civil freedoms, and they experienced more domestic conflict than non-MSO-2 countries.

The biggest difference between outcomes for these two categories (MSO-1 and MSO-2) is that when all MSO countries were clumped together (MSO-2), the differences in currency overvaluation between the two cases were even starker. The average level of currency overvaluation for non-MSO-2 countries was 3.58 – which was still high by World Bank standards. However, it was much lower than MSO-2 countries which featured a ratio of 43,100,000,000!

One surprising finding did emerge: the level of real currency appreciation for these countries was quite low on average. The highest level was with the MSO-1 countries, but it was only 1.09% – hardly a high level of real currency appreciation over time. The MSO-2 countries had even lower levels, at 0.31%. However, the non-MSO-1 and non-MSO-2 countries had negative levels of real currency appreciation, at –0.74% and –0.33% respectively. Looking at all mineral- or oil-exporting countries in the sample, the average level of real currency appreciation was relatively low at 0.05%. For all oil countries it was 1%, but for all mineral countries, it was negative at –0.43%. However, these differences were not statistically significant. This is an unexpected finding given that strong currency appreciation is often given as the primary reason for the Dutch Disease, which in turn usually explains much of the resource curse.

Looking at the differences between oil-exporting MSO-1 and non-MSO-1 countries, we see in Table 2.2 that most of the findings still hold, but with a few important differences. Although MSO-1 oil-exporting countries experienced average *negative* growth levels, and the non-MSO-1 countries experienced positive growth levels, the statistical difference was no longer significant (though the average absolute difference was about 1.56% growth per year). Nevertheless, for most of the other variables, the results were similar to the combined sample. The MSO-1 countries had lower per capita incomes, less value added in agriculture, less value added in manufacturing, higher currency overvaluation, lower levels of fixed investment per capita, lower levels of investment as a percentage of GDP, and more domestic conflict. These results remained statistically significant.

Table 2.2 Indicators for MSO and non-MSO countries: Oil, 1966–2000

	MSO-1	*Non-MSO-1*	*MSO-2*	*Non-MSO-2*
Growth	–0.1387	1.42	0.856%	1.092%
Real GDP/cap	$1,880.73***	$5,063.97***	$2,518.7***	$6,059.8***
Value added-Ag per cap	$85.15***	218.31***	$82.2**	$319.1***
Value added-Man per cap	$20.00***	106.41***	$36.7***	$143.3***
Currency ratio Unof/Of	1.17-E10**	3.053-E8**	6.34-E9***	1.02***
Real Currency Appreciation	6%	–1.1%*	0.31%	–0.33%
GDF Inv-cap	$72.49***	663.28***	$230***	$880***
GDF Inv % GDP	18.88%***	27.77%***	23.52%**	27.61%**
Debt/GDP	47.57***	177.98%***	126.06%***	63.16%***
Debt Service to Export Ratio	13.13*	16.88%*	16.14%	15.3%
Political/Civil Rights	5.48	5.73	5.63	5.67
Intrastate War	0.42***	0.14***	0.34***	0.09***

MSO-1: MSO of principal oil-exporting sector. MSO-2: All MSO-1 oil-exporting countries plus oil-exporting countries with MSO of only most capital-intensive industries. *Significant at 90% or higher; **Significant at 95% or higher; ***Significant at 99% or higher.

Table of differences in a few resource curse outcomes by ownership. Oil cases only.

One other difference for the subsample of oil exporters was that MSO countries (both MSO-1 and MSO-2) had very slightly higher levels of political and civil rights compared to non-MSO-1 countries – though the results were not significant. (Remember that for Freedom House the higher the number, the more autocratic.) In terms of the differences of real change in the appreciation of currency, MSO-1 countries did have higher levels, of 6% vs. negative 1.1%, but this was not significant beyond the 90% confidence level. For MSO-2 countries, they too have higher levels of real currency appreciation, at 0.31% vs. negative 0.33%, but this difference was also not significant. Again, negative currency appreciation was not expected for either category of countries, though the non-MSO countries (either 1 or 2) had negative currency appreciation for this period, on average.

One other quite unexpected, and significant, change did emerge for MSO-1 oil-exporting countries: they had lower levels of debt by either measure. Debt as a percentage of GDP was significantly lower for MSO-1 countries, though only debt per capita was statistically significant at the 95% level. This finding did not continue through the MSO-2 countries debt service to exports, where the MSO-2 countries had higher and statistically significant differences in debt% of GDP, while differences in MSO-2 debt as a percentage of exports was so small as to be negligible (though MSO-2 countries did still have the higher debt).

Thus, the oil-exporting MSO-1 countries did have worse resource curse outcomes for most variables compared to non-MSO-1 countries. However, the lower growth (negative) averages were not significant, nor were the differences in political and civil rights. Interestingly, they actually had lower levels of debt by either measure, though this was only significant for per capita debt. When clumping together all oil-exporting MSO countries (MSO-2), the findings were still similar to those found in the MSO-1 oil categories, with one or two notable differences. The MSO-2 countries still had had lower growth, but this time the levels were not negative, on average. Similar to the other oil-exporting category, the variables were not statistically different.

However, the MSO-2 oil countries also featured lower levels of income, less value added in agriculture, less value added in manufacturing, higher currency overvaluation, lower levels of fixed investment, lower levels of investment as a percentage of GDP, higher levels of debt relative to GDP, very slightly higher levels of debt service, and more domestic conflict. However, the debt service relative to exports was insignificant as were the differences in political and civil rights – which were negligible. The other big change can be seen in Table 2.1: currency overvaluation was much lower for all non-MSO-2 countries (whether oil or industry) in comparison to MSO-2 countries. In fact, the non-MSO oil countries had almost no overvaluation at all. The explanation for this is pursued in more detail in Chapter 3. Also, the lack of high real currency appreciation is surprising given the literature.

Finally, when examining only countries with significant mineral exports, the results are quite similar for the combined cases. First looking at MSO-1 vs. non-MSO-1, it can be seen in Table 2.3 that the mining countries with MSO suffered

Table 2.3 Indicators for MSO and non-MSO countries: Mining, 1966–2000

	MSO-1	*Non-MSO-1*	*MSO-2*	*Non-MSO-2*
Growth	–2.3%***	1.45%***	–1.83%***	1.8%***
Real GDP/cap	$1,719.78***	$2,127.79***	$1,970.5	$1,929
Value added-Ag per cap	$86.98***	$116.6***	$89***	$118***
Value added-Man per cap	$39.1***	$57.6***	$36.98***	$62.88***
Currency ratio Unof/Of	7.18-E10***	4.77***	5.96-E10***	5.61***
Real Currency Appreciation	–0.37%	–0.49%	–0.22%	–0.76%
GDF Inv-cap	$80.9***	$210.37***	$83.2***	$242.03***
GDF Inv % GDP	17.6%***	23.88***	17.7%***	24.54%***
Debt/GDP	123.24%***	73.48%***	121.35%***	69.1%***
Debt Service to Export Ratio	19.94***	10.56***	19.85%***	9.11%***
Political/Civil Rights	5.7***	5.0.***	5.8***	4.7***
Intrastate Conflict	0.089*	0.0408*	0.077	0.044

MSO-1: MSO of principal mineral-exporting sector. MSO-2: All MSO-1 mineral-exporting countries plus those mineral-exporting countries with MSO of only most capital-intensive industries. *Significant at 90% or higher; **significant at 95% or higher; ***significant at 99% or higher.

Table of differences in a few resource curse outcomes by ownership. Mineral cases only.

from worse mineral resource curse outcomes for almost every variable. They averaged –2.3% real growth for these years (with an absolute difference of 3.75% per year), lower GDPs per capita, less value added in agriculture or manufacturing, more debt by either measure, less investment by either measure, much higher currency overvaluation, lower levels of political and civil rights, and more intrastate violence. These findings were quite robust since each was significant at 95% or higher – aside from the intrastate conflict which was about twice as high in MSO-1 countries as non-MSO-1 countries, though it was significant only at the 90% level.

Including all mineral-exporting nations and then combining both forms of MSO (MSO-2), nearly identical results emerged. The MSO-2 countries had lower (and negative) growth rates (a difference of 3.6% per year), lower valued added in either agricultural or manufacturing, higher rates currency overvaluation, lower levels of investments by either measure, higher levels of debt by either measure, lower levels of political and civil rights, and more intrastate violence, though this was lower than the oil levels (MSO-1). However, the levels of per capita GDP were nearly identical (and not statistically significant), and the differences in intrastate conflict became insignificant in this match too.

Once again, we see the surprise concerning real currency exchange rates, they were negative on average for all categories of mineral-exporting countries – quite unexpected from the resource curse literature. We see more depreciation among the non-MSO countries than among the MSO countries, though these differences were not significant.

Overall Results

Looking across the three tables, MSO countries had worse performance vis-à-vis development for nearly every variable – or they were similar to the other resource rich countries. The only case in which an MSO category of countries had better indicators (that were statistically significant) was for oil-exporting countries and their lower levels of debt. For every other measure, MSO countries had similar or worse outcomes for these variables.

For example, countries that featured MSO of either their oil sector or their mineral sector (MSO-1) had *negative* growth rates for the period of 1966–2000 (between –0.138% and –2.3%). In none of the groups did the MSO-1 countries have positive growth rate averages. By contrast, the MSO-2 oil countries had very low, but positive, growth rates. Nonetheless, these levels were lower than that for non-MSO-2 oil countries. These countries featured MSO of industry, but not of the oil or mining sector. However, for mining alone, MSO countries (1 or 2) had *negative* growth rates, while non-MSO counties had positive growth rates, and the differences were statistically significant. Thus, the most noted resource curse variable was only negative for MSO of the major oil or mineral export sector (1), and it was positive for the non-MSO-1 countries.

We also see that non-MSO-1 countries had positive growth rates during this period (ranging between 1.4188% and 1.475%). This is an important finding showing that the *negative* growth attributed to mineral- or oil-exporting sectors correlates with the MSO of these sectors. The non-MSO countries did not experience high average growth during this period, but a record of low, but overall positive, growth is clearly more developmental than overall negative growth. However, as important as this finding is, it was not significant for oil. So, we see lower or negative growth for oil-exporting countries, which is consistent with the resource curse. We also see that non-MSO oil exporters experience positive growth, but the results are not statistically significant. Given the rapid price increases for oil between 1973 and 1986 (during OPECs heyday), it is actually quite surprising that more oil-exporting countries did not experience high (positive) growth rates.

Moreover, it appears that per capita incomes were consistently higher for non-MSO countries, whether they were oil exporters or mineral exporters. Only when less than majority state-owned minerals were combined with MSO of industry (MSO-2) were the levels between MSO-2 and non-MSO-2 incomes no longer significantly different.

Perhaps more importantly, the variables indicating a decline in rival export sectors were more associated with MSO. In every category, non-MSO (1 or 2) of either oil or mineral countries had more value added in both agriculture and manufacturing than did MSO (1 or 2), and these findings were robustly significant. In every case, the non-MSO countries had higher value added in agriculture and manufacturing.

Instead, however, of finding evidence of high levels of currency appreciation, we see low or negative levels of currency appreciation for some countries, and we see *currency depreciation*, not *currency appreciation*, for the non-MSO oil-exporting countries as well as for the MSO and non-MSO mineral-exporting countries. However, it seems that it was really the high levels of currency overvaluation which may be behind the decline in exporting from other sectors. A high level of currency overvaluation is the combination of a fixed exchange rate with a depreciating currency on the parallel market, but which is not allowed to depreciate on the market. These levels were only relatively low in countries with the CFA franc.[24] The levels of currency overvaluation (and its associated story of currency depreciation of the parallel currency markets) in these mineral- or oil-exporting countries should be a surprise given the expectations of the Dutch Disease. But as discussed elsewhere, a currency overvaluation would have a similar effect on rival exports as the amount of money paid to exporters in local currency would be greatly diminished – and it would have a similar effect on exports as would currency appreciation for exporters who are remunerated in local currency.

Thus, we see similar outcomes as those predicted by the Dutch Disease, but with a different cause: levels of currency overvaluation. Importantly, these levels were always much higher for the MSO-1 countries than the non-MSO-1 countries, though differences were even more extreme between the MSO-2 countries and the non-MSO-2 countries. This appeared whether the categories were combined or individual. Here is where the difference between MSO-1 and MSO-2 seemed the most significant. Any MSO seems to be associated with much higher levels of currency overvaluation.

Likewise, in terms of levels of investment, MSO countries, either 1 or 2, always had lower levels of investment, measured either in per capita terms or as a percentage of GDP. So, one of the primary movers in development, that is, investment, was found to be lower for nations where the state owned the major oil or mining sector, or if they owned most of the capital-intensive industries, compared with other oil- or mineral-exporting nations. This is ironic because one of the basic justifications for nationalization of multinational corporations (MNCs) mineral or oil sectors was to increase domestic investment for development and to stop MNCs from underdeveloping third world nations by extracting surpluses from these nations and repatriating these profits.

The story for debt is mixed, and a clear difference between oil- and mineral-exporting emerges. On the one hand, both the combined cases and the mineral-exporting countries show higher levels of debt for MSO-1 and MSO-2 countries, and these results were significant. However, for just oil, the MSO-1 oil-exporting countries had lower levels of debt as a percentage of GDP or as a percentage of exports, though only the former was significant at 95%. MSO-2 countries which exported oil, returned to having significantly higher levels of debt as a percentage of GDP, but these two categories of countries were in a virtual tie for levels of debt as a percentage of exports, though with very slightly lower levels. But, for the combined categories, or for just mining nations, MSO-1 and MSO-2 countries had higher levels of debt by either measure. Thus, much of the debt load may have been incurred through mining or industrial sectors concerns (or the international markets lent them less money).

The differences in levels of intrastate violence mostly showed a story of worse outcomes in MSO countries, though it seems this difference was most stark between MSO-1 oil countries than non-MSO-1 oil countries. In every case, the level of intrastate conflict was usually about twice as high (or higher). For the mineral-only country comparisons (Table 2.3) the differences became insignificant (90% for MSO-1 and non-MSO-1, and insignificant for MSO-2 and non-MSO-2).

The results for political and civil rights were more complicated. In the case of mineral-exporting countries, or in the combined categories, countries with MSO (1 or 2) had statistically lower levels of political and civil rights. In the case of oil, no statistically significant results emerged. So, the various impacts of oil upon the political economy of these nations might be more uniform and less driven by MSO. These finding are consistent with Ross': in terms of averages, both categories were rated as not free, though only just under partially free (5.5 or higher moves to not free).[25] By contrast, during the Cold War, and looking at 24 MSO-2 and non-MSO-2 (thus including MSO industries and mining) countries, non-MSO countries had significantly lower levels of multiparty regimes or political and civil rights.[26]

So, can this analysis prove that no resource curse occurred for countries without MSO of oil or mineral? Since we only examined differences among countries with significant mineral- or oil-exporting sectors, this conclusion cannot be reached. However, when looking at specific variables predicted to be part of the resource curse, we see, especially in the case of the minerals, that when the state had MSO of their mineral or oil export sector, these variables were nearly always much stronger or worse. In only a few instances was this not the case. The non-MSO countries were better off or equal to in regard to the key variables of the MSO countries. In addition, this finding was mostly supported by the oil-exporting countries. Only in the case of debt service for oil exporters, did a developmental indicator of importance move in the opposite direction in a significant way.

In sum, countries with MSO of minerals or oil appear to have experienced worse economic resource curse effects from 1966 to 2000. In each match, a significant difference has been found between oil- and mineral-exporting countries along the predictors of MSO. If the resource curse is independent of ownership, any findings should be random, occasional, or insignificant.

Next, we turn to look within case studies to see more details about the particular variables within oil-exporting countries first, then within mining countries. This ought to provide more control and understanding of the context of these variables. Some developmental elements are discussed as background associated with oil and mining sectors, though only insofar as they are common across cases. Moreover, by looking at time trends in each case instead of just a cross section, more inferences can be drawn, even as the cross section gives us prima facie evidence for the hypothesis.

Notes

1 Each included country had been colonized (aside from Liberia), became independent between 1960 and 1974, has "African culture," had low levels of industrialization, wealth, and education at the time of independence, and would be in the periphery of North–South relations. However, the units of analysis are not individual countries but groups of countries within a region sharing a common attribute.
2 The effects are held to be the result of both direct and indirect impacts of MSO, e.g., poor policies, poor management, and the politicization of the sectors associated with such ownership. See Quinn (2002) for policy effects of ownership in SSA during the Cold War.
3 A country is coded as a mineral or oil country if 30% or more of its exports for most years for either minerals or oil. Countries are included when they become a major oil or mineral producer. If, however, the exports fall below 15% for three or more years, they are no longer considered to be a major exporter. Sources include *Africa South of the Sahara* (various years). The levels of exports were taken from UN Commodity Trade Statistics Database (UNCTAD). (See https://comtrade.un.org.data/) Oil was SITC3. Minerals were SITC 27, 28, 68, 667, and 971. Each (either fuels (3) or summed minerals (27, 28, 68, 667, 971)) became the numerator and total exports (to world) was the denominator. Where these data were not available, minerals or oil were divided by total exports from *Africa South of the Sahara* (various years). If countries had large exports, but if *Africa South of the Sahara* did not have these exports listed among the top exports, they were excluded as they could have been re-exports or smuggled – and this raises different questions.
4 See, for example, van de Walle (2001) and Quinn (2016) for why things might be different after the end of Cold War.
5 Transparency International was only begun in 1995 and its African data was quite limited prior to 2000. Also, control of corruption for the World Bank only begins in 1996.
6 Bates (1981), World Bank (1989). For ties to MSO, see Quinn (2002).
7 Sachs and Warner (1995).
8 For example, see (Mauro 1995). Also see the discussion in Chapter 1 for view (and references) concerning the effect of investment on development.
9 Quinn (1993, 1999, 2002).
10 If it only had MSO of industry but not major oil or mineral export sector, it would not be included in this study. For such countries, see Quinn (2002).
11 Countries which were coded as having majority state ownership of oil or mining for most of the period were Angola, Congo, DRC, Mauritania, Nigeria, Sierra Leone, Togo, and Zambia. All other included countries were listed as not majority state-owned. Countries with MSO of industries but with minority state ownership in oil or mining were Republic of Congo and Guinea.
12 Quinn (1993, 2002) had them coded together in earlier work, which did not specifically identify, but included, mining and oil.
13 Feenstra, Inklaar, and Timmer (2015) [Penn World Tables 9.1]; variable names are GDP per capita, chain, growth chain, grgdpch.
14 World Bank (2002).
15 Although population came from Feenstra, Inklaar and Timmer (2015).
16 World Bank (2002).
17 Unless specified otherwise, real exchange rates come from Darvas (2021).
18 World Bank (n.d.).

19 Gleditsch, Wallensteen, Eriksson, Sollenberg, and Strand (2002). Data from Uppsala Conflict Data Program was also estimated, with no differences in findings. Years with conflict were summed through the period. Data was estimated with and without Rwanda with no differences in findings.
20 Since so much of the period was without mining post-1974, Rwanda was dropped after that date.
21 Privatization for most of the region really began about 1990, but most large-scale privatization was carried out post-2000. Few privatizations of oil or mining have been done at all, with the exception of mining in Ghana and Zambia. For privatization trends, see Nellis (2008), Quinn (2016), and Craig (2002).
22 Since there are only two measures on MSO (1 and 0), we use t-test instead of ANOVA.
23 They could also have MSO of industries, but just major export sector is enough to be MSO-1.
24 See the next two chapters about this currency union.
25 Ross (2012).
26 Quinn (1993, 1999).

References

Africa South of the Sahara. Various Years. Various Countries. New York: Europa Publications.

Bates, Robert H. 1981. *Market and States in Tropical Africa: The Political Basis of Agricultural Policies*. Los Angeles: University of California Press. https://correlatesofwar.org/data-sets/cow-war/

Craig, John. 2002. "Privatisation and Indigenous Ownership: Evidence from Africa." *Annals of Public and Cooperative Economics* 73(4): 559–576.

Darvas, Zsolt. 2021. "Timely Measurement of Real Effective Exchange Rates." Working Paper 2021/15, 23 December.

Feenstra, Robert C., Robert Inklaar and Marcel P. Timmer. 2015. "The Next Generation of the Penn World Table" *American Economic Review*, 105(10), 3150-3182, available for download at www.ggdc.net/pwt

Gleditsch, Nils Petter, Peter Wallensteen, Mikael Eriksson, Margareta Sollenberg, and Håvard Strand. 2002. "Armed Conflict 1946–2001: A New Dataset." *Journal of Peace Research* 39(5).

Mauro, Paolo. 1995. "Corruption and Growth." *Quarterly Journal of Economics* 110(3): 681–712.

Nellis, John. 2008. "Privatization in Africa: What Has Happened? What Is to Be Done?" In Gerard Roland, ed., *Privatization: Successes and Failures*. New York: Columbia University Press, 109–135.

Quinn, John J. 1993. "The Impact of State Ownership of Resources on Economic and Political Development in Sub-Saharan Africa." *Ufahamu* 21(1&2): 60–79.

Quinn, John J. 1999. "The Managerial Bourgeoisie: Capital Accumulation, Development and Democracy." In David G. Becker and Richard L. Sklar, eds., *Postimperialism and World Politics*. Westport: Praeger, 219–252.

Quinn, John James. 2002. *The Road Oft Traveled: Development Policies and Majority State Ownership of Industry in Africa*. Westport: Praeger.

Quinn, John James. 2016. *Global Geopolitical Power and African Political and Economic Institutions: When Elephants Fight*. Lanham: Lexington Books.

Ross, Michael L. 2012. *The Oil Curse: How Petroleum Wealth Shapes the Development of Nations*. Princeton: Princeton University Press.

Sachs, Jeffrey D. and Andrew M. Warner. 1995. "Natural Resource Abundance and Economic Growth." NBER Working Paper No. W5398, December. http://ssrn.com/abstract=225459

Sarkees, Meredith Reid and Frank Wayman. 2010. *Resort to War: 1816–2007.* Washington DC: CQ Press.

Transparency International: The Global Coalition against Corruption. 2024. www.transparency.orgUnited Nations Commodity Trade Statistics Database. n.d. http://comtrade.un.org/db/dqQuickQuery.aspx.

van de Walle, Nicolas. 2001. *African Economies and the Politics of Permanent Crisis: 1979–1999.* Cambridge: Cambridge University Press.

World Bank. 2002. *World Bank Africa Database CDROM.*

World Bank. n.d. "Worldwide Governance Indicators." https://info.worldbank.org/governance/wgi/#home

3 Oil Exporting, Majority State Ownership, and Resource Curse Outcomes in Paired Case Studies

> Oil creates the illusion of a completely changed life, life without work, life for free. Oil is a resource that anaesthetises thought, blurs vision, corrupts.
>
> —Ryszard Kapuściński, Shah of Shahs

> Formula for success: rise early, work hard, strike oil.
>
> —J. Paul Getty

Why should scholars be interested in studying the role of oil in Africa? First, petroleum is one of the world's largest resources: in 2022, the crude oil market represented around $2.7 trillion, and it was larger than all mining sectors combined.[1] In the same year, petroleum and its associated products constituted over 14.2% of all traded commodities.[2] Internationally, the number of oil-producing countries has increased recently, despite rising concerns about the effect of hydrocarbon usage on the larger environment. Over 100 countries produce oil, though five countries combined account for over half of the world's oil: the US, Russia, Saudi Arabia, Iraq, and Canada.[3]

Second, oil and gas production are becoming increasingly important in and for Africa. Countries in sub-Saharan Africa that have recently produced at least $100 per capita from oil include these: Equatorial Guinea, Gabon, Angola, Congo Republic, Nigeria, Sudan, Chad, and Cameroon.[4] Countries that had met this goal for over two-thirds of their time after independence and during the Cold War include Nigeria, Angola, Congo Republic, Gabon, and Cameroon.[5] Looking at production unweighted by population, the ten largest producers in Africa in 2017 were Nigeria (113 MT), Angola (88.7 MT), Congo (Republic) (14.5 MT), Equatorial Guinea (13.5 MT), Gabon (11.6 MT), South Sudan (7.3 MT), Sudan (5.2 MT), Ghana (5.0 MT), Chad (4.1 MT), and Cameroon (3.7 MT).[6] Equatorial Guinea, Sudan (and South Sudan), Ghana, and Chad are relatively new to exporting significant amounts of oil.

Third, more geopolitically powerful nations are starting to pay attention to African oil production. America has become interested in lessening its dependence

DOI: 10.4324/9780429423390-3

upon Middle Eastern oil, and importing more from Africa may serve this purpose. Much of this African oil is brought to the US for refining. In fact, between 2001 and 2013, 90% of US imports from Africa included unrefined petroleum.[7] China, too, has increased interest in and demand for African oil.[8]

Fourth, quite a lot of African oil is what is called sweet crude, which makes it of strong interest to the petroleum industry. Sweet crude is easier to refine, which decreases associated costs of production. In addition, most of Africa's crude oil is low in sulfur, which means that it is preferred in industrialized countries that have stiffer environmental regulations to meet.[9] Moreover, many MNCs prefer African oil since so much of it is found offshore; this plays into the strengths of international companies, given their lead in technology for deepwater exploration. Offshore production also lessens political risk associated with violence or civil strife that could negatively affect production in the developing world.[10]

State Ownership of Oil: In Africa and Elsewhere

Most oil sectors in developing countries have been majority state-owned.[11] Internationally, state-owned oil companies control over 73% of oil reserves and 61% of production, over 80% of all oil reserves are in government hands, and around 75% of the biggest 20 oil companies are state-owned national oil companies (NOCs).[12] This trend began in the 1960s, but it really accelerated in the 1970s. Aside from the US, Canada, and centrally planned economies, "from 1963 to 1975 public sector control in the oil industry rose from 9 percent to 62 percent in production, from 14 percent to 24 percent in refining, and from 11 percent to 21 percent in marketing."[13]

In addition, the OPEC nations, which have controlled around 69.3% or more of known reserves, have NOCs associated with production and distribution.[14] OPEC was created in an attempt to wrest control of oil prices and production away from large multinational oil companies, and most countries in OPEC have nationalized their oil industries. With the creation of OPEC, there was a gentlemen's agreement that members would have a NOC to have state involvement in decisions concerning oil and its production.[15] In the 1970s, national oil companies (which are usually majority or fully state-owned) were more prevalent, but they started to wane in the late 1990s.[16] African nations that belonged to OPEC during the Cold War include Nigeria and Gabon.[17] Only Nigeria was both a major producer as well as a long-term OPEC member.[18] Whether countries were members of OPEC or not, most had a national oil company, even if not majority state-owned. Nigeria formed the Nigerian National Oil Corporation (NNOC) in 1971, and Angola formed Sociedad Nacional de Combustíveis de Angola (SONANGOL) in 1976.[19] Gabon was late creating its own national oil group, the Gabon Oil Company (GOC), which it only did in 2011.

Both Angola and Nigeria have had majority state ownership (MSO) for most of the Cold War period and beyond. Cameroon and Gabon have not had MSO of their oil sector during any of this time. The Republic of the Congo is an interesting case because it would be classified MSO because it had MSO of most of its industries postindependence, though it did not have majority state control of its oil sector. In the former French colonies, continued close ties to France in the postindependence period may have played a role in this sector not being nationalized. Of the more recent producers of oil, Sudan, South Sudan, Ghana, and Equatorial Guinea, none has had MSO of the oil sector, even if some have NOCs working alongside international oil companies.[20]

Developmental Impacts of Oil and Gas and Majority State Ownership

In order to compare the developmental experiences of the cases, four oil-exporting countries are chosen: two with MSO of their oil sectors, and two with less than MSO of their oil sectors. These countries' experiences with oil will be overviewed along with their degree of state ownership. Then the developmental outcomes usually associated with the resource curse will be explored case by case and by comparing MSO oil countries to non-MSO oil countries.

As in Chapter 2, the data will be examined from 1966 (or after independence if later) through 2000.[21] This means that the period studied is before most of the privatization of the largest state enterprises that occurred post 2000. Although some significant effects of the international financial institutions (IFIs) occurred prior to 2000, most of the largest changes in trends were evident after 2000.[22] Likewise, Ross suggested that many of these resource curse effects were strongest during the Cold War period.

Majority State-Ownership Cases/ Majority State Ownership of Oil

Angola: Existence of a Major Oil Exporter

Angola is sub-Saharan Africa's second largest petroleum exporter. This sector first began its importance to Angola in 1955, when the Belgian company Petrofina discovered oil. This company was reorganized in 1966 as Fina Petróleos de Angola (PETRANGOL), with joint Angolan government and Petrofina ownership. (It needs to be remembered that Angola was still a colony at this time.) The oil sector expanded greatly in 1966 with the discovery of oil offshore at Cabinda, and by 1973 oil became Angola's main export.[23]

The petroleum sector grew rapidly following Angola's independence in 1975. In 1976, SONANGOL was created to work with and manage all petroleum production and distribution. By 1978, oil had come to represent 74% of exports and 38.1% of government revenue.[24] Through 1986, its importance continued, providing 95% of total exports and accounting for 35% of GDP as well as 40% of state revenues. By 2000, the importance of petroleum to the Angolan economy was still evident, with 90% of total oil exports accounting for 40% of GDP and 80% of state revenues.[25] According to the US Energy Information Agency (EIA), Angola has approximately 9.5 billion barrels of proved crude oil reserves.[26] In terms of oil production, in 1980, Angola produced 150 TBPD (thousand barrels per day), which grew steadily until 2000, when it reached 746 TBPD.[27]

Majority State Ownership

Angola began its independence in 1975 as an Afro-Marxist regime, and it began to nationalize much of its economy. The choice to nationalize was overdetermined: not only did the early leaders have a strong commitment to Marxism-Leninism, but also most of the Portuguese population (including managers and workers) fled soon after independence.[28] The state control over the economy was enormous: over 85% of industrial units and nearly all farms and plantations came under state control, including the nationalization of the petroleum sector.[29] The parastatal SONANGOL was established in 1976, and the petroleum law of 1978 mandated that the state was to be the sole owner of all of the country's petroleum deposits, with SONANGOL as the only concessionaire for oil development or exploration.[30]

SONANGOL was to manage all fuel production and distribution and to have at least 51% ownership within all joint ventures, though daily operations would be managed by foreign companies. To attract investment by foreign oil companies, SONANGOL split the petrol fields into 13 "exploration blocks" in which foreign interests could have a stake under production-sharing arrangements.

In 1991, with the end of the Cold War, Angola formally abandoned Marxism-Leninism and moved toward allowing some joint ventures to be less than majority state-owned.[31] Nonetheless, SONANGOL remains majority state-owned and is still the sole concessionaire for oil ownership. It can work with companies either in a joint venture with foreign companies or by granting them production-sharing arrangements (PSAs) (sometimes with majority government ownership of the joint venture, but not always). Although the PSAs left formal institutional ownership of the oil to Angola, the terms could be written so that the effective terms were similar to those of old rights of concessions. In 1992, one of the major joint ventures had a decline in the level of state ownership to 41% when SONANGOL sold 10% of its share to Elf-Aquitaine in the Cabgoc fields (this field provides approximately two-thirds of total output).[32] Since that time, more offshore blocs have featured less than MSO, some with only 20%, some with none.[33] Nonetheless, SONANGOL continues to own 100% of some other oil fields and 51% or more of all onshore joint ventures. Even with MSO, the private sector and foreign investors now have more managerial and operational control, usually through PSAs which were put into place to draw more foreign direct investment (FDI).[34]

Nigeria: Existence of a Major Oil Exporter

Oil is an extremely important sector for Nigeria. For most years of its independence, it has been the largest exporter of oil in sub-Saharan Africa, and it has usually been the fifth largest in OPEC. Oil was first discovered in 1956, and by 1970, oil represented 49.8% of all exports. From 1974 onwards, oil represented over 90% of export earnings. In 1983, Nigeria produced 1,246 TBPD and saw a slow and steady increase in production through 2000, when it saw a production level of 2,169 TBPD. Nigeria has both onshore and offshore production, mostly located near the Niger Delta. At the end of 2000, the economic contributions of oil accounted for

97% of export earnings, 20% of GDP, and more than 70% of government revenue. Its production levels averaged 1,838 TBPD between 1973 and 2000.[35] It is believed that Nigeria has about 37 billion barrels of proved oil reserves, the most in sub-Saharan Africa.[36]

Majority State Ownership

Following the first discoveries in 1956, petroleum in the Niger River delta was originally commercialized by Shell-BP, which began production in 1958. From 1960 to 1970, exploration and extraction rights were contracted through foreign companies.[37] In 1971, the state created the NNOC to have government as part owners in the concessions of foreign companies. In 1972, the Nigerian Enterprises Promotion Decree required that the state be granted 51% ownership in key sectors, especially petroleum.[38] Following the merger of the NNOC and the Ministry of Petroleum Resources, the Nigerian National Petroleum Corporation (NNPC) was formed in 1977 and sought to increase Nigerian state shareholding.[39] According to these terms, the "NNPC had 60% interest in the operations of Agip-Phillips, Elf-Aquitaine, Gulf, Mobil, Texaco and Pan Ocean, and had an 80% share in Shell (which accounts for one-half of total production)."[40] In 1989 and 1993, Nigeria sold small parts of their petroleum companies. For example, in 1993, NNCP sold part of the fields that had been nationalized from the British and given to other private companies. Nonetheless, most of the sector remained in state hands.[41]

Although the government announced the possibility of divesting major portions of its typical majority state-owned joint venture partnerships and choosing instead to seek production-sharing agreements, this drew much political fire. Most onshore production was in joint venture, with the NNPC having majority shares, while offshore exploration tends to be production-sharing agreements.[42] Some agreements were announced in 1999, but none had emerged in production by 2000. In addition, Jones Luong and Weinthal code Nigeria as majority state-owned for the whole time.[43]

Cameroon: Existence of a Major Oil Exporter

Beginning in 1977, four oil fields controlled by the French oil company Elf (now part of Total) began to produce, and petroleum grew to be the nation's principal export by 1980. In 1982, oil represented 43.1% of export earnings and 15.3% of GDP.[44] Oil production as a percentage of all exports grew rapidly during this period, until a significant fall in oil prices in 1985. In some years, the levels of oil as a percentage of exports dropped below 30%, but not by much or not for long. For example, in 1999, petroleum exports only accounted for 29.3%. However, from 1995 to 2000, fuel as an average of exports was 40.5%.

Look at Cameroon's oil production overall, it climbed from 1977 to 1985, when it hit a peak of 185 TBPD.[45] From 1985 to 1989, a decrease in production was evident, when it hit only 170 TBPD. Then from 1990 to 1994, production decreased to 108 TBPD, where it either plateaued or decreased. From 1997 to 2000, production continued to decrease to 85 TBPD in 2000. Nonetheless, Cameroon was a significant oil exporter for enough years to keep it in the study.

Less Than Majority State Ownership

Through maintaining a cautious growth rate of state participation in the economy, Cameroon has not sought to nationalize large parts of the economy. In 1982, Cameroon created the state corporation, Société Nationale des Hydrocarbures (SNH), which obtained a 20% stake in all petroleum-producing companies as well as joining companies in some joint ventures, including with Total, Pecten and Perenco.[46] Most production has been in joint ventures, with international oil companies holding a majority share of the joint venture.[47]

Since SNH had 50% of the joint venture, and 20% of the International Oil Company, some have suggested that therefore Cameroon has 60%: "SNH equity shares include participation in the Operating Committee of joint ventures and on the Board of directors of the IOC."[48] However, if we look at voting and decision-making, the government's 20% share of the larger company is not sufficient to force a decision against the interests of the majority shareholders at this level, nor could the 50% ownership of the joint venture result in this outcome at the other level. The ownership levels do not aggregate to a majority vote at either level of governance. Therefore, it is logical to code Cameroon as having less than majority share of this sector. Jones Luong and Weinthal also coded Cameroon's oil industry as foreign and privately owned from 1964 onwards.[49]

Gabon: Existence of a Major Oil Exporter

Gabon was for many years the third largest producer of petroleum in sub-Saharan Africa. The growth in the petroleum industry began in 1967 with the opening of the Gamba-Ivinga offshore oil deposit. In 1980, the petroleum sector's share of GDP reached 40.4% and represented 80.9% of export earnings. Continuing to 1985, the petroleum sector accounted for 83% of total export earnings, 40% of GDP, and 65% of state revenues. Between 1980 and 1989, its average production was 166.2 TBPD. Between 1989 and 1997, its growth in production was quite high, reaching its peak of 370 TBPD.[50] This is reflected in other data. For example, in 2002, the petroleum sector contributed 78.7% of total export revenues and 40.8% of GDP. More recently, Gabon ranked among the top five crude oil producers in sub-Saharan Africa. It reached peak oil production in 1997, with crude oil production at 370 TBPD. Production declined to about 315 TBPD by 2000.[51]

Less Than Majority State Ownership

Although exploitation of the oil fields began in 1956, significant expansion of the sector did not occur until the late 1960s. The primary producer was originally Elf-Gabon, which was a 25/75% joint venture between the state of Gabon and Elf-Aquitaine (now part of Total). In 1962, a mining code stated that the state was entitled to a 25% equity stake in any petroleum production venture.[52] Following the opening of the Rabi-Kounga fields, which was operated in association with Elf-Gabon and Amerada-Hess, Shell-Gabon became the biggest producer in 1993. In 1995, Energy Africa (a South African company) bought 40% interest in three fields bordering the Rabi-Kounga as well as several smaller offshore interests. Despite Gabon having had a national oil company, Société Nationale Petroliére Gabonaise, until 1987, it did not require MSO of companies operating in Gabon.[53] Since a law passed in 1984, all oil production is owned by the state, but private companies are contracted to extract the oil through a production-sharing contract.[54] Gabon is coded as not majority state-owned. As support, Jones Luong and Weinthal characterized Gabon's oil industry as foreign and privately owned from 1964 onwards.[55]

Resource Curse Outcomes

Growth

Angola had experienced relatively low growth for all of its postindependence years. During the postindependence/Cold War period (or from 1975 to 1989), it experienced an average *negative* 2.8% growth, which included the period of soaring prices for OPEC from 1979 to 1985.[56] Extending to 2000, its average growth rate was *negative* 1.8%. Similarly, Nigeria experienced poor growth. From 1966 until the end of the Cold War, its average per capita GDP growth was *negative* 3.66%, and from 1966 to 2000, it was *negative* 2.5%.

Cameroon's growth levels from 1966 to the end of the Cold War averaged slow but positive growth, at 2.35%.[57] In addition, from 1966 to 2000, its average per capital GDP growth rate was 1.6%. Gabon experienced a 3.6% (positive) per capita growth rate from 1966 to 1989; and from 1966 to 2000, it had a growth rate of 2.93%.

Returning to the main idea of the resource curse, we should remember that during the Cold War (as well as through 2000), both Angola and Nigeria had *negative* average levels of growth, while Cameroon and Gabon had positive levels (even if low). Negative growth clearly has enormously worse implications for development than low, but positive, growth.

Incomes/Wealth

During this period and looking at levels of wealth for these four countries during the Cold War, we see that Gabon had the largest per capita income at $8,429 (measured in 2011 dollars).[58] By the end of 2000, Gabon had an average of nearly $10,000 per capita (in 2011 dollars).

Nigeria had the second highest average wealth during the Cold War, at $4,547. Incomes dropped slowly from 1977 ($6,849) onwards, and then precipitously after 1985 to a low of $410 in 1998. Thus, its income in 1998 was only around 6% of what it had been 21 years earlier. In fact, between 1986 and 2000, the average income in Nigeria was $694.70. In 2000, however, its income was $764 per person.

Angola began with $3,877 in 1975, and its average during the Cold War period was $3,040 (which was lower than at independence). Thus, its income steadily fell through 1995, with an uptick until 1996, and then a plateau around $2,700 for several years, until 2000 saw a drop to around $2,300. The average level of income from 1975 to 2000 was $3,820. In 2000, Angola's per capita income was $2,274.

Cameroon's overall average per capita income level during the Cold War was $2,135. It began in 1966 with a per capita GDP of $1,629; and by 2000, it had climbed to $2,553. Like the other oil producers, it had slower, and sometimes even negative, growth between 1986 and 2000, but it did not experience as steep a decline.

Therefore, in terms of wealth (and growth) Gabon was clearly the richest during the whole period and experienced positive, but low, average growth. Although Cameroon started the lowest, it too had low, but positive, growth for most of the period. Despite having lower incomes than Angola and Nigeria for much of the period, by 2000, it had the second highest per capita income. Angola finished in 2000 with the third highest per capita incomes, but it had been higher than Cameroon for most of the period. Interestingly, Nigeria was nearly as rich as Gabon, until 1977, when negative growth rates pulled its level of wealth lower than the other three from 1986 onwards. Nigeria finished in 2000 with the lowest per capita incomes of the four. Thus, the MSO countries performed worse by these criteria than did the non-MSO countries.

Currency Appreciation

Part of the Dutch disease is the collapse of rival exporting economic sectors due to the currency appreciation associated with the booming mineral or oil sector. According to the theory, rival export sectors decline primarily because the appreciating currency makes their goods less competitive in other markets. Moreover, imports that could compete with domestically produced goods would be cheaper given the higher cost of domestic currency. This section examines the levels of currency appreciation in these countries. This section uses both the appreciation of the currency against the dollar (nominal) as well as the real exchange rate data where available.

Looking at Angola's currency set against the dollar, quite the opposite seems to have happened (at least looking at official exchange rates). With independence, Angola's currency, the kwanza, depreciated slightly for two years, (needing about 15% more kwanza to purchase a dollar in the second year than the first); however, a fixed exchange rate was introduced between 1978 and 1990.[59] Officially, no real currency appreciation (or depreciation) could have taken place. When the novo kwanza was introduced in 1990 and the fixed peg removed, it depreciated an average of 16% per year between 1990 and 1995. Inflation at the time was about 16%.[60] Then with the introduction of a new currency, the kwanza *readjusato* (1995–1999), the average *depreciation* against the dollar was 19.67% per year.

With the kwanza reestablished in 2000, the average depreciation was approximately 58.7% per year. The average annual percent growth of the CPI for those years was 716.5%.[61]

Looking at real exchange rate for Angola, the data appear to tell a different story. Angola's currency appreciated about 25% between 1975 and 1986, the time of the high prices of oil and strong OPEC pressures.[62] However, starting in 1987 to 1997, the *readjusato* depreciated an average of 6.4% over that period. From 1975 to 2000, its average appreciation was 7.6%, though clearly with a rising trend through 1986, and a decline until 1997, with a bump up in 1998–2000. This is closer to the predictions of the Dutch disease, though the implied upward rise was more a rise and fall associated with oil prices.

Looking at Nigeria's currency set against the dollar, we see a story more of currency depreciation than appreciation vis-à-vis the dollar, at least nominally. With the introduction of the naira in 1973 and until 1980, the percent change in exchange rates against the dollar showed only a slight depreciation of currency at 2.3%, though some years the exchange rate was fixed. Importantly, from 1973 to 1989, which was during the oil price boom, the average change per year was a depreciation against the dollar of 19.7% (officially). However, there was slight appreciation in the years 1978–80, at 5.2%. From 1990 to the present, the average depreciation per year was about 20.3%. Then from 2005 to 2008, the naira did appreciate against the dollar, but only for those years. These are lower numbers than Angola, but still, they represent official depreciation for most years. The annual percent growth of the CPI from 1975 to 1984 was 17.7%, and from 1985 to 1989 it was 23.2%.[63] By contrast, inflation for Nigeria from 1991 onwards was over 400%.[64]

Examining the real exchange rate data, we see Nigeria did have a slight increase in appreciation of its currency over this period. From 1967 to 1989, it appreciated by 1.4% on average. However, like Angola, it appreciated during the higher prices between 1973 and 1986 an average of 7.8%. However, this soon fell to an average depreciation of 20% between 1986 and 1993. For the longer period of 1966–2000, the average appreciation was only 5.4% (leaving out 2000 and the new denomination of bills). So here we do see some evidence of the real exchange rate appreciating, at around 5%.

Cameroon's currency mostly depreciated against the dollar. From 1966 to 2000, it experienced an average depreciation of 4.5% per year, but from 1967 to 1989, it was 1.8%. Although this level of depreciation is low, it is not *currency appreciation.* Cameroon's currency did have a brief period (1979–1981) where it appreciated against the dollar. The average appreciation from 1979 to 1981 was 4.9%, but for the next five years, it depreciated an average of 16.6% per year.

Looking at real exchange rates Cameroon had a slight appreciation in its currency, to the tune of 0.6% between 1970 and 1989. Taking this average through 2000, Cameroon's average appreciation was –0.4%, which is a very slight depreciation of its currency, on average. So, we see either the smallest appreciation or very slight depreciation for this currency during our period of study. We do not see a significant level of appreciation.

Since Cameroon has been a member of the Central African Economic and Monetary Community (CEMAC—Communauté Économique et Monétaire de l'Afrique Centrale), politicians in Cameroon have not had direct control over the value of this currency.[65] CEMAC includes five other Central African nations, and France backs the currency, (the CFA franc), and it is fully convertible. Membership in the franc zone prevented the manipulation of the exchange rate by the African elites, as France holds a veto of all major decisions affecting the currency.[66]

Like Cameroon, Gabon also was in the CEMAC currency union, and would have the same levels of currency appreciation, depreciation (of official exchange rates), or overvaluation vis-à-vis the dollar as Cameroon. Thus, the average currency depreciation of Gabon against the dollar was low. From 1966 to 2000, it was an average of 4.5% per year. During the Cold War period, it was 1.8% annual depreciation.

Using its real exchange rate, the index of real exchange rate for Gabon between 1964 and 1989 was 0.2% appreciation. Through 2000, this average was –0.87. These are incredibly low levels of appreciation, or even negative over these periods. We do not see evidence of significant changes in purchasing power predicted by the Dutch disease literature. But, again, our cases for non-MSO belonged to a common currency union. Regardless, significant increases in domestic prices in each period could have made the real exchange rate quite different.

Therefore, for official exchange rates, we see an overall depreciation of the currencies of these oil exporters vis-à-vis the dollar. And since oil is denominated in dollars, this is not an unreasonable measure to look at. Angola and Nigeria experienced quite a bit more depreciation of their currencies vis-à-vis the official exchange rate, on average, but neither was part of a currency union. So, both had autonomy with printing money and setting the price of their currency with pegs or their control over the supply of money. However, looking at real exchange rates for these two MSO countries, they experienced more appreciation during higher oil prices, and Angola appeared to have more overall appreciation than Nigeria.

Thus, there is some evidence that the appreciation of currency associated with the export of natural resources was more evident in the two MSO countries than in the non-MSO countries, according to these measures.

Currency Overvaluation

As discussed earlier in this work, an indirect measure of either currency appreciation or currency depreciation in countries with a pegged currency is currency overvaluation. This requires comparing official exchange rates to parallel market rates. Where the currency has appreciated even though it is pegged to the dollar, it will become more valuable on parallel markets and fewer of them will be needed to purchase dollars.[67] By contrast, a depreciation of the value of a pegged currency will lower its price on the parallel markets, which means more of the local currency is needed to purchase dollars, indicating currency overvaluation. Where the values align, parallel markets will be unlikely to emerge. Also as discussed in Chapter 1, currency overvaluation results in a lower level of remuneration in the local currency for exported goods, and a cheaper cost for foreign currency for those lucky enough to obtain this scarce hard currency. Any effects of real appreciation of the currency would be exaggerated by an additional increase in currency overvaluation for those are paid in local currency.

Looking at Angola, we see that it experienced an overvalued currency for most of its independence period.[68] The annual average of the ratio of the parallel exchange rate to official exchange rate from 1983 to 1994 was 34.85.[69] These numbers are quite high, as currency that had no divergence between the two would have a ratio of one. During this later period, the kwanza was quite overvalued. Given this level of overvaluation, and the implicit subsidy for imports for those able to obtain hard currency, the incentives to import were exceedingly high and those to export low.

Turning next to currency overvaluation and Nigeria, using available data, we see that in Nigeria the annual average of the ratio measuring currency overvaluation from 1975 to 1984 was approximately 2.09, which means the currency was overvalued by slightly more than twice.[70] From 1984 to 1989, the average ratio was 2.56; and from 1990 to 1998, it was 2.4. From 1978 to 2008, it averaged 2.39.

Looking at Cameroon and Gabon by these same measures, we find the ratio of parallel markets to official markets to be close to the ratio of one. Since both Cameroon and Gabon share the same currency, both will be examined at the same time. During the Cold War (and up until 1994), no large difference existed between black market rates and official rates for the CFA. Since the CFA monetary union had a currency that was convertible upon demand, and as it was backed by the French treasury, no significant or prolonged differences should have existed between official and unofficial markets. In fact, the average level of currency overvaluation of the CFA franc from 1978 to 1986 was under 1.9%. In addition, from 1978 to 1987, it was 2%. (1.02 was the ratio of unofficial to official.)

Using another metric, the World Bank argued that the currency was overvalued by 50% in the 1990s, but given the measurement of currency overvaluation as the ratio of black market to official markets, and with French convertibility, it would not show up in this measure.[71] Importantly, even if the CFA had been overvalued by 50%, this would clearly not be the result of an appreciating currency tied to natural export commodities. It would have been merely less currency overvaluation, in the face of currency depreciation against a peg. The largest depreciation of the CFA occurred after the death of Houphouët-Boigny, when the CFA had a 96% depreciation.[72] Even after 1994, the average depreciation was only 0.3%. This is not high, but, importantly, it is not currency appreciation as per the Dutch disease thesis.

In sum, the countries with the highest levels of currency overvaluation were those with MSO. Since both Cameroon and Gabon were in currency unions, we cannot know what the rates would have been had they had independent monetary policies. Though, we have to remember that either of these countries could have left the currency union. In other studies of MSO vs. non-MSO countries, and leaving out CFA countries, between 1966 and 1986, MSO countries had an average of about 211% currency overvaluation, and non-MSO countries had an average of about 38%.[73] Both showed overvalued currencies, though the MSO rates were much higher.

Diversification of the Non-Oil-Related Economy

The natural resource curse thesis suggests that other parts of the economy which export will fall away. We will examine aspects of manufacturing and agriculture to see to what degree these alternative sectors suffered, flourished, or merely endured at the time.

Manufacturing

In Angola, the average percent of manufacturing in GDP was low for most of the years, at least compared to the other three countries (data is missing for many years). Data show that it represented 3.97% of GDP from 1995 to 2000.[74] Earlier data is available for per capita output of manufacturing, and here Angola averaged $48 of value added in manufacturing per person between 1985 and 1989, even if this declined slightly to $46 averaging through 2000.[75] However, looking at another measure of manufacturing, Angola's average registered value added per capita was $35, though it began at $70 in 1985. This steadily declined, down to $21 by 1995/96. Then it slightly increased to $27 in 2000. This showed a steady decline in value added domestically for most of the period. In addition, we need to remember that beyond MSO of oil, most manufacturing in Angola had become majority state-owned soon after independence.

In terms of manufacturing exports (as a percentage of all exports) during the Cold War, the percentage began at about 11% for the early available data (1978–1981), but it began to fall thereafter. From 1986 to 2000, it averaged 2.2%. This clearly shows the economy moving away from the export of manufactured goods as predicted by the resource curse literature. In per capita terms, during the Cold War, Angola averaged $31 per person for exports of manufactured goods. However, from 1986 onwards, this number dropped to the high single digits, at an average of $8.40 per person.

For Nigeria, the average value added in manufacturing as a percentage of GDP began at a high of 20.3% in 1981 (first data), and held relatively steady through 2000, with an average of 19% for those years. In terms of per capita value added, Nigeria averaged about $11.86 during the Cold War period. It actually started and remained quite low: at around $7 per capita in 1996, rising to around $14, from 1990 through 2000.

As far as the exports of manufacturing goes, Nigeria had quite low numbers.[76] Less than 1% of its exports was comprised of manufactured goods. This could be a sign of import substitution industrialization rather than a lack of manufacturing per se. For the whole time through 2000, the average was about 0.7%. In terms of per capita value of manufactures exported, during the Cold War, Nigeria exported less than $1 per person per year, though this rose to $6.13 through 2000. This number was significantly lower than for the other counties.

In Cameroon, manufacturing value added averaged about 10.5% of GDP during the Cold War, increasing to 12.4% up through 2000. In per capita terms, during the Cold War, Cameroon averaged $65 value added per person. Unlike the two MSO countries just discussed, this value in Cameroon increased from around $30 and rose to an average above $100 from 1983 to 1985. This number would decline slightly to an average of $86 from 1986 to 2000. Most manufacturing in Cameroon involves the processing of agricultural goods and raw materials. Despite the fact that many firms were state-owned, private firms were allowed to compete.

In terms of the percentage of exports composed of manufacturing, this average in Cameroon during the Cold War was 8.9%. This average rose slightly to 9% through 2000. In per capita terms, manufacturing represented $17 per person in the Cold War and remained there, with an overall average of $17.54 overall. This is hardly an elevated level, but it is higher than Nigeria's and quite similar to Angola's overall average, and it did not decline over time as Angola's did.

In Gabon, its manufacturing value added as a percentage of GDP during the Cold War averaged about 6.2%, with this decreasing slightly to 5.6% up to 2000. However, as discussed above, this could reflect oil price changes affecting the overall denominator as much as productivity in manufacturing, so looking at per capita levels; it averaged $356 during the Cold War, which decreased slightly to $322 up through 2000. In per capita terms, Gabon averaged $268 in value added in industry, with a slight decline in value for most of the period, falling from around $270 to around $230. Nonetheless, these numbers were much higher than the other oil case study countries.

In terms of exports, Gabon averaged about 5% of its exports being comprised of manufactures through 1989, and 4% through 2000. In per capita terms, Gabon's exports were relatively high, averaging $131 per person during the Cold War, with an overall average of $199 through 2000.

In terms of exporting manufactured goods, which is more at the heart of the Dutch disease, here we see evidence of the resource curse predictions hitting Angola and Nigeria quite strongly. Angola showed a significant decline for most of this period, despite starting relatively strongly.[77] Its per capita exporting of manufactured goods also declined over time. Cameroon and Gabon seemed to have steady levels of manufacturing exports, even if they were not very high, though on a per capita basis, Gabon was quite high. Nigeria seems to be in a league of its own with very low levels of manufacturing as a percentage of its exports – never reaching 2% – and its per capita levels of manufacturing exported is even lower. Nigeria exported the least amount of manufactured goods, either in per capita terms or as a percentage of exports. It should be of note, however, that many of its industries were majority state-owned, some by the federal government and some by state governments.[78] This is consistent with the hypothesis that MSO makes the natural resource curse worse.

Agriculture

Agricultural exports should be part of the natural comparative advantage of most African states, especially with most countries having a relative abundance of land relative to both capital and people – with countries in the Great Lakes region as a partial exception.[79] Given the relative abundance of land relative to labor and capital in most of the region, the examination of agricultural exports is a reasonable place to look for Dutch disease effects.[80]

Like most countries in sub-Saharan Africa, Angola has much promise from its agricultural sector, even if only about 3% of its land has recently been cultivated due to poor infrastructure and unrest associated with civil war.[81] Nonetheless, around the time of the end of the Cold War, approximately 43% of Angolans worked in agriculture, through it came closer to 50% more recently with the end of the conflict.[82] In fact, most of Angola's population engages in subsistence agriculture.[83] During the Cold War, agriculture represented between 43 and 50% of gross domestic product.[84] In value added per capita, the average in Angola was just under $64. It was $93 per person in 1985 and fell to the low 30s in 1993/94. It rebounded slightly to right around $50 by the end of the 1990s, though it tells us a story mostly of decline of agriculture during the period.

In terms of exporting, Angola has clearly lost much of its ability to export agricultural products. Before the war, Angola had been one of the largest exporters of coffee and sisal. In fact, coffee had been the third largest export commodity, but after years of war, coffee is no longer a significant export.[85] Before the civil war, Angola was self-sufficient in food, aside from wheat.[86] For the period for which data is available (beginning in 1978), agriculture made up an average of 45% of merchandized exports for Angola in 1978/79, through dropping rapidly each year, to about just about 2% around 2000. Clearly, the emergence of oil as a major export played a decisive role in agriculture's relative decline – especially in years with high oil prices and/or high oil exports. In terms of value of agriculture exports, Angola experienced an annual average decrease in the value of total agricultural exports of –18.7% from 1975 to 1989.[87] In addition, from 1990 to 1997, it experienced an average decline in value of exports of –7.6% per year. Overall, from 1975 to 1997, the average value change in agricultural exports was –14.8%.

Looking at volume of agricultural exports (to take away potential issues of price fluctuation), Angola experienced an average 12.8% annual decline of agricultural exports between 1975 and 1980. They continued to experience a 14.2% average annual decline in food exports between 1980 and 1985, as well as a 12.5% annual decline from 1986 to 1988.[88] This would mean that from 1975 to 1988 Angola experienced an average decrease in the volume of agricultural exports of 15.7% per year. Looking at agriculture as a percentage of merchandized exports, Angola averaged less than half of a percent in 1978/79 when the data is first available. This number continued to decline, with an average of 0.1% from 1987 to 2018. In per capita terms, agricultural exports averaged about $1.25 per person up to 1989, and through 2000, the average dropped to $1. The overall average was about $0.50.[89]

In Nigeria's early independence history, agriculture produced over half of the GDP and more than three-fourths of its exports.[90] In fact, during the first decade after independence, Nigeria was the leading exporter of palm oil and palm oil products and the second largest exporter of cocoa as well as a leading exporter of cotton, groundnut, rubber, hides and skins.[91] However, between the rise of petroleum and Nigeria's pursuit of inward-oriented policies, its agricultural sector declined significantly. In fact, by the mid-1980s, Nigeria became heavily dependent upon food imports. Despite these falls in levels, agriculture remains important to most Nigerians: in 1990, about 50% of all employment was with agriculture. In terms of value added, from 1981 to 1989, Nigeria averaged about 18% of GDP, and up to 2000, this rose to about 21.3%. In per capita terms, Nigeria had an average value added per person of around $100 in the mid-1960s, which fell to around $65 in the early 1980s. This climbed back to between high and low 80s right to the end of 2000, resulting in an overall average was $87.56[92]

Looking at agricultural exports from Nigeria, we can see that the percent share of merchandized exports during the Cold War averaged 2.6% of exports. It started in 1966 at 10.6%, though this declined to less than 1% in the late 1980s. Extending to 2000, the average of agricultural exports as a percentage of overall exports was 2.1%. In per capita terms, the value of agriculture exported by Nigeria was $3.02 per person during the Cold War, and this declined to $2.50 through 2000.

The average change in the value of agricultural exports from 1975 to 1989 for Nigeria was about –3.8% per year. This trend changed direction and did turn positive from 1990 to 1997, with an average of 12.9%. By 1996, Nigerian exports were finally passing the value of 1980 exports. Looking at just volume and not price, agricultural exports from Nigeria experienced a 3% annual decline between 1975 and 1980. This decline was even larger from 1980 to 1985: it experienced an annual average decrease in the volume of agricultural exports of 17.2%. From 1986 to 1989, we did see the needle move in the opposite direction, even if it came nowhere near to prior levels, with an average annual increase of 1.8%.[93] This meant that during the Cold War, or from 1975 onwards, Nigeria experienced an average annual decline in the volume of agricultural exports of 7.7%

Agriculture in Cameroon has been an important aspect of its economy, and it is more diversified than many other countries. Export crops include coffee, cocoa, palm oil, bananas, and sugar cane.[94] With the privatization of a banana monopsony, Cameroon became a more important exporter of the crop. In addition, forest products have long been important and were normally second only to oil exports. From 1991 to 2000, approximately two-thirds of all workers were employed in the agricultural, forestry, or fishing sector. In terms of value added, during the Cold War, agriculture, forestry and fishing averaged 28.2% of the value added to its GDP. This declined slightly to 25.4% through 2000. In per capita terms, and in 1999 dollars, from 1966 to 2000, Cameroon averaged $236 per person in this sector. In 1966, it was $190, and by 2000, it was $286 per person. Cameroon was amazingly stable by these numbers, with a slight upward trajectory overall.

As a percentage of merchandized exports, agriculture in Cameroon seemed to be steady most of the years, averaging between 16% and 18% of exports. During the

Cold War, it was 16.6% and 17.6% through 2000. Measuring agricultural exports on a per capita basis, Cameroon averaged $33 during the Cold War, and $34 on average through 2000. Looking at the average change in the value of agricultural exports, Cameroon had an average growth or 3.4% per year from 1975 to 1989. From 1990 to 2000, this level was lower at an average growth in value per year of 0.5%. This resulted in an overall average from 1975 to 2000 of 2.4% growth in value per year.[95] By contrast, looking at volume of exports, we see that Cameroon experienced a slight decline in agricultural exports at an average of –0.15% from 1975 to 1989.

For Gabon, forestry is more important as an export than tradition agricultural crops.[96] In the late 1990s, over 75% of Gabon was covered by virgin forests.[97] The World Bank estimates that 20% of land is used for agriculture, and this number has not changed much from the 1960s. Timber has long been the second largest source of foreign earnings, even if manganese has been rising in importance. For example, by 2000, timber represented 12% of export earnings, while petroleum represented 80% and manganese nearly 4%.[98]

Agriculture provided employment for about 40% of Gabonese around the end of the Cold War. Even with so much of the population engaged in agriculture, this sector only represented about 8% of value added for the GDP. During the 1960s, the value added of GDP grew to 25% in 1966. This indicator dropped to about 13% in 1973, and then to about 5.5% in 2018.[99] Therefore, the average for the Cold War period was 28%, and 25% from 1966 to 2000. In per capita terms, from 1966 to 2000, Gabon had an average value added per capita in agriculture, forestry and fishing of $465, with a slight decline from 1980 (first year of data) from $590 to around 340 in 2000.[100]

In terms of exports, approximately 16% of Gabon's exports were raw agricultural exports during the Cold War period, which this dropped a bit to 14% through the year 2000. Using other measures of agricultural exports, Gabon had an average of $347 of agriculture exported per person from 1966 to 1989 and an average of $383 through 2000. In terms of percent change in value of agricultural exports, Gabon averaged an *increase* of 8.5% in the value of agricultural exports per year from 1975 to 1989.[101] Looking at this data through 1997, Gabon continued to have an average increase in value of agricultural exports of 8.4% per year. Looking at volume of exports during the Cold War, Gabon's volume of agricultural exports grew from 1975 to 1980 at an average rate of 12% per year. From 1981 to 1985, it declined an average of 3% per year, and from 1986 to 1988, it declined to an average of 11.5%. Therefore, during the Cold War, it had an average annual change of 1.7% increase in volume of agriculture, forestry or fishing exported.

During the Cold War period, and beyond, Cameroon and Gabon had a larger percent of their agricultural exports as a part of merchandized exports than either Angola or Nigeria. They also had higher per capita value added overall, with an average increase over time – quite the opposite of the Dutch disease predictions. They also had higher per capita exports in agriculture, which could show a viable agricultural sector. Of the two, Gabon clearly had the largest per capita value of exports; however, as percentage of exports, they were tied at about 16%. More of

Cameroon and Gabon economy's value came from agriculture compared with the two MSO countries. Nevertheless, in terms of keeping competing export sectors, the non-MSO countries were more successful in the agricultural sector, meaning that the purported Dutch disease effects were less severe.

Diversification of the Economy: Horizontal or Vertical Linkages to Oil

Refining Oil or Capturing Natural Gas

Although the natural resource curse story is one of declining traditional export markets, a deepening of the comparative advantage of the natural resource with upstream or downstream development could lessen the loss of other export markets with the creation of a new one. The refining of oil, as well as the capturing and exporting of natural gas, could join the new resource and comparative advantage for beneficial developmental ends for petroleum-producing nations.

Refining Oil

The refining of oil can be considered a vertical link with oil exporters' comparative advantage in the resource itself. Despite having low levels of capital or technology, MNCs could export out of their comparative advantage in this area and combine them with the host country's comparative advantage in having natural resources.

Despite being a major oil producer and despite having a refinery since the 1950s, Angola has imported refined petrol/gasoline to meet most of its needs. During the 1970s, Angola routinely exported 90% of its output as unprocessed crude, but 10% was held back as feedstock for the Luanda refinery.[102] Despite this one refinery, Angola imports over 80% of its refined fuel products.[103] Although Angola has some investment in upstream refining, in the early 2000s, it only had one refinery at Luanda, which can produce 65,000 bpd when operating efficiently.[104] The refinery was not majority state-owned (as of 1989), even if it was managed by SONANGOL. In addition, the price for the output of the refinery was subsidized by the state, leading to a reform recommendation by the World Bank in 1989.[105] Between 1985 and 2000, it averaged a production of 30,500 barrels a day (mb/d) of refined petroleum. This number rose steadily from 27 mb/d to the high 30s by 2000.[106] During the civil war, the refinery seemed to meet most domestic needs. With the end of the war, demand increased dramatically so it will likely not be able to meet rising demands.[107]

Unfortunately, many large clients of the refinery did not always pay their bills[108] (e.g., the army, cement manufacturers), given their ties to the political elite. In addition, the refinery itself was run as cost plus, which usually reduces incentives for efficiency. Incentives for improved efficiency were further eroded with sales having to go through SONANGOL, which enjoys a monopoly on both marketing and distribution of petroleum products in Angola.[109]

Nigeria has not diversified very much into oil refining enough to meet domestic needs – let alone enough to export. In 2015, it was estimated that they imported

223,400 barrels per day of refined petroleum products (esp. gasoline), the largest in sub-Saharan Africa.[110] In fact, the Nigerian National Petroleum Corporation imported approximately 90% of its gasoline needs.[111] By way of contrast, it was estimated that they exported 2,332 barrels a day of refined petroleum products. The government-owned NNPC has managed (and has 100% ownership in) four oil refineries and these facilities often run at less than 50% of full capacity.[112] In fact, around 40% seemed to be the top capacity, and some months registered 0%. Output was only 14.4% of potential capacity in 2014, which was down from 22% in 2013.[113] A lack of maintenance for more than a decade for these majority state-owned refineries was cited as the primary reason for the low capacity of output.[114] Overall, they averaged output of 226 mb/d between 1986 and 2000.[115]

Cameroon also built a refinery to help process oil in 1981, with its refinery in Limbe, and it was managed by SONARA, which is 66% owned by the Cameroonian government.[116] This refinery is only able to process lighter crudes, and it has been unable to refine some of the domestically produced oil. Between 1986 and 2000, it refined approximately 27,000 barrels per day, which is below the maximum output of the refinery, but it was above 50% of its total capacity.[117] Even so, Cameroon imported approximately 2,043 barrels per day of refined petroleum products in 1990, suggesting that domestic demand well exceeded local production.[118]

Gabon has one refinery that often runs below capacity (around 60%), and it capacity is estimated to be at 24,000 barrels a day.[119] This refinery, the Sogara (Société Raffinage du Gabon) refinery, which began production in 1967, is located at Port-Gentil and it is 25% state-owned.[120] According to one source, Gabon imported an average of 10,680 barrels per day in 2015.[121] Back in 1975, a second refinery was opened by Elf-Gabon on the same site and named the Compagnie Gabonaise de Raffinage (COGER). This would close within 10 years, in 1985 (when the prices of oil collapsed).[122] It was 30% owned by the government and 70% owned by Elf-Gabon.[123] Between 1986 and 2000, Gabon refined an average of 15,784 barrels a day.[124]

Thus, Nigeria had the most refineries and the most (potential) capacity, though the actual output of these refineries often ran below 50% of full capacity, and sometimes around 45%. Moreover, Nigeria imported over 90% of its refined fuel needs, which was often subsidized at great losses. Angola too usually had more relatively potential capacity, but their refineries also produced at only 40% of that which was possible. Moreover, it imported 80% of the needed refined fuel. Both Cameroon and Gabon only had one refinery, and Gabon had the lowest potential capacity for refining. Interestingly, both countries' refineries usually ran at an average of 60% capacity.

Natural Gas

The processing of natural gas for oil-producing countries could be seen as an extension of part of its comparative advantage. This is because natural gas often is extracted, or emerges, at the same time as petroleum is extracted. This gas has to be processed to remove impurities. Initially it was ignored or considered too costly to capture, so it has been vented or flared instead. Despite having low levels of capital or technology, MNCs could export their comparative advantage in these areas and combine them with the host country's comparative advantage in having that natural resource.

During the Cold War, Angola did not have liquid natural plants, and the first ones to be created were well after the Cold War. Angola first announced plans to create such plants were in 1998.[125] Most of their natural gas has been flared. The USEIA lists Angola with an average of 0 mb/d of natural gas from 1980 to 2000.[126]

Nigeria had quite a large reserve of natural gas, perhaps the largest in sub-Saharan Africa.[127] The first move to capture its natural gas came in 1989, when the company Nigeria LNG was commissioned to harness available natural gas in Nigeria (LNG is 49% owned by the state).[128] During the Cold War, however, no such production was available, and most of the natural gas associated with oil extraction was just flared. In fact, Nigeria has flared around 75% of the gas associated with oil production.[129]

Cameroon has only recently become involved with natural gas, and therefore it did not have any natural gas plants during the Cold War period or through 2000. Its first plans to build natural gas plants were begun in 2002.[130] Gabon does not have much capacity to use natural gas, and it either flares or reinjects 80% of natural gas produced as a byproduct.[131] Even still, natural gas does supply about 15% of domestic electricity needs.[132] For all of the countries involved, natural gas production does not seem like it was a practical concern during the Cold War period through the 2000s.

Investment, Debt, and Inflation

Investment

From 1976 to 1985, Angola's investment rate as a percentage of GDP was 5.6%.[133] In terms of gross domestic fixed investment, as a percentage of GDP, Angola averaged about 14.84% of its GDP in investment from 1985 to 1989.[134] On a per capita basis, from 1985 to 1989, its average was $132.70 (in 2011$). From 1985 to 2000, it had a similar, but slightly higher level at 18.32%. On a per capita basis, this rose to $142.9 per year through 2000.

Nigeria had an average level of fixed investment of 18.6% during the Cold War, with another source placing it at 17.8%.[135] Measured in per capita 2011 dollars, this averaged to $48.83. Including years through 2000, the average level of investment was similar at 19.04% and the per capita level average was $46.69.

Cameroon featured an average of 20.95% during the Cold War (1966–1989). From another source, from 1975 to 1986, it was 16.1%.[136] On a per capita basis, it was $219.66 (in 2011$). From 1966 to 2000, it was 19.52%, representing an average of $172.20 per person.

During the Cold War, Gabon had levels of gross domestic fixed investment of 40.45% between 1970 and 1989, yet another source placed it at 26.7% of GDP. Nonetheless, Gabon had quite high per capital investment: $2,169.73.[137] From

1970 to 2000, it was slightly lower at 35.23%, with also a lower per capita investment average of $1,682.73.

For this set of numbers, it is clear that the non-MSO countries had higher levels of gross domestic fixed investment as a percentage of GDP and on a per capita basis. Gabon's levels of investment were by far the greatest: they were more than double the levels for either Angola or Nigeria. Next in order would be Cameroon, even if its levels were only a few points higher for the measure of investment as a percentage of GDP, but its per capita levels were much higher than the two MSO countries. Angola and Nigeria were quite similar vis-à-vis the percentage of GDP, even if Angola had higher levels of investment per capita. The early arguments for nationalization were exactly to increase domestic investments that were being drained away by neocolonial powers – these policies seem to have had the opposite effect.

Debt

In terms of debt as a percentage of exports, Angola's levels during the Cold War (1980–89) were 147.8% of GDP. From 1990 to 2000, it increased to 245.7% of GDP. The overall percentage through 2000 was 202.9% of its GDP in debt stock. This number started low at 23.3% in 1980 and grew to 230.4 in 1989. Then it would grow and peak in 1993, and then decline to 130% in 2000. In terms of debt relative to GDP, it was 66.6% from 1980 to 1989, 168% from 1990 to 2000, and 131.6% from 1980 to 2000. This number also grew slowly from 44% in 1985 to 78.5% in 1989. This jumped to 174% in 1992, and then it rose to over 200% in 1993–1995. Debt as a percentage of GDP would stay in the 100s through 2000.

In Nigeria, the percentage of total debt relative to exports during the Cold War was 117%. In 1970, it was 62.4% and this rose to about 300% between 1985 and 1989. It remained in the high 200s and low 300s until 1996, when it leveled off at around 150–200%, for an average of 1990–2000 of 244.8%. Debt relative to GDP was lower: it started at about 7% of GDP in 1970 and rose to over 100% by 1985. During the Cold War period, the average was only 40.8%. By 1996, it lowered to just below 100% with the average of 105.8% from 1990 to 2000. For the period of 1970–2000, it averaged 63.9%.

In Cameroon, during the Cold War, the average level of debt relative to exports was 124.7% from 1970 to 1989. This began in 1970 with the debt representing nearly half of exports, at 47%, though this rose to 230% of exports by 1989. Looking at it as a percentage of GDP, Cameroon's debt was lower with an average of 30.2%. This began at around 10% in 1970 and rose to the high 30s in 1979 and stayed about there through 1988. From 1999, it jumped to nearly 60% and another jump to the hundreds occurred 1994–1998. The average debt to GDP level for Cameroon for 1998–2000 was 87.8%.

For Gabon, its total debt as a percentage of exports from 1970 to 1989 was 88.5%, which is the lowest of these four. The level in 1970 was 38% and this grew to 80% by 1989. It was not until 1986 that the number exceeded 100%. Moreover, from 1990 to 2000, the level of debt was 142%. The high point of this level was 1988, and it lessened gradually to 108% in 2000. Their debt as a percentage of GDP was also lower than the other comparison countries. The average from 1970 to 1989 was 47%, and the average from 1990 to 2000 was nearly 90%.

Even with the more mixed comparisons for debt, the best performer was a non-MSO country, and the worst was an MSO country. As a percentage of exports, and through 1989, Angola had the highest levels of debt, followed by Cameroon, then next Nigeria, and then Gabon. The actual distance between Nigeria and Cameroon was small, but this gap would widen in the 1990–2000 period. Looking at debt as a percentage of exports, Angola had the highest levels, then Nigeria, then Cameroon, and then Gabon. So, Gabon had consistently lower levels of debt by either criterion, Angola had the highest, and rank order of Nigeria and Cameroon flipped depending on the measure.

Inflation

Inflation was linked with MSO in prior studies, so we will look to see if it varies significantly by ownership for oil in particular. Inflation should be expected for exporters of natural resources as per the natural resource curse. Since so much inflation would be linked to oil prices, most major oil exporters should experience similar levels of inflation – if it is mostly driven by oil prices and not poor policy.

Angolan numbers were only available from the World Bank form 1991 onwards, though one source suggests that inflation for an average of former Portuguese colonies, including Angola was about 20%.[138] Looking at the period of 1990 and to 2000, inflation rates were high: starting with 81% in 1991, it increased to over 4,000% in 1996, and then it went to double digits through 2000; it averaged 1,042.3%, which was astronomical.[139] Unlike most countries in sub-Saharan Africa, Angola did not have any structural adjustment programs through 1996.[140]

During the Cold War, Nigeria's average level of inflation was 15.9%. For the years 1988 and 89, these rates were above 50%. Since the rate of inflation from 1990 to 2000 was 28.5%, the average for the longer period was 12.3%.

In Cameroon, from 1969 to 1989, the average level of inflation was about 9.2%, and this declined slightly through 2000, at an annual average of 7.9%. Gabon's levels were similar, but slightly lower than Cameroon's levels. During the Cold War (1966–1986), Gabon had an average annual inflation rate of nearly 7.8%, and this decreased slightly through 2000, at an average level of 6.4%.

We see with the inflation numbers that Angola and Nigeria had higher levels of inflation, with Angola's rates quite a bit higher than the other three cases, especially in the 1990s. Moreover, most African countries showed a significant improvement in their fiscal balance/levels of inflation/levels of currency overvaluation in the post-Cold War years, and we see this reflected in these countries, though Angola's turn was nearly a full ten years later.[141] Nonetheless, even during the Cold War, the non-MSO countries had single digit numbers, while Nigeria usually had double digit, and from the limited data we have from Angola, it was around 20% during the 1980s, and it also experienced three and four digit inflation rates for some years.

Sociopolitical Outcomes

Some suggest that other costs are associated with the natural resource curse which are more of a political or social nature, and less directly economic. As discussed in prior chapters, countries with consistently high levels of oil exports are associated with less democracy. We will look to see if MSO is correlated here. In addition, levels of civil conflict will also be examined.

Levels of Democracy/Freedom

Most countries in sub-Saharan Africa had been one-party states or no-party states (i.e., military) within a decade after independence until the end of the Cold War. With the new period, the region had a significant regionwide shift in political institutions in the early to late 1990s for several reasons. First, few countries had had significant development under these authoritarian regimes. Second, with the end of the Cold War, the ideological support for state socialism was greatly diminished. Third, with the dissolution of the USSR and the inward-looking period that followed, as well as with China undergoing significant, yet partial, economic liberalization, no powerful nations were left to be strong defenders of Communism or state socialism at the international level. In addition, the US appeared to be an unrivaled superpower, supporting increasing political and economic liberalization worldwide. Finally, the World Bank and IMF had become more active in linking economic aid to economic reforms, and Western nations became more active in linking political aid to political reform. Although the oil-producing countries often had the fewest increases in rights in the wake of these changes, all at least adopted the appearance of more liberal political regimes.

Angola

Unlike some other former Portuguese colonies, ideological and ethnic divisions fragmented the nationalist groups fighting for independence, with the Movimento Popular de Libertação de Angola (MPLA), the União Nacional para a Independência Total de Angola (UNITA), and the Frente Nacional de Libertação de Angola (FNLA) all struggling to rule after independence.[142] Angolan independence was birthed while a military struggle was fought by these three competing groups. Later, the MPLA, which was Marxist-Leninist in outlook, held the capital, and came to be recognized by the Organization of African Unity (OAU). However, a civil war raged for over 27 years, especially with UNITA, which held much of the hinterland. In each of the former Portuguese colonies, an Afro-Marxist regime established one-party states.[143]

The levels of political and civil rights for Angola have been an average of 6.2 (where above 5.5 is not free) from independence onwards. It was rated as a six or seven from independence until 1991, when there was a slight liberalization reflected when other parties were allowed to run with the adoption of multiparty elections. With its renunciation of Marxism-Leninism, Angola experienced a partial political liberalization and held founding multiparty elections in 1992.[144]

From 1992 until 2000, its average level of civil and political rights was 5.8, which places it still in the "not free" category of states, despite more electoral competition. Like many African countries that moved away from one-party states to one-party dominant states, it was led by the former dominant party.[145] In 1992, the MPLA obtained 58% of all seats.[146] The MPLA has continued to win a comfortable majority in all subsequent elections.[147]

Nigeria, also, did not emerge from decolonization with a single dominant political party. Three major political parties, each partially reflecting regional, ethnic, and religious differences and loyalties emerged.[148] Before the 1966 coup, the major parties were the Northern People's Congress (NPC), the National Council of Nigerian Citizens (NCNC), and the Action Group (AG). The NCNC began as a truly national party, but it would later become associated with Igbo aspirations and the Southeast. Each party would derive most of their support from the major ethnic groups in each region: NPC (Hausa/Fulani), AG (Yoruba), and NCNC (Igbo).[149]

Nigeria's political history has been marked by a seesaw back and forth between corrupt electoral systems and corrupt military rule. For the whole period for which Freedom House data is available (1972 onwards), Nigeria had an average of 4.6, which is considered to be partly free. However, within Nigeria we see more variance than with other countries. During the Cold War period, the average was 4.5, while for the post-Cold War period it was 4.55. From 1979 to 1983, it was rated as free (2.5), though from 1984 to 1989, and 1993 to 1997, it was mostly rated unfree. Otherwise, Nigeria was usually rated as partly free outside of these abovementioned periods. In 2000, however, it was coded at four, which was partly free.

Cameroon came into a one-party system soon after independence, as did most sub-Saharan African countries. All the same, it did have a brief period of multiparty competition until 1966.[150] From then until 1990, it was under one-party rule, with two longstanding rulers: first Ahmadou Ahidjo as president from 1961 to 1982, and Paul Biya ruled the single party regime until 1990. With the founding elections in 1990, Biya narrowly won, as did his former dominant party. With subsequent elections, Cameroon has since become a one-party dominant system with Biya at the helm through 2000. From 1972 to 1975, Cameroon was ranked at partly free at five for those years. By contrast, from 1976 onwards, Cameroon had been ranked as Not Free, hovering between 5.5 and 6.5.[151] For the whole period, its average level of political and civil rights was 5.9. During the Cold War, its average was 5.9. Since the end of the Cold War, its average has been six.

Gabon also became a de jure one-party state soon after independence. From 1960 to 1968, it was a one-party dominant system which became a one-party state from 1968 to 1990, when a constitutional amendment made Gabon a multiparty state again.[152] Elections were held for the legislature, but the chief executive's office was not contested until 1993. When these were held, the incumbent Bongo Ondimba won with 51.2% of the vote.[153] After the death of the longtime leader, elections were held and his son Ali Bongo Ondimba won the next election in 2009. The levels of freedoms in Gabon during the Cold War have been an average of six. From 1990 to 2009, its average level of freedom increased to 4.5 (which is party free). With the ascension of Bongo's son to the presidency from 2009 onwards, the average level of political and civil rights was 5.6, which is not free. Nonetheless, the entire post–Cold War average was 4.9 (which is partially free).

Therefore, these countries with significant oil resources were either partly free or not free during the Cold War, with the occasional exception of Nigeria, which alternated between brief periods of democracy and strong authoritarianism. None of the other oil-exporting countries was reliably free or party free for either period. In addition, countries that had oil-exporting sectors were found to be less likely to liberalize in the post-1990s Cold War period, with some variance.[154] Even though we see Angola liberalized a bit, it has remained rated as not free.[155] Nigeria remained about the same, as did Cameroon, but Gabon did move to partly free.

Civil Conflict

As discussed in prior chapters, mineral resources are often linked with an increase in civil violence and unrest, both as a target of acquisition for rebels and political outsiders, as well as a means of financing a rebellion, should they be the type of resource that can be captured by rebels. Also, with the general knowledge that democratic politics were less prevalent in countries with MSO, and that democracy is known to reduce the likelihood of civil conflict, it should follow that MSO of oil had an indirect effect on domestic conflict, post nationalizations.

In the case of Angola, it had a history of civil war associated with its inception. It was birthed with a domestic struggle for independence by separate movements seeking to evict the Portuguese colonizers, though these groups would contest power once the Portuguese were gone. Three significant rebel groups formed to combat the Portuguese: the MPLA, UNITA, and the FNLA. As per Hodges, the minerals resources had nothing to do with the start of the civil war, but their existence allowed the conflict to extend and expand significantly.[156] The wars of independence lasted from 1961 to 1975, with an estimate of 79,000 battle deaths.[157]

Postindependence, the longest running aspect of the civil war was the MPLA, which had access to oil wealth through the state-owned oil, and UNITA, which had access to alluvial diamonds to fund their insurgency, as well as controlled the central highlands, which provided a safe haven.[158] In fact, most Angolan diamond fields were located in territory held by UNITA throughout most of the civil war.[159] It is estimated that UNITA raised over $3 billion in the 1990s alone.[160] The diamonds were not state-owned, even if the single purchaser (a monopsony) was state-owned. However, given the fact that diamonds were in the hands of the rebels, the state could not control these diamonds, even with MSO of the monopsony.

Angola experienced civil war from 1975, the year of independence, until 1994, and again from 1998 through 2002.[161] Therefore, it has experienced near nonstop civil war from independence through 2000. Eighty-five percent of its postindependence time was marked by civil war.

Another source has Angola experiencing continuous civil war from 1975 to 2002, with an estimated 1,000,000 people having been killed, with 160,500 of these battle deaths.[162] Both sides of the civil conflict had access to natural resources to fund their side, and neither had to build significant public goods or institutions to maintain their rule during the costly civil war. In fact, the oil fields in the north of the country became a military target of UNITA, even to the point where the MPLA government needed the protection of Cuban soldiers to protect it.[163] This shows the zero-sum nature of this sector, that a military victory by one side or the other could sway the outcome of the conflict and enrich the side that holds it. Additionally, the failure of the government to redistribute the earnings from oil in a (perceived) fair fashion prompted much of the domestic unrest. Nonetheless, the civil war had a larger impact on onshore production than on offshore production. It cannot be said that state-owned oil caused the civil war, but Hodges says that both it and diamonds prolonged the conflict.[164]

Nigeria also experienced significant unrest, and the link between oil and conflict was strong, especially in the early years. Within a few years of independence, the region in Nigeria that had most of the oil reserves attempted to secede from the nation – leading to a civil war that ran from 1967 to 1970. In this conflict, over 500,000 people died, of which 75,000 were battle deaths.[165] Nigeria was also experienced civil conflicts from 1980 to 1981.[166] From independence through 2000, Nigeria spent about 15% of this time in civil war.[167] We need to keep in mind that Marshall's data (2006) would have Nigeria experiencing intercommunal, as well as intrastate violence (civil war); Nigeria can be listed as experiencing such conflict for 60% of its time from 1966 to 2000. The oil sector was still privately owned at the time of the civil war, so state ownership did not directly have an impact on the early civil war, though this sector had clearly been politicized. The nationalization of the petroleum sector made it the prize of whoever ran the country.

Neither Gabon nor Cameroon experienced any years of civil war during this period.[168] Gabon has not had any significant domestic violence events listed in these sources. Cameroon did experience significant civil conflict in its bid for independence from France between 1955 and 1960.[169] Cameroon had an estimated 30,000 deaths and 4,300 battle deaths during the decolonization period.

Therefore, of this group, Angola had the most conflict in terms of postindependence civil war years, followed by Nigeria. In the case of Angola, state-controlled oil helped fuel the conflict, but so too did alluvial diamonds accessible to the rebel group UNITA. In the case of Nigerian civil war, the start of the war cannot be attributed to state ownership in any way as the conflict predated the nationalization of the oil sector. However, Nigeria did have six of eight coups coming after the nationalization of oil. Oil in Cameroon and Gabon did not seem to have any negative effects vis-à-vis civil war or civil conflict. However, each did report one attempted coup.

Conclusions

We can see that nearly all the variables strongly linked to resource curse were stronger in the MSO oil countries than in the non-MSO countries. Even when the rank order was not perfectly maintained, the worst performer by any particular variable was always an MSO country and the best performer was a non-MSO country – and usually both MSO countries were worse off than the non-MSO countries.

Starting with the primary variable of interest for the resource curse – economic growth – the two oil countries with MSO of this sector (Angola and Nigeria) featured *negative* per capita economic growth during this period. Although Cameroon, as a non-MSO country, had low levels of growth, its rates were positive. Gabon featured the highest level of growth among these oil-exporting countries.

Looking at the second variable of interest, wealth, the rank order was not maintained until the very end of the period. For much of the period, Angola's incomes were higher than those in Cameroon were, but by 2000, Cameroon had become wealthier than Angola. Nonetheless, Gabon was clearly the richest in per capita GDP, and Nigeria recorded the lowest for much of the period.

One finding from this research that might surprise resource curse scholars is the lack of currency appreciation for the nominal exchange rate against the dollar, on average, for any of the cases for most of the period. Importantly, currency appreciation is considered by many to be the key mechanism that produces much of the resource curse problem: the Dutch disease.

However, using real exchange rates, we do see both Angola and Nigeria experienced more years of currency appreciation than did either Cameroon or Gabon. As discussed in Chapter 1, an export boom is held to lead to currency appreciation, which then makes alternative export sectors less competitive in foreign markets, and then they wither.[170] Nonetheless, a more complicated outcome was seen here. Both Angola and Nigeria (the two MSO nations) had real exchange rate appreciation, on average, but both had relatively low levels. Neither Cameroon nor Gabon experienced average currency appreciation in their real exchange rates. Given that both were in monetary unions, this might explain this partially, but their relatively lower levels of inflation also likely played a role.

However, both of the MSO countries had quite high levels of currency overvaluation – both of which would create incentives against exporting from other parts of the economy – especially if the exporter is paid in local currency. By contrast, neither of the non-MSO countries featured this.

Another primary predictor of the resource curse, and related to the above point, is the decline over time of alternative export sectors. Manufacturing and agriculture are often identified as the most likely alternative sources for exports or value added in sub-Saharan Africa. We see in the oil case studies that the MSO countries featured either lower levels, or declining levels, of manufacturing exports during the period of study. In fact, the strong prediction of the resource curse is that alternative sectors will decline over time – not that they would not have existed prior to a booming mineral export sector. MSO countries also experienced declining levels of agricultural exports. However, to be fair, during the Cold War, manufacturing, as a percentage of exports, was low in all the mineral- and oil-exporting countries, though not all had similar declines. Again, this analysis is about differences in degree of change over time, and those with MSO saw the greatest declines.

We also saw similar outcomes for levels of investment, debt, and inflation – with one exception – the non-MSO countries outperformed the MSO countries. The exception was lower levels of debt for the MSO oil countries. The finding that investment was lower in the MSO countries should be surprising for some – given past arguments that the nationalization of such resources should have stopped MNCs from draining profits away to their home countries. One should have expected the reverse to be true. For inflation, the non-MSO countries had much lower levels. This comparison could be found to be problematic as both countries were members of a currency regime. However, either Cameroon or Gabon could have left the French-backed currency union.

The countries with MSO also had more years of conflict than the two non-MSO countries. Discerning cause and effect is problematic, as MSO could either help give incentive to capture the state as well as for continuing any conflict once begun, especially if diamonds are involved.[171] Angola had both oil and alluvial diamonds that helped fund different sides in a civil war.[172] Nigeria had significant conflict over its oil sector, given Biafra's decision to leave the larger state of Nigeria, and it had most of the oil reserves. Clearly, the oil had not yet been nationalized, but the struggle over oil access was quite zero sum: had Biafra been successful, the rump of Nigeria would have been left with very few oil resources. Neither Cameroon nor Gabon had significant civil disturbances post decolonization through the end of the Cold War.

One outcome where no significant differences were found was in levels of political and civil rights. None of these countries was fully free for most of the Cold War period through 2000, and most countries were not free for most of it. Nigeria and Cameroon had periods of being party free after the end of the Cold War, and Nigeria even had brief periods of being ranked as free, though they did not last. No significant differences were apparent for this category, and this is reflected in Table 2.2, which showed no statistical difference between the two categories. However, most other categories were clearly significant.

Notes

1 See Mining (2017); also summary of "Crude Oil Market Report" (2023). Ross (2012) suggested that it was worth over $2.3 trillion in 2009 (p. 3). "Mining, by Contrast." https://finance.yahoo.com/news/mining-global-market-report-2023-123400878.html#:~:text=The%20global%20mining%20market%20grew,(CAGR)%20of%206.1%25.
2 Ross (2012, 3). However, in the middle of the coronavirus pandemic, oil prices were even briefly negative as oversupply exceeded storage capacity. See, for example, Ambrose (2020).
3 USEIA (2020).
4 From Ross (2012, 21–22). Listed in order of production per person. Data from 2009.
5 Ibid.
6 Pariona (2020). MT, million tons.

7 Meltzer (2016).
8 Schraeder and Crouzel (2005), Taylor (2010).
9 Taylor (2010, 134).
10 Ghazvinian (2007, 4), cited in Taylor (2010, 134).
11 Krasner (1985), Ross (2012), Quinn (2002).
12 Victor, Hults, and Thurber (2011), Marcel (2009).
13 Tordo (2011, 18).
14 Mason and Polasky (2005, 322).
15 Tordo (2011, 17).
16 Mason and Polasky (2005).
17 Nigeria joined in 1971. Gabon joined in 1975, left in 1995, and rejoined in 2016. Angola would join after 2000, in 2007. More recently, Equatorial Guinea joined in 2017, and Congo joined in 2018.
18 Tordo (2011, 18).
19 Tordo (2011, 17). Later joiners also had NOCs: Equatorial Guinea formed GEPetrol in 2002, and Chad formed SHT in 2006.
20 See Jones Luong and Weinthal (2010, appendix B).
21 van de Walle (2001) and Quinn (2016) both show major shifts in economic policy post–Cold War, and this was even more so after 2000. However, if a country is independent afterwards, it is included from the start of independence.
22 van de Walle (2001).
23 Hodges (2001, 143), see also Collelo (1991)
24 *Africa South of the Sahara* (1978), Angola; unless stated otherwise, like the data for the dependent variables, the data for each country comes from *Africa South of the Sahara* (various years).
25 USEAI (n.d.), Angola.
26 Ibid.
27 Oil production numbers come from EIA, unless otherwise stated.
28 *Africa South of the Sahara* (various years), Angola.
29 Young (1988, 165–184).
30 Hodges (2001).
31 For end of Afro-Marxism, see Schraeder (2004, 132–134).
32 *Africa South of the Sahara*; despite these changes over time, Jones-Luong and Weinthal (2010), who have explored issues of majority state ownership, but mostly in the former Soviet Union, have also coded most major oil exporters by ownership. They code Angola from 1970 to 2010 as majority state-owned. However, they call it state ownership without control, however with majority state ownership of the sector.
33 See, for example, USIEA (2006).
34 Jones Luong and Weinthal (2010); also United States International Energy Agency (2006, 19), Angola.
35 USEIA (2006), Nigeria.
36 USEIA (2006), Nigeria. Although from a later date, 2015.
37 Much of this section is taken from NNPC (2006).
38 Schatz (1977), Biersteker (1987).
39 Forrest (1993); see also *Africa South of the Sahara* (1987), Quinn (2002, 81), Rood (1976).
40 *Africa South of the Sahara* (2000, 832).
41 *Africa South of the Sahara* (2008, 890).
42 USEIA (2006), Nigeria, analysis.

43 Jones Luong and Weinthal (2010, appendix B). Nigeria's nationalization and Indigenization decrees were not until 1972; see Quinn (2002, 80). Also, they coded it as state ownership with control from 1970 to 1990, and as state ownership without control from 1991 to 2010.
44 Such data from *Africa South of the Sahara* (1988) and various years.
45 Data on oil production comes from USEIA. www.eia.gov/international/data/country/CMR/petroleum-and-other-liquids/annual-petroleum-and-other-liquids-production?pd=5&p=00000000000000000000000000000000vg&u=0&f=A&v=mapbubble&a=-&i=none&vo=value&&t=C&g=none&l=249--40&s=94694400000&e=1546300800000.
46 USAID (n.d.).
47 Gauthier and Zeufack (2011, 31).
48 Ibid., 11, fn #9.
49 Luong and Weinthal (2010).
50 Bozec (2018). Also data from USEAI (n.d.), Gabon, petroleum and other liquids.
51 Ibid.
52 Akitoby and Coorey (2012, 198).
53 Gary and Karl (2003).
54 Akitoby and Coorey (2012, 199).
55 Jones Luong and Weinthal (2010, appendix B).
56 Growth and per capita GDP from Feenstra, Inklaar, Timmer (2015) [Penn World Tables 9.1] , real GDP expenditure side chained PPPs per capita 2011 US$. Growth used this variable, transformed by percent change and averaged for periods 1966–1989, 1990–2000, and 1966–2000. For Angola, the starting year was 1975. Unless stated otherwise, growth and RGDP come from this source.
57 Growth numbers are incomes calculated from Feenstra, Inklaar, Timmer (2015) [Penn World Tables 9.1].
58 Unless stated otherwise, data from Feenstra, Inklaar, Timmer (2015) [Penn World Tables 9.1], real GDP expenditure side chained PPPs per capita 2011 US$.
59 Calculated from World Bank (n.d.) official exchange rate (LCU per US$, period average). Unless specified elsewhere, all data on official exchange rates come from here.
60 World Bank (2000, table 3-3).
61 Ibid.
62 Unless stated otherwise, values for real exchange rates in this chapter come from Darvas (2021). World Bank numbers were missing for some countries and more years.
63 World Bank (2000, table 3-3), Nigeria.
64 World Bank (n.d.). Nigeria, inflation.
65 For background, see Central African Economic and Monetary Community (CEMAC) (n.d.). Also Hadjimichael and Galy (1997).
66 Ibid.
67 Often called black markets or illicit markets.
68 Bates (1981), Lofchie (1989).
69 World Bank (n.d.).
70 These numbers are from World Bank (2000, table 3-8).
71 Wilson (1993)
72 Ibid.
73 Quinn (2002, 39).
74 Unless stated otherwise, data for this section comes from World Bank (n.d.), individual countries.
75 World Bank (2002).

76 See more detailed description of Nigeria's inward orientation, see Quinn (2002).
77 Hodges (2004) reminds us that the data is not always accurate.
78 Forrest (1993), Lewis (1994), Nellis (1986), Rood (1976), Schatz (1977).
79 For a discussion of abundant and scarce sectors, see Rogowski (1989).
80 Assuming Heckschire-Ohlin principles are at work. For an overview of Heckscher-Ohlin, see Caves and Jones (1973); for political effects (and Stolper-Samuelson), see Rogowski (1989); for the application of both to Africa, see Quinn (2002).
81 *Africa South of the Sahara* (2011).
82 World Bank (n.d.), Angola, employment in agriculture (% of total employment). 1990.
83 Begu et al. (2018).
84 World Bank (1989b, table 3).
85 Bhagavan (1986, 27–28).
86 Food and Agriculture Organization (2012). .
87 World Bank (2000, table 8-7).
88 World Bank (1992).
89 Calculated by multiplying share of Merch X by value of Merch X (with deflator for 2010) and then dividing by population. This was followed for each country. World Bank (n.d.).
90 *Africa South of the Sahara* (1996).
91 Gbaiye (2013).
92 In 1999 dollars.
93 World Bank (1992, table 8-9).
94 *Africa South of the Sahara* (2011).
95 World Bank (2000, table 8-7).
96 Some sources combine these sectors together in one measure, some measure them separately.
97 *Africa South of the Sahara* (1996, 2004).
98 *Africa South of the Sahara* (2004).
99 This included forestry as well as fishing.
100 In 1999 dollars.
101 World Bank (2000, 8–7). In current US dollars.
102 World Bank (1989a).
103 Reuters (2018a).
104 Ibid.
105 World Bank (1989a).
106 USEIA (n.d.).
107 USEIA (2006).
108 Ibid.
109 Ibid.
110 CIA Factbook (n.d.).
111 Reuters (2018b).
112 Adeyemo (2018), Ogbuigwe (2018, 181–192), who argues that refineries are 100% state-owned.
113 USEIA (n.d.).
114 Ibid.
115 Ibid.
116 Barrel Full (n.d.).
117 USEIA (n.d.), production.

118 Cameroon Digital Portal. https://cameroon.opendataforafrica.org/kenlbw/cameroon-crude-oil-and-petroleum-products-import-and-export-1986-2012.
119 USEIA (n.d.), Gabon.
120 *Africa South of the Sahara* (2011). However, according to another source, it was 51% owned by the government (in 1980). See *Minerals Yearbook 1981* (1981, 367).
121 CIA Factbook, refined petroleum products – imports is the country's total imports of refined petroleum products, in barrels per day (bbl/day)
122 Oxford Business Group (2012).
123 Minerals Yearbook (1980, 368). Though the Gabonese government owned 25% of Elf Gabon.
124 USEIA (n.d.).
125 Reed (2009, 90).
126 USEIA (2006).
127 USEIA (n.d.), Nigeria. It was estimated to have 37 billion barrels of proven reserves in 2015.
128 Nigeria LNG(n.d.) . www.nlng.com/Our-Company/Pages/Profile.aspx.
129 UNDP (2016).
130 Business in Cameroon (2019).
131 USEIA (n.d.), Gabon.
132 *Africa South of the Sahara* (2011), Gabon.
133 Dollar (1992, 523–544, appendix).
134 For investment, data comes from World Bank (2002). Gross domestic fixed investment, per capita, gross domestic fixed investment as a percentage of GDP 2002 from World Bank (2002).
135 Dollar (1992).
136 Ibid
137 Ibid.
138 Barro (1996), although he suggests that the numbers for Angola were rough estimates.
139 For a brief overview of history with IMF, see Jensen (2016).
140 In fact, Angola was one of few with no IMF agreements through the 1990s; see Clapham (1996, 171).
141 van de Walle (2001, 69); for a description of partial economic reforms, see Quinn (2016). In fact, by 2007, inflation for most African countries was only 7% (excluding a few outliers).
142 Unless noted otherwise, background for this section from *Africa South of the Sahara* (various years), Angola. For an overview of Portuguese policy, see Bender (1978).
143 For decolonization see Hargreaves (1988); also Gifford and Louis (1982); for Afro-Marxist regimes, see Keller and Rothchild (1987).
144 For transitions away from authoritarianism and founding elections, see Bratton and van de Walle (1997); also Lindberg (2006).
145 Ishiyama and Quinn (2006, 317–340); see also Quinn (2016).
146 African Election Database (n.d.), Angola.
147 For an in-depth discussion of pros and cons for various terms for one-party dominance, see Bogaards (2004); also Doorenspleet and Nijzink (2013).
148 For early Nigerian political parties, see Ajayi and Ekoko (1988), Coleman (1958), Sklar (1963), Sklar and Whitaker (1964).
149 For background, see Metz (1991).
150 *Africa South of the Sahara* (various years); African Election Database (n.d.), Cameroon.

151 Freedom in the World (various years). Also, 1972 is the earliest date available from Freedom House (n.d.).
152 *Africa South of the Sahara* (1996).
153 *Africa South of the Sahara* (2011).
154 Quinn (2016, chapter 8).
155 Freedom in the World (various years).
156 Hodges (2001).
157 Marshall (2006, annex 1a).
158 For an analysis of diamonds' role in Angolan civil war, see Sherman (2000); for an analysis of Angola's economy more generally, see Hodges (2001), also Frynas and Wood (2021) .
159 Sherman (2000, 707).
160 Ibid.
161 According to the Correlates of War dataset, see Sarkees and Wayman (2010).
162 Marshall (2006).
163 For arguments linking minerals, oil, and conflict in Angola, see Jedrzej and Wood (2001).
164 Hodges (2001).
165 Marshall (2006).
166 Marshall (2006) puts the period of conflict from 1980 to 1985 instead of COW's 1980–1981, which would increase the years of conflict. Marshal also has 1986–1993 with intercommunal violence.
167 Sarkees and Wayman (2010).
168 Marshall (2006).
169 Ibid., annex 1a.
170 Ross 2012; van der Ploeg (2006).
171 Collier and Hoeffler (2004), Lujala et al., (2005), Ross (2006).
172 Le Billon (2001), Hodges (2001).

References

Adeyemo, Ifeoluwa. 2018. "No Nigerian Refinery Worked up to 50% Capacity in 2017: NNPC." *Premium Times*, May 22. www.premiumtimesng.com/news/headlines/269289-no-nigerian-refinery-worked-up-to-50-capacity-in-2017-nnpc.html.

Africa South of the Sahara. Various Years. Various Countries. New York: Europa Publications.

African Election Database. n.d. Various Countries.

Ajayi, J. F. Ade and A. E. Ekoko. 1988. "Transfer of Power in Nigeria: Its Origins and Consequences." In Prosser Gifford and Wm. Roger Louis, eds., *Decolonization and African Independence: The Transfer of Power, 1960–1980*. New Haven: Yale University Press, 245–269.

Akitoby, Bernardin and Sharmini Coorey. 2012. "Oil Wealth in Central Africa: Policies for Inclusive Growth." In Bernardin Akitoby and Sharmini Coorey, eds., *Oil Wealth in Central Africa Policies for Inclusive Growth*. Washington, DC: International Monetary Fund, 197–212.

Ambrose, Jillian. 2020. "Oil Prices Dip below Zero as Producers Forced to Pay to Dispose of Excess." *The Guardian*, April 20.

Barrel Full. n.d. Limbe Refinery Project. n.d. http://abarrelfull.wikidot.com/limbe-refinery-project.

Barro, Robert J. 1996. "Inflation and Growth." *Review: St. Louis Federal Reserve*, May/June. https://files.stlouisfed.org/files/htdocs/publications/review/96/05/9605rb2.pdf.

Bates, Robert H. 1981. *Market and States in Tropical Africa: The Political Basis of Agricultural Policies*. Los Angeles: University of California Press.

Begu, Liviu Stelian, Maria Denisa Vasilescu, Larisa Stanila, and Roxana Clodnitchi. 2018. "China-Angola Investment Model." *Sustainability* 10(8): 29–36.

Bender, Gerald J. 1978. *Angola under the Portuguese: The Myth and the Reality*. Los Angeles: University of California Press.

Bhagavan, M. R. 1986. Angola's Political Economy 1975–1985. Uppsala: Scandinavian Institute of African Studies. www.diva-portal.org/smash/get/diva2:277672/FULLTEXT01.pdf.

Biersteker, Thomas J. 1987. *Multinationals, the State and Control of the Nigerian Economy*. Princeton: Princeton University Press.

Bogaards, Matthijs. 2004. "Counting Parties and Identifying Dominant Party Systems in Africa." *European Journal of Political Research* 43: 173–197.

Bozec, Jean-Pierre. 2018. "Gabon 2018 Hydrocarbons Law Reform: Appetite for New Incentive." *Into Africa*, May.

Bratton, Michael and Nicolas van de Walle. 1997. *Democratic Experiments in Africa: Regime Transitions in Comparative Perspective*. Cambridge: Cambridge University Press.

Bureau of Mines. 1980. *Minerals Yearbook*. Washington, DC: Bureau of Mines.

Bureau of Mines. 1981. *Minerals Yearbook*, vol. 3. Washington, DC: Bureau of Mines.

Business in Cameroon. 2019. "Cameroon: Natural Gas Can Contribute 20–30% of the Energy Mix, SNH Says." May. www.businessincameroon.com/energy/2911-9729-cameroon-natural-gas-can-contribute-20-30-of-the-energy-mix-snh-says.

Business Research Company. 2023. "Crude Oil Market Report." www.thebusinessresearchcompany.com/report/crude-oil-global-market-report.

Cameroon Digital Portal. n.d. https://cameroon.opendataforafrica.org/kenlbw/cameroon-crude-oil-and-petroleum-products-import-and-export-1986-2012.

Caves, Richard E. and Ronald W. Jones. 1973. *World Trade and Payments: An Introduction*. Boston: Little, Brown.

Central African Economic and Monetary Community (CEMAC) n.d. https://cemac.int/node/32.

CIA Factbook. n.d. "Importation of Refined Petroleum Products." www.cia.gov/library/publications/the-world-factbook/fields/268rank.html.

Clapham, Christopher. 1996. *African and the International System: The Politics of State Survival*. Cambridge: Cambridge University Press.

Coleman, James S. 1958. *Nigeria: Background to Nationalism*. Berkeley: University of California Press.

Collelo, Thomas, ed. 1991. *Angola: A Country Study*. Washington, DC: GPO for the Library of Congress.

Collier, Paul and Anke Hoeffler. 2004. "Greed and Grievance in Civil War." *Oxford Economic Papers* 56(4): 563–595.

Darvas, Zsolt. 2021. "Timely Measurement of Real Effective Exchange Rates." Working Paper 2021/15, 23 December.

Dollar, David. 1992. "Outward-Oriented Developing Economies Really Do Grow More Rapidly: Evidence from 95 LDCs, 1976–1985." *Economic Development and Cultural Change* 40(3): 523–544.

Doorenspleet, Renske and Lia Nijzink, eds. 2013. *One Party Dominance in African Democracies*. Boulder: Lynne Rienner.

Feenstra, Robert C., Robert Inklaar and Marcel P. Timmer. 2015. "The Next Generation of the Penn World Table." *American Economic Review* 105(10): 3150–3182.

Food and Agriculture Organization. 2012. Angola Country Programming Framework 2013–2017. Luanda: FAO. www.fao.org/3/a-bp627e.pdf.

Forrest, Tom. 1993. *Politics and Economic Development in Nigeria*. Boulder: Westview Press.

Freedom House. n.d. Freedom in the World. Various Years. https://freedomhouse.org/report/freedom-world.

Frynas, Jedrzej George and Geoffrey Wood. 2021. "Oil and War in Angola." *Review of African Political Economy* 28(90): 587–606. www.jstor.org/stable/4006839.

Gary, Ian and Terry Lynn Karl. 2003. *Bottom of the Barrel: Africa's Oil Boom and the Poor*. Baltimore: Catholic Relief Services.

Gauthier, Bernard and Albert Zeufack. 2011. *Governance and Oil Revenues in Cameroon*. Oxford: Revenue Watch Institute.

Gbaiye, Oluwaseun G., Adeyemi Ogundipe, Evans Osabuohien, Oluseyi O. Olugbire, Odunola A. Adeniran, Kofo A. Bolaji-Olutunji, Oluwakemi D. Awodele, and Oluwatomi Aduradola. 2013. "Agricultural Exports and Economic Growth in Nigeria (1980–2010)." *Journal of Economics and Sustainable Development* 4(16): 1–5.

Ghazvinian, John. 2007. *Untapped: The Scramble for Africa's Oil*. New York: Harcourt.

Gifford, Prosser and Wm. Roger Louis, eds. 1982. *The Transfer of Power in Africa: Decolonization 1940–1960*. New Haven: Yale University Press.

Global Gas Flaring Reduction Partnership. n.d. www.worldbank.org/en/programs/gasflaringreduction.

Hadjimichael, Michael T. and Michel Galy. 1997. "The CFA Franc Zone and the EMU." IMF Working Paper No. 97/156. Washington: International Monetary Fund.

Hargreaves, John D. 1988. *Decolonization in Africa*. New York: Longman.

Hodges, Tony. 2001. *Angola: From Afro-Stalinism to Petro-diamond Capitalism*. Bloomington: Indiana University Press.

Hodges, Tony. 2004. *Angola: Anatomy of an Oil State*, 2nd ed. Oxford: James Curry.

International Tanker Owners Pollution Federation Limited. n.d. "Cameroon." www.itopf.org/knowledge-resources/countries-territories-regions/countries/cameroon.

Ishiyama, John T. and John James Quinn. 2006. "Phoenix from the Ashes: The Formerly Dominant Parties in New Democracies in Africa." *Party Politics* 12(3): 317–340.

Jensen, Søren Kirk. 2016. "Can the IMF Help Angola Deepen Its Reform Agenda?" *Chatham House*, April.

Jones Luong, Pauline and Erika Weinthal. 2010. *Oil Is Not a Curse: Ownership Structure and Institutions in Soviet Successor States*. Cambridge: Cambridge University Press.

Keller, Edmond J. and Donald Rothchild. 1987. *Afro-Marxist Regimes: Ideology and Public Policy*. Boulder: Lynne Rienner.

Krasner, Stephen D. 1985. *Structural Conflict: The Third World against Global Liberalism*. Berkeley: University of California Press.

Le Billon, Philippe. 2001. "Angola's Political Economy of War: The Role of Oil and Diamonds, 1975–2000." *African Affairs* 100(398): 55–80.

Lewis, Peter. 1994. "Development Strategy and State Sector Expansion in Nigeria." In Barbara Grosh and Rwekaza S. Mukandala, eds., *State-Owned Enterprises in Africa*. Boulder: Lynne Rienner, 63–82.

Lindberg, Staffan I. 2006. *Democracy and Elections in Africa*. Baltimore: The Johns Hopkins University Press.

Lofchie, Michael F. 1989. *The Policy Factor: Agricultural Performance in Kenya and Tanzania*. Boulder: Lynne Rienner.

Lujala, Päivi, Nils Petter Gleditsch, and Elisabeth Gilmore. 2005. "A Diamond Curse? Civil War and a Lootable Resource." *Journal of Conflict Resolution* 49(4): 538–562.
Luong, Pauline Jones and Erika Weinthal. 2010. Oil Is Not a Curse: Ownership Structure and Institutions in Soviet Successor States. Cambridge: Cambridge University Press.
Marcel, Valarie. 2009. "States of Play: National Oil Companies Control Ever More of the World's Oil. But They're Not All Alike." *Foreign Policy* 174: 104.
Marshall, Monty G. 2006. *Conflict Trends in Africa, 1946–2004: A Macro-Comparative Perspective*. London: Department for International Development.
Mason, Charles F. and Stephen Polasky. 2005. "What Motivates Membership in Non-Renewable Resource Cartels? The Case of OPEC." *Resource and Energy Economics* 27(4): 321–342.
Meltzer, Joshua P. 2016. "Deepening the United States-Africa Trade and Investment Relationship." January 28.
Metz, Helen Chapin, ed. 1991. *Nigeria: A Country Study*. Washington, DC: GPO for the Library of Congress.
Mining. 2017. "Just How Big Is the Oil Market?" https://oilprice.com/Energy/Crude-Oil/The-Oil-Market-Is-Bigger-Than-All-Metal-Markets-Combined.
Nellis, John R. 1986. *Public Enterprise in Sub-Saharan Africa*. Washington, DC: The World Bank.
Nigeria LNG. n.d. www.nlng.com/Our-Company/Pages/Profile.aspx.
Nigerian National Petroleum Company Limited. 2006. www.nnpcgroup.com/history.htm.
Ogbuigwe, Anthony. 2018. "Refining in Nigeria: History, Challenges and Prospects." *Applied Petrochemical Research* 8: 181–192.
OPEC. n.d. "About US/Member Countries." www.opec.org/opec_web/en/about_us/25.htm.
Oxford Business Group. 2012. *The Report: Gabon 2012*. https://oxfordbusinessgroup.com/reports/gabon/2012-report
Pariona, Ameber. "Top 10 Oil Producing Countries in Africa." *WorldAtlas*. www.worldatlas.com/articles/top-10-oil-producing-countries-in-africa.html.
Quinn, John James. 2002. *The Road Oft Traveled: Development Policies and Majority State Ownership of Industry in Africa*. Westport: Praeger.
Quinn, John James. 2016. *Global Geopolitical Power and African Political and Economic Institutions: When Elephant Fight*. Lanham: Lexington Books.
Reed, Kristin. 2009. *Crude Existence: Environment and the Politics of Oil in Northern Angola*, vol. 12. Los Angeles: University of California Press.
Reuters. 2018a. "Angola's SONANGOL Plans to Build Refineries, End Fuel Imports." *Financials*. February 1.
Reuters. 2018b. "Nigerian State Oil Firm Spent $5.8 Bln on Fuel Imports since Late 2017." February 20. www.reuters.com/article/nigeria-oil/nigerian-state-oil-firm-spent-5-8-bln-on-fuel-imports-since-late-2017-idUSL8N1QA6LR.
Rogowski, Ronald. 1989. *Commerce and Coalitions: How Trade Affects Domestic Political Alignments*. Princeton: Princeton University Press.
Rood, Leslie L. 1976. "Nationalisation and Indigenisation in Africa." *Journal of Modern African Studies* 14(2): 427–447.
Ross, Michael L. 2006. "A Closer Look at Oil, Diamonds, and Civil War." *Annual Review of Political Science* 9: 265–300.
Ross, Michael L. 2012. *The Oil Curse: How Petroleum Wealth Shapes the Development of Nations*. Princeton: Princeton University Press.
Sarkees, Meredith R. and Frank Wayman. 2010. *Resort to War: 1816–2007*. Washington DC: CQ Press.

Schatz, Sayre. 1977. *Nigerian* Capitalism. Berkeley: University of California Press
Schraeder, Peter J. 2004. *African Politics and Society: A Mosaic in Transformation*, 2nd ed. Belmont: Thompson, Wadsworth.
Schraeder, Peter J. and Ivan Crouzel. 2005. "La guerre contre le terrorisme et la politique américaine en Afrique." *Politique Africaine* 2: 42–62.
Sea Alarm. n.d. www.sea-alarm.org/web/wp-content/uploads/2010/07/Gabon-2014.pdf.
Sherman, Jake H. 2000. "Profit vs. Peace: The Clandestine Diamond Economy of Angola." *Journal of International Affairs* 53(2): 699–719.
Sklar, Richard L. 1963. *Nigerian Political Power: Power in an Emergent African Nation.* Princeton: Princeton University Press.
Sklar, Richard L. and C. S. Whitaker, Jr. 1964. "Nigeria." In James S. Coleman and Carl G. Rosberg, eds., *Political Parties and National Integration in Tropical Africa.* Berkeley: University of California Press, 597–654.
Taylor, Ian. 2010. *The International Relations of Sub-Saharan Africa*. London: Bloomsbury.
Tordo, Silvana (with Brandon S. Tracy and Noora Arfaa). 2011. "National Oil Companies and Value Creation." World Bank Working Paper 218, 18.
United Nations Development Programme. 2006. *Niger Delta Human Development Report.* Abuja: UNDP.
United States International Energy Agency. 2006. *Angola: Towards an Energy Strategy.* Paris: OECD/IEA.
US Energy Information Administration. 2020. "Oil: Crude and Petroleum Products Explained." www.eia.gov/energyexplained/oil-and-petroleum-products/where-our-oil-comes-from.php.
US Energy Information Administration. n.d.a. "International/Data Petroleum and Other Liquids." www.eia.gov/international/data/world/petroleum-and-other-liquids/annual-petroleum-and-other-liquids-production?pd=5&p=000000000000000000000000000000000bg&u=0&f=A&v=mapbubble&a=-&i=none&vo=value&t=C&g=0000000000000000000000000000000000000000000000001&l=249-ruvvvvvfvtvnvv1vrvvvvfvvvvvvfvvvou20evvvvvvvvvvnvvvs0008&s=94694400000&e=1546300800000&
USAID. n.d. "Cameroon, Minerals." www.land-links.org/country-profile/cameroon/#minerals.
USEAI. n.d. "Angola." www.eia.gov/beta/international/country.php?iso=AGO.
van de Walle, Nicolas. 2001. *African Economies and the Politics of Permanent Crisis, 1979–1999.* Cambridge: Cambridge University Press.
van der Ploeg, Frederick. 2006. "Challenges and Opportunities for Resource Rich Economies." Centre for Economic Policy Research No. 5688.
Victor, David G., David R. Hults, and Mark C. Thurber. 2011. *Oil and Governance: State-Owned Enterprises and the World Energy Supply.* Cambridge: Cambridge University Press.
Wilson III, Ernest J. 1993. "French Support for Structural Adjustment Programs in Africa." *World Development* 21 (3): 331–347.
World Bank. 1989a. "Angola: Issues and Options in the Energy Sector." Joint UNDP/World Bank Energy Sector Assessment, May.
World Bank. 1989b. *Sub-Saharan Africa: From Crisis to Sustainable Growth.* Washington, DC: World Bank.
World Bank. 1992. *African Development Indicators 1992*. Washington, DC: World Bank.
World Bank. 2000. *African Development Indicators 2000*. Washington, DC: World Bank.

World Bank. 2002. *Africa Database 2002 CDROM.*
World Bank. n.d. "World Development Indicators WDI." https://databank.worldbank.org/source/world-development-indicators
Young, Tom. 1988. "The Politics of Development in Angola and Mozambique." *African Affairs* 87(347): 165–184. www.jstor.org/stable/722399.

4 Mineral Exporting, Majority State Ownership, and Resource Curse Outcomes in Paired Case Studies

There is no honest man – not one – that can resist the attraction of gold!

—Aristophanes

The desire of gold is not for gold. It is for the means of freedom and benefit.

—Ralph Waldo Emerson

Why should scholars of development be concerned with the issues associated with mining in sub-Saharan Africa? First, mining is a major economic sector internationally. Although oil is larger in overall valuation, mining still represents an exceptionally large segment of the international market. Worldwide, major metal mineral commodities have been worth over $638 billion or so annually.[1] Another source places the value of such production at just over a trillion dollars.[2] These data do not include either diamonds or coal, which were worth $15.6 billion and $366 billion, respectively.[3] This represented a combined value of at least $1.02 trillion per year for this sector.[4] Nonfuel mining in particular is a major source of exports for many developing countries.[5] In 2016, more than 21 countries had nonfuel mining exports accounting for 50% or more of their exports.[6]

Not only is mining important for Africa, but Africa is also important for mining. The region is home to around 30% of the world's known mineral reserves, despite only representing about 5% of world's production.[7] It is also the major, or a significant, producer of many minerals: Africa has 95% of known reserves of chromium, 88% of platinum, 82% of manganese, 66% of phosphate, 60% of diamonds, 55% of gold, 45% of aluminum, 44% of vanadium, 42% of cobalt, 15% of uranium, 6% of coal, 5% of copper, and 2% of iron.[8]

Moreover, mining also represents a significant source for exports for many African countries. For example, between 1990 and 1999, it represented over 50% of exports for such countries as Guinea, the Democratic Republic of the Congo (DRC), Zambia, Niger, Botswana, Namibia, and Sierra Leone.[9] For many countries in the region, minerals exports comprised between 15% and 50% of all exports,

DOI: 10.4324/9780429423390-4

including such countries as Mauritania, Central African Republic, Mali, Togo, Ghana, South Africa, and Tanzania. Finally, mineral exports made up between 5% and 15% of all exports for such countries as Zimbabwe, Senegal, Angola, Gabon, Cameroon, Madagascar, Sudan, and Burkina Faso.

In addition, minerals in Africa have become more important internationally, given the rise and industrialization of China and India following the end of the Cold War. African countries have long had relationships with the OECD countries and their MNCs, but other countries are finding African minerals to be more important to their developmental needs. China and India have become significant importers of African minerals, but Chinese investment in African mines is of particular importance, given the potential geopolitical balancing between a rising China and the West and her allies. Minerals comprise almost 80% of African exports to China.[10] Indian trade was also on the increase, though it only represents about a third of the value of Sino-African trade.[11]

Environmental Issues with Mining

As mentioned in Chapter 1, mining has quite a few negative impacts on the environment and can be a source of significant pollution. Given that its nature is a bit different from that of oil, and not all countries have the same ores, only a brief description will be offered here. To begin with, mining means extracting and bringing potentially poisonous resources above ground where they can interact with air and drinking water. For example, potential contaminants from slag heaps can spread when rainfall hits them and washes them downstream or away from the heaps. Also, any ores stored or piled above ground can begin to oxidize, become acidic, and impact local water and soil. Heavy metals, which are often the most toxic, are more abundant in deeper soil and can be introduced into the local agriculture and water ecosystems through extraction.

The process of extracting metals from ores often uses hard chemicals that can be harmful to both workers and the environment. In poorer nations, especially, governments are less likely to restrict or closely monitor these practices. For example, mercury and cyanide have been used to extract gold from ore. In fact, the Ghanaian government has been strongly criticized for its poor regulation of the use of such chemicals in artisanal mining.[12] The associated mercury pollution is a particular problem for water tables, given its high levels of toxicity.[13] The release of arsenic into ground and surface water can also be linked to mining processing.[14] Likewise, the smoke from mines can impact local inhabitants. In addition, arsenic in dredged up dirt can come into the food supply around mining areas.[15]

Not only can water become contaminated, but significant air pollution concerns can also come from blasting, digging, and hauling of toxic compounds dredged up with the mining process.[16] The control, abatement, and reduction of pollution requires both technological ability and strong political will – in conjunction with strong political institutions. Oftentimes, the technology to limit pollution resides in the hands of the MNCs and not local governments, the former will likely have different interests concerning pollution and the public goods.[17]

As discussed in Chapter 1, the pollution associated with mining involves both short and long-term issues. On the one hand, shorter-term pollution is involved during the active phases of mining. On the other hand, the extraction of these non-renewable resources can result in later pollution issues long after the company has closed. For example, mines are rarely filled back in and often flood. The water from the flooded mines can seep out into rivers or drinking water. Thus, governments and companies must make plans to avoid pollution during the period of active mining as well as after the operational life of mines. Otherwise, countries can find themselves dealing with a legacy of cleanup costs associated with pollution and other environmental issues long after the closing of the mines.[18] Plans need to include how to handle toxic materials drawn up from the soil which normally are not involved in the local agricultural or human ecosystems. Unlike agriculture, which is potentially renewable for generations (unless the soil is exhausted or desertified), or industry, which could continue if demand continues, mines will eventually run out and leave a legacy of degradation. Even if more resources are left underground, the longer the mining operation continues, the more costly the extraction, and the more rehabilitation that will have to be done after the closing of the mines.

Finally, radioactive materials dredged up by mining have their own set of environmental and safety concerns, all of which are more difficult for developing and poor nations to deal with. For example, uranium mining has unique hazards associated with its production. Radon gas is created by the decay of U-238, and it is a known cause of lung cancer. Such mines require special ventilation to keep workers safe.[19] In addition, radium is often found near uranium, and it emits ionizing radiation that can penetrate the skin and bones of workers, potentially causing cancers. Uranium itself is toxic beyond its radioactivity. If ingested, it can cause kidney failure. Radium, too, is often found near uranium ore, and it can enter miners' bones and lead to early death.[20] These issues are of course more severe for developing African nations with no comparative advantage in the technology preventing environmental damage associated with radioactive substances.

Transportation Issues and Mining

Beyond issues such as pollution, mining often involves high transportation costs for ores, especially copper, iron ore, and coal. Copper producing countries, for example, have strong needs for efficient transportation as copper is relatively high weight to low value, especially compared to output like gold or diamonds. Given this high weight to value ratio, copper must be transported by land or sea – it cannot be flown out profitably.

Zambia, which exports copper, is a landlocked country and must ship its copper out by rail through neighboring countries. In the early years, Zambia exported its copper through Rhodesia (later Zimbabwe). In 1973, the border through Smith's Rhodesia was closed which closed a significant route.[21] Then in 1975, the Benguela

Railway, which passes through Angola, and which was the main alternative route, became unreliable due to the Angolan civil war. Zambia then wanted to export its copper through Tanzania by opening the Tanzania-Zambia Railway (TAZARA). This means of export, however, did not prove sufficiently efficient, so Zambia broke with the frontline states and began to export its copper through South Africa.[22] This longer distance to the sea necessarily increased the price of Zambian copper. Despite Zambia's percent metal to ore being among the world's highest in the 1960s at 3% (compared to 2% in Chile and 1% in the US), these transportation problems made Zambian copper quite expensive once on the market.[23]

Over time, more and more Zambian copper transport has been by road. But here too, costs have been high. Poor maintenance of the roads, damaged by overweight freight, and long delays at borders added to the cost of exports. Although little copper should be transported by truck given its weight to value ratio, the poorly run state agency for Zambian rail helped lead to this outcome.[24] In theory, bulk exports of copper semis (semi-manufactures like wire) would be cheaper (and more environmentally friendly) by rail. The government tried to curb this trend by mandating that rail had to be at least 30% of the form of transit.[25] This law has come under criticism by copper firms.[26]

The DRC is also a copper exporter and faces high prices to bring its output to market. Even if the DRC is not technically landlocked, and it has one of the most important rivers in Africa, copper cannot easily be exported through the main seaport. The copper belt contains nearly all the mines, and this is found in Katanga. DRC's national line (la Voie Nationale – VN) could link its copper mine in the Southeast to its Atlantic port at Matadi, but it is comprised of several rail/river connections that have not been well maintained over time. Copper can move from Katanga (AKA Shaba) to Ilebo by rail, Ilebo by barge to Kinshasa, and from Kinshasa by rail to Matadi.[27] Each leg has been managed by a parastatal, and times have slowed from 50 days in the 1970s to 90 days by 1984.[28]

As a result of these distances and costs, Zaire (DRC) has exported about 37% of its copper and 90% of its cobalt through South Africa, though some intelligence experts estimated copper exports in 1980s were really between 67% and 71%.[29] The main reason that copper was shipped through South Africa was DRC's outdated and poorly maintained equipment and infrastructure – which were due to the lack of prior investment, lack of skilled workers, and overall poor management by the parastatals in charge.[30] In fact, internal shipping costs were estimated to be 8–9% more per ton than they were through Tanzania or South Africa.[31] However, the government prefers to use domestic lines as it saves scarce forex (foreign exchange).[32] Zaire/DRC had exported through the Benguela rail system which passed through a corridor of Angola; however, with onset of Angola's civil war, this option was eliminated in 1975.[33] More recently, copper has been shipped east via Dar es Salaam in Tanzania, and it used to be shipped through Beira in Mozambique. This line was destroyed during the latter's civil conflict.

Since Botswana's top export is gem-quality diamonds, it does not need a rail system to export such a low weight and highly valuable commodity. As a landlocked nation, its rail has to connect to other countries. Despite diamonds being of highest value, Botswana has copper mines and also exports copper-nickel matte, representing approximately 22% of its exports.[34] Beyond diamonds and copper, Botswana has coal, which is mostly used for the production of domestic electricity. Rail lines carrying mining output led to South Africa or to Beria or Maputo. The original colonial rail links were made to link South Africa, to the two Rhodesias, and to the Belgian Congo (DRC).[35]

After independence, Botswana built segments of rail lines to Morupule and Selebi-Phikwe in 1972 for coal, nickel, and copper. They also created segments to Sua Pan to carry soda ash. Botswana would begin the nationalization of rail in 1974, which was completed by 1987. Botswana railways was initially owned by a parastatal, but for most of the Cold War period, it was not majority owned by the government.

Niger is also a landlocked nation and must export its goods through other neighboring nations. Niger had no railway system as of 2000, and the Niger River is only navigable for four to five months a year.[36] So, the yellow cake had to be shipped by road through Niger and Benin until it reached a rail station in Parakou, Benin. Then it has traveled by rail to Cotonou, where it then was then shipped to France. Transportation of uranium yellow cake (magnesium diuranate and sodium diuranate) out of Niger requires special treatment, given the radioactive nature of the export.[37] Many safety regulations have had to be met at each part of the mining, processing, and shipping of the product.

State Ownership of Mining: Worldwide and in Africa

As with oil sectors, worldwide trends in the nationalization of mining sectors have mostly taken place in formerly colonized nations. With the geopolitics of the bipolar world in the wake of WWII, and with most colonies obtaining independence by the mid-1960s through the mid-1970s, developing nations found they had relatively more autonomy internationally during the Cold War.[38] The US usually took a pragmatic foreign policy vis-à-vis nationalization and did little in the face of the nationalization of US companies for fear of increasing zeal for communism in the country of concern – as long as these countries did not raise the Communist flag.[39] At that point, they would get America's interest, but not in a positive way vis-à-vis these new leaders.

Much of the move for governments taking over mining sectors emerged out of the ideologies and realities of colonization and the rise of nationalist movements seeking independence. Between America condoning such actions and with socialist and dependency views of international economics arguing for state-owned or -managed economies, national leaders could easily justify the nationalization of mining resources.

As more newly independent nations gained more relative autonomy vis-à-vis the great powers during the Cold War, the trend was to nationalize economic resources following WWII, though it was strongest in the 1970s.[40] In fact, from 1960 to 1974, the United Nations documented 875 cases of nationalization in 62 countries throughout the world: of these, 340 (or 39%) were in sub-Saharan Africa.[41] Aside from the petroleum sector, this region led all others in the "instances of nationalisation of mining, agriculture, manufacturing, trade, public utilities, banking and insurance."[42] Specifically for mining, in the 1960s, 32 acts of nationalization of MNC in mining were made from 1970 to 1976.[43]

By 1975, several years after the decolonization of most of sub-Saharan Africa, the DRC (then Zaire), Ghana, Mauritania, Sierra Leone, Togo, and Zambia had nationalized their largest mining export sectors at levels of 51% or greater.[44] As for the type of mining involved, Zaire (DRC) and Zambia exported mostly copper, Ghana gold, Mauritania iron ore, Sierra Leone diamonds, and Togo phosphates. In addition, both Angola and the DRC nationalized their diamond sectors, though these sectors did not consistently rise to 30% or more of exports. Ghana, too, nationalized its gold mining sector, but it did not represent 30% or more of exports during our period.

Developmental Impacts of Mining and Majority State Ownership

To compare the developmental experiences of the cases, two countries will be chosen if they have had (1) significant mineral exporting during the period of study, and (2) majority ownership of these sectors for most of this period. Then their experience vis-à-vis predicted resource curse policy outcomes will be compared to two countries which had (1) significant mineral exports during this period, and (2) less than majority state ownership (MSO) of their main mining sectors. Their relevant experiences associated with mining will be outlined as will be the degree of state ownership, usually through acts of nationalizations. Then, as in Chapter 3, the developmental outcomes usually associated with the resource curse will be explored on a case-by-case basis.[45]

As discussed in prior chapters, mining countries are examined from 1966 through 2000. In this way, some control is taken for some of the important shifts in partial political and economic liberalization undertaken by most African countries, though with fewer shifts for oil and mining countries.[46] Significant effects of the International Financial Institutions (IFIs), especially the World Bank and IMF, on African economic management changed in the 1990s, but they were especially evident by 2000.[47] Most African nations had "adjusted" their economic policies to be more in line with the so-called Washington Consensus, and the variance of these policies would be less dramatic after 2000.

Majority State Ownership of Mining

Zambia: Existence of a Major Mineral Exporter

Beginning the 1920s, two major companies dominated the Zambian mining industry: Zambian Anglo-American Corporation Groups and Roan Selection Trust Group, both of which were later nationalized. Copper was important for Zambia for the entire period of independence to 2000. In fact, copper accounted for about 60% of government revenues soon after independence.[48] These companies were nearly always the most important creators of foreign exchange, accounting for over 95% from 1968 until 1973. Mining accounted for about one-quarter of Zambia's GDP.

Following a decline in world copper prices in 1975, by 1983 copper production contributed only 15% of GDP compared to 33% in 1970; nevertheless, its share in exports remained high.[49] In 1980, the export of copper and cobalt[50] constituted 96% of Zambia's exports.[51] Copper's contribution to GDP for the same year was only 17%, and its contribution to government revenue was only 6%. These numbers for GDP and revenue were down from the high in 1969 of 48% of GDP and 59% of government revenue. The percentage value of exports was about the same – 97%. By 1991, copper extraction contributed 93% of foreign exchange earnings, falling to 68% in 1994, and falling again to 52% in 1996. By 2000, the proportion of foreign exchange earned by copper export dropped to about 54%.[52] In fact, copper production in Zambia peaked in 1969, with 720,000 tons, and it continued to decline to 250,000 tons by 2000.[53] Nonetheless, Zambia is clearly within the category of mineral exporter for the period.

Majority State Ownership of Mineral Sector

In 1969, President Kaunda announced the nationalization of the two major copper groups to a level of 51% shareholding buyout by the state.[54] The costs of this acquisition were assessed at book value and were to be paid out of future profits.[55] Full nationalization was achieved in 1973. These two nationalized companies were later consolidated into Zambia Consolidated Copper Mines (ZCCM) in March 1982, and the level of state ownership rose to 60.3%.[56] This level of ownership remained constant until the mid to late 1990s. At the beginning of the 1990s ZCCM was the fifth largest copper producer in the Western world.[57]

Unlike most petroleum-exporting countries, after the end of the Cold War period, a few countries have had considerable experience with the privatization of their mineral sectors. This was rarer during the Cold War. Zambia began privatization plans following multiparty elections in 1991, partially due to the deteriorating economic situation. Moreover, the mines were not sufficiently capitalized, and the new democratic governments did not have deep pockets to recapitalize this sector. Output would decline, while production costs soared.[58]

Like other African countries, a significant political and economic liberalization process began to unfold near the end of the Cold War. This process usually accelerated in the late 1990s or early 2000s. While initial ZCCM privatization plans began in 1992, the basic process started in 1996. By 2000 most mining assets had been privatized.[59] So Zambian mining can be considered MSO from 1969 to 2000 (though it had begun to divest in 1996).

Democratic Republic of the Congo/Zaire

Existence of a Major Mineral Exporter

The DRC (Zaire), too, has been highly dependent on copper for revenue and GDP since independence. Mining traditionally generated 60–70% of export earnings and 70% of the national budget.[60] In 1981, mining, of which copper is the greatest part, comprised 86% of export revenue.[61] In the year of 1974, copper comprised 68% of exports, cobalt 5%, and diamonds 5%.[62] Turner and Young point to the fall of copper prices as one of the significant factors leading to the beginning of the fall of the Zairian (Congolese) state.[63] In the 1990s, just before the civil war, mining accounted for around 75% of exports, rising to 92% in 1992, and then falling to around 60% in 1994.

By the end of 1998, the mining sector nearly collapsed under the weight of the civil war, but artisan diamond mining continued.[64] Nearly all foreign exploration activity and development-oriented feasibility work stopped. Regardless of the decline in foreign activity, the 80% state-owned Société Minière de Bakwanga continued to export diamonds. Then, during the second phase of the war, Rwanda and Uganda started exporting mineral resources extracted from the occupied territories in the DRC.

Majority State Ownership of Mining

In the DRC, the state came to own the most important and lucrative sectors in the country, with the copper sector as the largest piece. Mobutu nationalized its copper industry, Union Minière du Haut-Katanga (UMHK) within seven years of independence, in 1967.[65] This act was one of the first major nationalizations of mining in the postcolonial period. The UMHK had been responsible for around 50% of government revenues and around 70% of its foreign exchange earnings.[66] Mobutu initially only demanded 60% ownership and offered to sell the remaining 40% to other international actors, but when no foreign partners emerged to claim the other 40%, the state came to control 100%.[67] The parastatal which replaced the UMHK was Gécamines (Générale des Carrières et de Mines), and it was responsible for over 90% of copper output during the 1980s. It was also responsible for cobalt, zinc, and coal.[68]

After years of corruption and misrule of both the country and the copper sector, Gécamines found itself under economic pressure, and in 1991 announced that it could no longer fulfill their contracts to supply copper to foreign clients.[69] In 1995, international pressure to privatize invoked attempts at reform, but given Mobutu's need for money to maintain his power, some parts of Gécamines were sold off in 1995, though most of the sector remained under MSO.[70]

With the start of the refugee crisis in Eastern Zaire emerging from the Rwandan Genocide, a civil war would be sparked in 1997, and the Alliance des forces démocratique pour la liberation du Congo-Zaire (AFDL), led by Laurent Kabila would come to control the territory in Katanga (AKA Shaba), where Gécamines operated.[71] During the years following Mobutu's fall, mining rights and ownership became a bit of an international and regional political football, being kicked around on short notice, reflecting changed political fortunes and alliances.

During the rebellion, once Kabila's forces conquered territory, any mining sectors that came under AFDL control had new mining contracts issued. For example, Kabila signed an agreement with an American-owned company, American Mineral Fields International (AMFI), which would have given this company exclusive rights to conduct feasibility studies to rehabilitate some key mines held by Gécamines.[72] In early 1998, after Kabila gained control of the capital, some 15 mining contracts were cancelled by the Congolese government with the justification that investment into the mines concerned had not been forthcoming as the companies had been dragging their feet.[73]

The civil conflict would reignite in August of that year, which discouraged private investment in Congolese mining. With the initiation of a second rebellion, which had the backing of his erstwhile allies of Rwanda and Uganda, and which was now directed at him, Kabila turned to the Southern Africa Development Community (SADC) for backing, and Zimbabwe answered this call by supplying significant military support in August. In fact, their troops were among the first to arrive.[74] In September of the same year, Gécamines signed a joint venture agreement with Ridgepoint, a Zimbabwean company, in which 80% of the Central Mining Group of Gécamines was transferred to this company. Ties with Zimbabwe became tighter when Billy Rautenback, from Zimbabwe, was appointed Managing Director of Gécamines.[75] The contracts and with whom they were signed were often honored in the breach. Despite Gécamines' strong control, its move into joint ventures in 1998 meant that its MSO of the sector was in decline. Nonetheless, we can consider DRC/Zaire to have been MSO for most of the Cold War period through 2000.

Botswana: Existence of a Major Mineral Export

Botswana has a significantly large diamond-mining sector. In fact, Botswana is the third largest mineral producer in all of Africa.[76] For diamonds, Botswana is the largest, producing over 24 million carats-weight of diamonds in 2018.[77] In 2002, mining represented 36% of the GDP, with the diamond sector comprising the largest part of domestic mining.[78] In terms of exports, diamonds represented 82% of exports, and copper-nickel matte represented 6% of exports.

Ironically, the existence of a large-scale mining industry came as a surprise to newly independent Botswana. In fact, a British survey in 1965 (one year before independence) found no evidence for a lucrative large-scale mineral sector. Large-scale mineral exploitation began in 1971 with the Orapa diamond mine, although the mine had been discovered several years before, in 1967. In 1972, diamonds comprised 43.5% of total exports, rising to over 50% in 1976.[79] By 1982, the contribution of mining to export earnings rose to 75%. Two other mines opened in 1982 and 1983, resulting in a total rise of output of 164% from 1981 to 1986. Botswana has a copper mineral sector in addition to diamonds. The copper exports were significantly less in terms of export earnings or contribution to GDP than those from diamonds. From 1990 to 1999, mining represented an average of 70% of Botswana's exports.[80] Importantly, most of Botswana's diamonds are kimberlite diamonds, which means that it requires significant investment and planning to extract them. Almost none of the production is artisan.

State Ownership of Mineral Sector

Unlike so many other mineral-exporting countries, Botswana has less than MSO of this sector, with exactly 50% ownership. By law, Botswana can demand between

15% and 25% of the stock of mining companies without payment, and it can purchase up to 50%.[81] In fact, the parastatal De Beers Botswana Mining Company (DEBSWANA) was jointly owned by the state of Botswana and De Beers Mining Company, which is the sole diamond mining interest in the country. The state enjoys minority ownership, not majority ownership, of the next largest extractive industry: copper-nickel. The government owns 15% of Botswana Roan Selection Trust. Moreover, Botswana has been known as a pragmatic capitalist country in its approach to development.[82] Very few of the main parts of the economy have MSO, with the partial exception of the Botswana Development Corporation (BDC). The BDC is government-owned and -managed, and it invests in the economy to jump start industrial and commercial companies. Nevertheless, it contains the goal of divesting government ownership or control once the company is viable. The BDC was begun in 1970, but with the goals of encouraging private sector development.[83]

Niger: Existence of a Major Mineral-Exporting Sector

Niger became an important producer of uranium mining in 1971 with its mine at Arlit.[84] A second mine opened in 1978 at Akouta. In 1971, uranium ores represented 18.7% of manufactured exports, and this rose to 34% in 1973. This level then reached and remained above 50% until 2000, when it dropped to about 40%.[85] Although mining contributed significantly to the exports of Niger (usually around or above 40%), it has not represented as much of the domestic GDP. For example, mining comprised only about 13% of its GDP in 1980.[86] Niger is the seventh largest exporter or uranium, representing about 5.4% of world production. The mines have traditionally employed between about 1,500 and 1,800 people.[87]

State Ownership of the Mineral Sector

Like Botswana, Niger has less than MSO. When mining began, the main mining company was named the Société des mines de l'Air (SOMAIR), and the majority shares were held by the French company Campagnie générale des mateires nucleares (COGEMA), which was linked to the French government's atomic energy commission.[88] The government of Niger owned 37% through its Office nationale des resources minières du Niger (ONAREM). Most other companies that have been formed saw government ownership at levels of between 31% and 33.35%.[89]

Resource Curse Outcomes

Growth

From 1966 to 1989, Zambia experienced an average growth rate of –2.4%. Extending this to 2000, Zambia experience an average annual growth of –1.8%. Therefore, Zambia had *negative* overall growth rates during the Cold War period. Many point to the relative collapse of copper prices post-1974 as being the most important explanation for this negative growth, however, two of the worst years for economic growth occurred before the copper price collapse (but after nationalization!).[90]

The DRC also experienced average growth of –0.74% per year from 1966 to 1989. Extending the numbers through 2000, the average was much worse, at –3.54 per year. Clearly, the civil war that started in the 1990s further negatively impacted the economy. For example, during the two wars (1996–1997 and 1998–2003) the average growth was –4.3% per year. Nonetheless, during the time of our study, the DRC experienced negative growth.

Botswana, by contrast, had quite strong (*positive*) growth numbers during the Cold War, at an average of 11.4% growth from 1966 to 1989, even if its average growth slowed slightly when the years through 2000 are included, at 9.4%. This was quite an extraordinary performance for any sub-Saharan African nation during these periods.

Niger, more like the MSO countries, experienced *negative* economic growth during the Cold War, with an average level of –2.3% per year from 1966 to 1989, and –2.05% from 1966 to 2000. This made its average more like the MSO countries from this and the prior chapters.

Therefore, only Botswana, a country without MSO, had average positive growth for the period. The DRC's growth was negative prior to the wars beginning the 1990s, and this became even worse during the conflicts later in the decade.[91] Nevertheless, in terms of resource curse effects on growth, Zambia, the DRC, and Niger seem to have suffered the most during the Cold War period. Only Botswana had positive growth during this period. Nonetheless, since each non-MSO country produced and exported distinct types of minerals, and since price per commodity can influence the political economy of ownership, it is hard to make direct comparisons.

Incomes/Wealth

Zambia had an average per capita income level for the Cold War period of $2,418. This average fell to $2,000 when examining the longer period of 1966 through 2000.[92] Although Zambia had relatively higher initial incomes, these fell significantly, especially after 1975. In fact, from 1977 onwards, incomes fell to under $2,000 per person and stayed below this level through 2000. Per capita incomes even fell to under $1,000 for 1994/95 – just before the commencement of privatization. Zambia actually started independence with more wealth than most countries in the region. It began with about the same per capita GDP as did South Korea in 1960.[93]

Zaire (DRC) began the period with high per capita incomes of an average of $2,196 from 1966 to 1989. However, its GDP per capita fell during this period. For example, in 1966 it was $2,788, but from 1976 to 1983, per capita incomes were usually under $2,000. From 1994 to 2000, incomes fell even further, to below $1,000 per person. So, the overall average from 1966 to 2000 was $1,773.

Botswana started as the poorest of the group in 1966, with a per capita income of only $507. This level would climb to a $2,137 Cold War average. The discovery of diamond and their exporting by 1972 clearly changed Botswana's wealth profile. Between 1990 and 2000, its average GDP per capita was $7,694, making it one of the richest countries in sub-Saharan Africa. For the 1966–2000 period, its average income was $3,883.

Niger also began the period being among the poorer countries in the region. In 1966, its per capita income was $1,524, and the Cold War average was $1,166. Continuing through 2000, the average fell to $1,036. Niger saw a slow and steady decline of incomes for most of this period: by 1984, per capita incomes fell to under $1,000 and stayed there through 2000 at under $700.

Here, we see again that Botswana was the best performer in terms of rising incomes, despite it starting at much lower incomes than did either Zambia or the DRC. Of the two non-MSO countries, Niger's per capital incomes seem closer to the prediction for the resource curse, while Botswana does not fit this at all. Although Zambia, DRC, and Niger all had declining incomes, Zambia and DRC's fell the most, despite later rebounds. Niger started out the as one of the poorest nations, and, similar to the MSO states, and it too saw incomes decline, but this was not until the beginning the early 1980s.

Currency Appreciation and Non-Mineral Economic Sectors

As discussed in prior chapters, the Dutch disease has been one of the major explanations for the resource curse. The argument holds that the country's currency appreciates greatly given the inflow of money associated with natural resource exports. This combined with the domestic expansion of the booming sector and resources and talent flowing into it, and out of other sectors, results in the collapse of alternative exporting sectors. Therefore, each mining country is examined for evidence of currency appreciation as well as any decline in the exporting sectors of manufacturing or agriculture.

The Zambian kwacha has been in circulation since 1967, when it replaced the Zambian pound.[94] From 1967 to 1989, the Zambian currency experienced an average annual *depreciation* of 13.3% against the US dollar. During its first few years, the kwacha was pegged to the dollar and could not appreciate or depreciate against the dollar.[95] From 1971 to 1975, the kwacha did briefly appreciate against the dollar – to the tune of about 22% over this time. After 1975, and with the fall of copper prices, the currency then began to depreciate against the dollar and continued to do so through the end of the Cold War. Taking the average through 2000, the average annual *depreciation* was 7.9%, so the total period shows an overall average nominal *depreciation* of 32.3%. Despite a brief period of currency appreciation, the kwacha mostly experienced currency depreciation. On a side note, some have suggested that the brief appreciation was actually due to Zambia's currency peg to the pound at the time of America's devaluation of the dollar in 1971 (when the US abandoned the prior Bretton Woods currency regime).[96]

Looking at real exchange rates, which were available from 1971 onwards, we do see a slight depreciation through 1989 at –1.3%.[97] Taking this average through 2000, it was –1.5%. Even with real exchange rates, the predicted appreciation of currency associated with the Dutch disease is not evident for most of the period when Zambia had control over its own currency exchange rates.

Looking at the DRC/Zaire after the end of the civil wars, the zaire was introduced as the currency of Zaire by Mobutu in 1967. For its first two years, it averaged a *depreciation* of 77%, though it became pegged to the dollar from 1969 to 1975. Therefore, for these years, it had zero depreciation/appreciation vis-à-vis the dollar (officially). Looking at a longer time, from 1967 to 1989, the country's currency experienced an average annual *depreciation* of 47.6%.[98] Taking this to 1993, the last year of the "old" Zaire, the average annual depreciation was 309.8%. Then from 1995 to 1998, the average depreciation rate was about 322%.[99] Therefore, for most of the period, aside from the peg to the dollar, no significant appreciation of the nominal exchange occurred – rather depreciation was the strong syndrome.

Real exchange rates also tell a similar story. From 1968 to 1993 (starting one year after the interdiction of the new zaire), the average real depreciation was 2.4%.[100] The currency had an average appreciation from 1974 to 1997 of –0.03%. This is a relatively low level of depreciation of the real exchange rate. Nonetheless, the DRC did not experience real currency appreciation.

From independence until 1976, Botswana was in a de facto monetary union with South Africa.[101] From 1976 onwards, it established its own currency, the Pula. Even with the launching of its own currency, and despite its significant diamond exports, Botswana experienced a general *depreciation* of its currency against the dollar. From 1966 to 1989, it averaged 5.2% annual depreciation of its currency, and it was 7.6% from 1977 to 1989.[102] From 1977 to 2000, the numbers are similar, with an average annual currency depreciation of 8.2% (only looking at years with the Pula).

Looking at real exchange rates, the rate of appreciation from 1976 to 1989 was –1.4%, which was a depreciating currency. Though 2000, this was 0.6% rate of depreciation. This is clearly a slight, not high, level of depreciation, but it is not appreciation.

Not unlike Cameroon and Gabon, Niger has long been part of a French-backed currency union. In the case of Niger, the union was called the West African Monetary Union (WAMU).[103] Originally, the organization was the Union monétaire ouest-africaine (UMAO) which came into force in 1974. This currency was used by members of the regional trade zone, the Communaute économique de l'Afrique de l'ouest (CEAO). Both were replaced in 1994 by the Union économique et monétaire ouest-africaine (UEMOA). Membership in the Franc zone prevented the manipulation of the exchange rate by the political elites of any particular African country as France held a veto of all major decisions affecting the currency. The external veto clearly means that no direct control over currency valuation by the elites was effective.[104] From 1946 to 1994, the CFA (Communauté française d'Afrique) was pegged to the French Franc at 1 FF to 50 CFA.[105]

During the Cold War, the average level of currency *depreciation* for Niger's currency (the CFA) was 1.8% from 1966 to 1989. Extending this through 2000, the average annual currency depreciation vis-à-vis the dollar was 4.6%. The link to the French Franc, and later the Euro, is key to understanding these levels – much more than Niger's mineral export sector. Niger did have a brief period of currency appreciation against the dollar, but this was more likely due to the strong Franc. We do see an average appreciation of 6.7% from 1986 to 1992, though this would not have been due to Niger's uranium given the currency union's peg to French prices driving valuation more than African prices.[106]

Using real exchange rates, we see an average, but low *depreciation* from 1965 to 1989 of 0.2%. Similarly, through 2000, there were low levels of depreciation, 1.3% (or –1.3% appreciation). In sum, Niger also experienced currency depreciation both nominally and in real terms – not currency appreciation.

Quite contrary to predictions of the resource curse, all of these mining nations experienced an average currency depreciation for most of the Cold War period through 2000.[107] Countries did have some brief periods of appreciation against the dollar, but not for most of the period under question.

Currency Overvaluation

Looking at currency overvaluation for Zambia, the average level was 72% from 1966 to 1986.[108] From another source, from 1975 to 1984, it had an average currency overvaluation of 69%.[109] From 1985 to 1989, the average ratio increased to an average of 2.85, so it was about 185% overvalued. Finally, from 1990 to 1997, the ratio was 2.24. This means the parallel market paid 124% more than the official rates.

For Zaire (the DRC) from 1966 to 1986, the average overvaluation was 142%.[110] From 1975 to 1979, the ratio was 2.94, so it was 194% overvalued.[111] Later, from 1980 to 1985, the ratio was 1.3, and from 1986 to 1990, it was 1.10.[112] Between 1992 and 1993, its levels were off the charts, with an average ratio of 2,513,980![113] Then, from 1994 to 1997 (end of data), the average level of currency overvaluation was down to around 8.75%.[114]

Botswana had one of the lowest levels of currency overvaluation compared to most other African countries outside of the CFA zones. Its average rate from 1966 to 1986 was 11.2%.[115] From 1985 to 1989, its average level of overvaluation increased to about 34%.[116] Then, from 1990 to 1997, it was only overvalued by about 9%.

For Niger, few differences existed between the black markets value for its currency and the official value: the CFA was freely convertible, pegged to French currency, and guaranteed by France. From 1975 to 1984, the ratio of parallel to official market exchange rates was an average of 1.03, so only 3% overvalued. From 1985 to 1989, it was similar, and only at 1.01%. From 1990 to 1997, the average was .99, so it was slightly undervalued, by this estimation.

Prior to the devaluation of the CFA Franc 1994, the World Bank and IMF had suggested it was overvalued by 40–50% in the 1980s, though France was reluctant to revalue the peg until 1994.[117] Even if the zone had been overvalued by 40–50% in the 1980s and early 1990s, this was still much lower than the MSO countries in our sample.[118]

So, it seems that MSO countries experienced much higher levels of currency overvaluation than the non-MSO countries (and not currency appreciation as noted above). And as currency overvaluation seem to mimic the Dutch disease, and it was worse in MSO countries, then they would appear to suffer from a greater extent of the resource curse.

Diversification of the Non-Mineral-Related Export Economy

As mentioned in Chapter 3, the natural resource curse thesis suggests that other parts of the economy which export, or which are import competing, will fall away due to currency appreciation as well as the overdevelopment of the booming sector. We examine the performance of manufacturing and agriculture to discern the degree to which resource curse outcomes manifested in each case.

Manufacturing

Zambia's manufacturing sector was initially established primarily as an import substitution industrialization (ISI) approach and as such was not intended to contribute to exporting – rather it was meant to replace imports to save hard currency in the long run and to develop industry in these countries through "learning by doing."[119] These sectors were initially mostly centered upon vehicle assembly plants, chemical plants, sugar refineries, and textile factories.[120] Other traditional ISI manufacturing sectors included food, beverage, tobacco, textiles, wood, paper, chemicals, mineral products, metals and other easily manufactured goods.[121]

During the Cold War, Zambia's levels of manufacturing as a percentage of GDP mostly increased, starting at 7.81% in 1966 and cresting at 33% in 1992, though these data clearly included mining as part of manufacturing.[122] Consequently, this is not capturing only the activity sectors outside of mining. In 1993, this level declined to about 25%, and it dropped to high single digits the subsequent two years. From 1994 to 2000, manufacturing was between 9% and 10% of GDP. Part of the decline was associated with the low utilization levels that were often below 50% in the 1980s.[123] In per capita terms, value added from industry was about $42 per person from 1966 to 2000. In 1966, it was $32 per person, rising to $51 in 1974, and then hovering around the low $40s from 1989 through 2000.

Despite being such a large part of the economy, non-mining manufacturing has not been a strong exporting sector for Zambia. For example, manufacturing represented less than 1% of exports in 1980.[124] In 1982, only 4% of all exports were composed of non-mineral materials. Looking at a longer period, from 1966 to 1979, manufacturing exports only represented 0.4% of all exports.[125] From another source and different time periods, between 1983 and 1993, manufactured goods represented about an average of almost 7%.[126] By 1999, it had climbed to 16% in 1999, though some of this included the partial refining of copper (and hence not really non-mineral exports), depending on the source.

Similarly, during the Cold War, the DRC attempted industrialization through ISI industries. These produced mostly consumer goods, such as beer, cigarettes, and textiles – it even had a vehicle assembly plant.[127] Most of these were established while copper prices were high. By the late 1980s, given the distortions created by the inward-oriented policies and state ownership, and including pressures on hard currency, most were running only at 30% of production capacity.[128] In 1988, manufacturing only accounted for 1.7% of GDP.[129] Another source reports that it represented about 11% of GDP in the 1980s.[130] Some suggest the discrepancies in the data are due to decline: with manufacturing as a percentage of GDP declining from 10% in 1975 to 2% 1982.[131]

In the DRC, manufacturing did not amount to large percentages of total exports. Between 1965 and 1978, manufacturing represented about 6% of exports.[132] This would increase during the post–Cold War period (between 1990s and 1996) to 13.6%.[133] But we must be careful here because this could be explained by the drop of traditional mineral exports rather than any strong uptick in rival sectors.[134] In fact, later data showed that 89.5% of all exports were of primary commodities, of which 85.3% was mining.[135] The lion's share of nonprimary commodities were industrial diamonds (worked or not) (about 60%). Therefore, it is likely that industrial diamonds were the main component of these higher numbers rather than the export from ISI manufacturing. In fact, of the consumer goods listed, all were less than 1% of exports. Only chemicals and specific manufactured items other were above 1% of exports for two or more of these years.

In Botswana, the manufacturing sector has historically comprised almost 6% of its GDP. For the Cold War years, value added from manufacturing was 5.9%, and this was similar through 2000, at 5.7%. In terms of value added per capita in industry, Botswana averaged around $111 from 1966 to 2000. It began at $26 and rose to $100 by 1975 and stayed above 100 for most years until 1987. But by 1988, it was above $150 for most years.

In terms of exports, in 1999, 7.5% of exports were textiles, vehicles, and parts, and this fell to 3.5% in 2001.[136] It should be noted that the data on Botswana is mixed and inconsistent in terms of exports of manufactured goods. The World Bank African database gives the average of 0% of exports for the years from 1997 to 2000.[137] This shows a gradual increase, at least in value added, if not exports.

Most manufacturing in Niger consists of the processing of agricultural goods as well as some traditional import substitution industrialization sectors. The type of manufacturing included peanut oil extraction, a brewery, cotton ginneries, rice mills, four mills, and tanneries.[138] During the Cold War, manufacturing represented about 5.2% of value added to its GDP.[139] Extending this to 2000, the average became 5.6%. Post–Cold War, this average increased to 5.8%. In per capita value-added terms, Niger averaged only $14, which is among the lowest levels. The first data from 1985 was $19, and this slowly declined to about $14 per person by 2000.

In terms of exporting, during the Cold War, manufactures represented 3.7% of all exports, and this dropped slightly to 3.5% through 2000.[140] In fact, according to *Africa South of the Sahara*, Niger's exports of beverages and tobacco (manufactures), basic manufactures, and machinery and transport equipment, constituted 33% of exports in 1998, with this number including re-exports.[141] Later, from 1999 and 2000, and excluding re-exports, these averaged at 6.1% and 13.8%, respectively.

Hence, during the Cold War, manufacturing as a percentage of exports was low in all of these countries. Despite overall lower levels, clear variance is apparent. It was highest in Botswana, then Niger, then the DRC, and then lowest in Zambia. None of these countries featured a booming (non-mineral) manufacturing export sector and Niger had particularly low per capita value added according to one set of numbers. With the end of the Cold War, manufacturing seemed to rise across the board, though it is still hard to disentangle ores and diamonds processing from non-mineral exports. Nonetheless, the evidence does indicate a slight correlation between low manufactured exports and MSO.

Agriculture

Agriculture has been quite important to Zambia, but not as much as during the colonial period. From 1965 to 1987, Zambia devoted 7% of its land to cropland.[142] In 1973, agriculture represented 11% of GDP, and it grew to around 34% by the early 1990s.[143] Unlike many other countries, Zambia emerged from independence with large commercial farms, which often accounted for around 45% of agricultural output.[144] Much of the farming in Zambia was for domestic or regional consumption, with Zambia often producing enough maize (corn) for domestic consumption. During the Cold War, between 75% and 79% of the population worked in agriculture.[145] From the 1990 onwards, approximately 66% of Zambians worked in agriculture.[146]

With another category of production, Zambia had an average of 13.5% value added for agriculture, forestry, and fishing as a percentage of GDP between 1966 and 1989, and this increased to 14.7% through 2000.[147] Looking at value added per capita in agriculture, we see that Zambia had an average of $62 per person through 2000. It started at $74 per person for value added to this sector and continued a slow decline to about $60 in 2000.[148]

In terms of agricultural exporting, Zambia saw clear declines in the volume of such exports from independence through the end of the Cold War. Tobacco used to be among its most lucrative exports. Unfortunately for this sector, the volume of tobacco exports declined steadily from 1965, with 9,119 metric tons exported, to 1982, with only 2,573 metric tons exported. This number rebounded slightly to 3,600 metric tons by 1987, representing approximately 40% of prior levels.[149]

In volume of all agricultural exports, Zambia averaged a decline of 18.7% per year from 1975 to 1980.[150] In fact, in 1981, Zambia only exported 6,000 metric tons of agricultural goods, which was among the lowest in sub-Saharan Africa. Only the Seychelles and the Comoros showed lower numbers for that year! Zambia did see an average increase in volume from 1980 to 1985 of 31% per year; however, this only brought them up to 30,000 metric tons, placing Zambia among the ten lowest agricultural exporters that year. As a percentage of merchandise exports, the trends for agricultural are similar: agriculture only comprised an average of 0.15% of exports per year during the Cold War.[151] During the late 1970s, Zambia experienced an average annual decline in agricultural exports of 2.6%.

Agriculture has long been quite important to the DRC's economy, even if it has not always represented a high percentage of its GDP. For example, during the Cold War, the percentage of the population that worked in agriculture fell from 75% to 68%. From the 1990s onwards, the average was 70%.[152] During this early period, the value added from agriculture averaged 23.7%.[153] Extending through 2000, the annual average contribution to GDP was 30.6%. Unlike other countries, the DRC's value added peaked in the 1990s at an average of 46.6%, with a high of 56% for 1994 and 1995.

Agricultural represented about 40% of all DRC's exports in 1960, but this fell to 12.5% by 1994.[154] During the Cold War, agriculture represented an average of about 15.5% of all exports.[155] The percentage rose slightly post-1974/75 (when copper prices were falling), where the average was over 25%. This would later fall to an average of 6.5% from 1988 to 1997. Only coffee would sometimes be listed as a significant agricultural export, ranging between 4.2% and 25% (depending on the prices of both coffee and copper), with agriculture representing 40% in one particular year.[156]

In terms of value, agricultural exports as a percentage of exports declined in the DRC at an average of 1.7% per year from 1975 to 1980 as well as declining 8.5% per year between 1980 and 1985. The negative direction continued through 1997, with an average from 1990 to 1997 of negative 3.9% in the value of agricultural exports.[157] In terms of volume (to discount the effect of prices only), from 1975 to 1980, the volume of agricultural exports from the DRC declined an average of 6.5% per year; from 1980 to 1985, it continued a decline in exports at an average of 2.7%. From 1986 to 1988, the decline in volume of agriculture continued, but at an average of 12.6% per year.[158] Nevertheless, as we saw earlier, the overall direction of agricultural exports in both volume and value was negative for most recorded years. In the late 1990s with the civil war, these numbers would be even worse.

Botswana is somewhat unusual for the region as its agriculture sector is mostly comprised of cattle. Given its geography, which contains a large desert and vast savannah, its land is better suited for grazing than for crop production. Over 80% of agricultural GDP is from cattle, and over 78% of agricultural land in the country was dedicated to pastureland.[159] Prior to a robust diamond sector, beef had been the most valuable export.[160] Unlike many other parts of Africa (aside from white settler colonies), large commercial farmers dominate production. For example, in 1975, 15% of farms hosted three-fourths of all cattle.[161] Even in "normal" crops, there was great inequality in ownership and output. During the 1970s, 20% of farmers produced about 60% of agricultural output, and 50% of farmers only produced 10% of output.[162] During the Cold War, agriculture represented 21% of Botswana's GDP, though this dropped to about 16% through 2000. Up to 1974, agriculture generated more than 30% of GDP.[163] But by 1982, the percentage dropped to single digits, and from 2000 onwards, it has always been under 3%.[164]

Despite the declining numbers for agriculture as a percentage of GDP, the percent change in value of agricultural exports in Botswana over time was normally positive. In fact, the average change in value for agricultural exports increased from 1968 to 1989 by nearly 9% per year.[165] In addition, the average through 1997 was 7.3%. From another source, the value of agricultural exports increased annually by an average of 5.2% between 1975 and 1984; it also increased an average of 2.7% from 1985 to 1989, and it increased an average of 5.9% per year from 1990 to 1997.[166]

In terms of export volume, Botswana saw a negative growth in volume of agricultural exports of 10% from 1975 to 1980. It had a rebound of 10.4% average growth from 1980 to 1985, but it experienced another decline of 28% from 1986 to 1988. One must remember that Botswana is often affected by severe droughts, which clearly can impact the agricultural output independent of any government policy. In fact, Botswana experienced major droughts during the years 1982–1987, 1992, and 1995.[167] However, given the rising value of exports through these years, the economy has not suffered from an apparent Dutch disease in the agricultural sector even if it has underperformed due to climate.

Niger, like Botswana, faces significant challenges in agriculture related to geography and climate. Despite Niger being larger than Nigeria in land mass, two-thirds of the country is desert, large parts of which are uninhabitable.[168] One source suggests that only 35% of all land is available for settled farming.[169] One other thing to consider with Niger and agriculture is that Niger faces severe desertification and loses an average of 200,000 ha per year. Like Botswana, the agricultural sector of Niger is dominated by livestock rearing, which accounted for 14% of GDP in 1988. Despite such challenges, the agricultural traditional sector usually employs more than 80% of the working population.[170]

During the Cold War, agriculture in Niger represented an average of 51% of value added to the GDP, with numbers falling from around 70% in the mid-1960s to around 35% in 1989. Extending the average through 2000, the average was 48%. In addition, from available data, agriculture employs approximately 90% of all workers.[171]

In terms of exports, the value of agricultural exports grew from 1975 to 1984 by an average of 8.4% per year.[172] However, from 1985 to 1989, these exports decreased by an annual average of 7.5%, and the countries continued to see an average decline of agricultural value from 1990 to 1997 of 4.1%. It should be remembered that Niger, like much of the Sahel, experienced significant droughts in 1983–84, 1987, 1990, and 1995–97.[173] According to one source, Niger was the African country most impacted by the Sahel droughts of the 1970s and 1980s.[174] Not only does it suffer from frequent droughts, but it also has experienced significant issues with pests. For example, Niger suffered from a major locust invasion in 1988.[175] Nonetheless agriculture makes up an important part of exports. For example, in 1985, live animals, vegetables, and hides/skins represented approximately 16% of exports by value.[176] Of these, live animals represented nearly 12% of this 16%. Uranium, in the same year, represented 79% of exports.

We see similar numbers for agricultural exporting, where Niger experienced an average growth of 5.5% per year from 1975 to 1980, a negative average for the years of 1980–85 of 3.3%, and a greater average loss of 14% from 1986 to 1988, in which several years of drought were evident.[177] We should note, however, that according to some scholars, much of Niger's export of cattle may be done off the books, thereby underestimating its true value.[178]

As such, a booming mineral sector reduces the percentage of value agriculture has for the GDP, but a truer measure is volume and value added per capita over time as well as agricultural exports trends. And despite having the toughest geographies, Botswana and Niger had longer periods of positive growth in value added and growth in export volume, while Zambia and the DRC saw this sector becoming a fraction of what it once was, despite having much greater potential in agricultural output and volume, and many fewer droughts. Here the competing sector of agriculture in the MSO countries had a stronger "resource curse effect."

Diversification of the Economy: Horizontal or Vertical Linkages to Mining

Refining Mineral or Other Mining Ventures

Like other copper producers, Zambia also mines cobalt. In fact, most cobalt is found as a byproduct of either nickel or copper mining.[179] Interestingly, most of the cobalt in the world comes from Zambia and the DRC.[180] For Zambia, cobalt represented between 17.5% and 20.6% of total exports from 1996 to 1998.[181] Zambia was the second most important producer of cobalt in 1987, representing about 11.5% of world production that year.[182] In addition, Zambia mined smaller quantities of zinc, lead, gold, silver, selenium, marble, emeralds, and amethysts.[183]

Zambia does engage in some value added beyond mere copper mining, but mostly by changing ores to refined copper. In fact, refined copper constituted around 90% of its exports in the 1980s.[184] Zambia had three smelters during most of the period under study, more than elsewhere in Africa.[185] Even with this capacity, Zambia rarely refines more than 5% of its output beyond blister.[186] According to a World Bank analysis, Zambia cannot likely capture much value added by moving into more sophisticated copper fabrication in the short to medium term.[187] Aside from nickel, many other metals needed to produce alloys with the copper elements are not mined in Zambia and would have to be imported.[188]

Like Zambia, the DRC also extracts cobalt, though it also mines diamonds and zinc. In addition, in the north and east, the DRC also has cassiterite, wolframite, gold, and columbo-tantalite.[189] These latter minerals plus diamonds are mainly mined by small scale enterprises and/or artisan labor – making output difficult to track and regulate. The DRC did have smelting plants for copper, but most of its exported copper is less refined than Zambia's. The Shituru refinery usually processed about 225,000 tons per year.[190] However, unrest in the region damaged production ability. Moreover, non–copper mining represented about 17% of all exports in 1982. More recently, Zaire started to export crude petroleum in 1981, though it only represented about 15% of all exports in 1981–82. Copper, plus other mining, plus oil represented 75% of exports.[191]

Interestingly, the DRC had a white elephant associated with what could have been an otherwise wise investment decision involving mining and refining.

Quite publicly, Mobutu launched the Maluku steel mill in 1972. The economic logic of its viability was linked to the building of the Inga-Shaba dam that could provide sufficient energy for the making of steel and the smelting of copper in Shaba. Unfortunately, the plan was ill-conceived, even at the time: the iron ore deposits were too far away and too expensive to mine, and the plant rarely achieved even 10% capacity.[192] It was finally closed in 1980.[193] The Inga-Shaba dam was completed in 1982, but it rarely operated at full capacity and neighboring countries were reluctant to purchase electricity from Mobutu's Zaire. In 1990, for example, the dam only generated 14% of its total potential.[194]

Botswana too has other minerals to mine beyond diamonds, such as copper, nickel, iron ore and coal. Of these, only copper and nickel received significant investments during most of the Cold War period. The Selebi-Phikwe mine project was initiated while copper prices were very high. The plant required massive infrastructure development, which the government provided. Production was begun in 1974 and total production was to have been reached in 1975. However, between the slowness of achieving full production and the fall in the world price for copper, the economic results were poor. In 1975, for example, it faced operating losses of $23 million. With the drastic fall in (inflation adjusted) copper prices just the year before, and a series of technical difficulties, Botswana saw a drastic shortfall in production. These troubles resulted in the mines running at well below capacity.[195] Even when production improved in 1977 and 1978, the mines continued to incur economic losses due to low prices for copper and nickel.[196] Botswana would see the opening of two other mines in the late 1980s. As a percentage of exports in 1987, diamonds represented 85% of the value of exports, and copper represented about another 4%.[197] This number for copper and nickel matte was similar to the contribution of agriculture for the same year.

Botswana does have a smelter in country, which was built in the 1970s to help process its nickel and copper mining. Bamangwato Concessions Limited's (BCL) original nickel smelter was built during the 1970s.[198] The parent company of BCL is 15% owned by the government of Botswana, but majority shares belong to Anglo-American and Amex Corporation.[199] The approximately 4,200 employee operation produces around 50,000 tons per annum (tpa) of granulated high and low sulfur matte that contain nickel, copper, cobalt, iron, and sulfur, as well as precious and platinum group metals. By the 1990s, it was able to process 1,142 tons of nickel and 1,051 of copper.[200] The sector has both made and lost money over the years, mostly based upon the price of copper and nickel.

Botswana does not process most of its mined diamonds. Nonetheless, through ownership and taxation, it captures the lion's share of this segment of its diamond sector.[201] Botswana also sells and markets rough diamonds to companies licensed by the government.[202] In 1971, it created the Botswana Diamond Valuing Company (BDVC) to participate in appraising the value of its diamonds. In addition, Botswana opened its first diamond polishing and cutting factory, owned by the Diamond Manufacturing Botswana, in 1976.[203] However, De Beers was not very supportive of this aspect of the business – although three such factories were established between 1980 and 1990, none recorded a profit.[204]

The uranium which is mined in Niger is exported with little processing. In fact, its uranium only goes through one processing step: from ore to yellow cake.[205] It is milled in country at either the SOMAIR uranium mill or at the COMINAK mill.[206] This yellow cake contains less than 1% U-235. The rest of the processing of the ore takes place in the importing country.[207]

Niger has recently also found gold and oil. The gold finds were beginning to draw international interest around 2000. This resource remained unexploited during the Cold War. The government also wanted to begin oil exploration and passed legislation to facilitate this in 1991.[208] Niger also has other minerals, such as cassiterite, iron ore, calcium phosphates, and gypsum. Even with these potential sources of mineral production and exports, in the early 1990s, no other minerals were listed as significant sources of exports. The data are unclear as much as 13% of exports were not attributed to particular sectors (or listed as miscellaneous), and many exports from Niger were actually re-exports.[209]

The DRC, by contrast, has more diversification of minerals exports compared many others countries. Nonetheless, it has had little by way of upstream value added. Aside from a few smelters, Congo's attempts at processing and other development projects have been widely viewed as ineffective white elephants beset by corruption and inefficiency. Zambia has several smelters for its copper, which does add some value added. Botswana has a smelter for its much smaller copper sector, while Niger does not refine its uranium – given the highly sensitive and dangerous potential of uranium. Here Zambia, as an MSO country, had some success in smelting, but its ability to move far up the manufacturing ladder is limited by a lack of access to other alloys, as well as its high transportation costs.

Levels of Investment, Debt, and Inflation

Investment

Zambia began with having a large share of gross domestic fixed investment as a percentage of GNI. From 1970 to 1989, it averaged 23% of GNI. This number would fall, however, from nearly 30% in 1970 to 10.8% in 1989. This number rebounded slightly from 10.8% in 1989 to 18.28% in 2000. During later years, from 1990 to 2000, this average was only 14.5%. In per capita terms, Zambia started with some of the highest numbers, at $448 per person in 1970, but this declined an average of 12% per year until 1989, when it arrived at $34 per person. It rose slightly from 1990 to 2000, with an average of nearly $50 per person in the second period. The overall average (1970–2000) was $146, but a downward trend clearly existed during the Cold War period. The partial privatization starting in 1996 may be responsible for some of the rebound in savings near the end. Nonetheless, Zambia did not invest enough in its copper mines after nationalization, which many say lead to an overall decrease in production of 24% between 1982 and 1990.[210]

The DRC had low levels of gross domestic fixed investment during the Cold War period. From 1966 to 1989, it averaged 13.5% of gross national income. From 1990 to 1997, this declined to an average of 6.85%. For the longer average (to

2000), investment represented 11.8% of GNI. In per capita terms, from 1968 to 1989, it averaged $51 per person per year. Post–Cold War to 2000, this fell to $15.72 per person, resulting in an overall average of $41.68 per year.

Looking at investment in Niger, from 1966 to 1989, gross fixed investment averaged 14.71% per year. Investment rose slowly through 1980, going from 8% to 20% through 1983. Then it declined to low double digits through 1989 with lower uranium prices. Uranium prices were in decline until 1973, and then they rose significantly through 1979, and fell from the 1980s through 2000.[211] However, investment as a percentage of GNI was single digits for most years between 1990 and 1996. After the end of the Cold War and through 2000, it averaged 9% of GNI. For the whole period, it averaged 12.6%. In per capita terms, the Cold War average for Niger was $51.15 up to 1989, and $20.39 from 1990 to 2000, for an overall average of $35.

Botswana had relatively high levels of gross domestic fixed investment during the whole period. During the Cold War, from 1966 to 1989, its level of investment was 33% per year of GNI. From 1990 to 2000, this fell slightly, to about 25.7% of GNI per year. Examining the period from 1966 to 2000, it averaged 30.7% investment of GNI per year. This is quite high. In per capita terms, from 1982 to 1989, it averaged $570 per person (in 1995 dollars) from 1982 to 1989. This increased to about $812 per person 1990–2000, for an overall average of $710 for this longer period.

From this group we see that Botswana had the highest levels of savings of these countries. During the Cold War, it had the highest average percentage of investment as a percentage of GNI and the highest per capita investment. Moreover, the numbers for investment continued to grow for most of this period – indicating no negative effects on investment were associated with its booming mineral sector. Through 2000, Botswana still had the highest levels of saving, but the averages shrank a bit for both categories. Niger and the DRC had quite similar numbers for percentage of GNI and per capita for investment, though Niger had begun as one of the poorest countries in sub-Saharan Africa. Also, Niger had only slightly better numbers for investment as a percentage of GNI relative to the DRC.

Zambia is a special case, as its numbers were so high for the start of the period (numbers started at 1970), but its trajectory was negative during the Cold War period. In fact, it was the only country to have an average negative percentage change in fixed investment as a percentage of GNI, and it had the steepest fall in per capita incomes – falling from second highest at nearly $500 per person down to $34 per person in 1989. Even Niger had higher numbers in 1989, at $42 per capita. However, Zambia had negative trends in investment as a percentage of GNI, even if it had had the second highest numbers overall. Nonetheless, in 1989, it had a lower percentage than any of the other four countries, at 10.8%, compared to DRC (14.3%), Niger (13.7%), and Botswana (30.9%).

So, one non-MSO country did not appear to have negative impacts on its investment levels (Botswana), and one MSO (Zambia) country started strong by this metric. Zambia's numbers, however, dropped amazingly quickly during the Cold War period (Zambia). Niger and the DRC had similar performances, although

Niger had slightly better investment numbers during the Cold War period. It might also be appropriate to remind the readers that nationalization was meant as a means of capturing profits and creating more investment domestically, and this clearly did not happen in these cases.

Debt

High levels of debt for countries was also one of the negative policy outcomes associated with the resource curse. Starting with Zambia, we see that total debt as a percentage of exports was relatively high at 301.7% from 1970 to 1989. It began at 81% in 1970. However, this quickly increased to over 700% by 1986. This lowered to just above 400% for 1989. From 1990 to 2000, the average was just shy of 600%, with only one year (1997) below 500% (494%). As a percentage of GDP, it was high with an average of 116.7% from 1970 to 1989. It began at about 50% in 1970 and rose through 1986 to 339%. From here it gradually declined to 164% by 1989. From 1990 to 2000, the average of total debt to GDP was 204%, and most years were in the high 100s or low 200s.

The DRC also had high levels of debt relative to its exports. The average for 1970–1989 was 232.6%, but this built from a low in 1970 of 42.6%, rising to over 300% from 1985 to 1989. The average from 1990 to 2000 greatly increased to 742%. The DRC's debt load was lower when reported as a percentage of GDP. During the Cold War, it was 40%, starting quite low in 1970 at 7%, rising to about 100% between 1985 and 1989. From 1990 to 1998, the average rose to 178%.

Niger's levels of debt as a percentage of exports were lower than either Zambia's or the DRC's. Its Cold War average ratio of debt to exports was 187%. Beginning at about 50% in 1970, it rose to over 400% by 1986. It remained at the 300% level from 1987 to 1989. Niger's debt rose to represent 463% of exports from 1989 to 2000. These are high levels, yet still lower than the DRC's or Zambia's levels. Looking at total debt as a percentage of GDP, Niger's had an average level of 37.7% between 1970 and 1989. From 1990 to 2000, this number rose to 81%.

Botswana had relatively lower levels of debt by either measure during these years. The level of debt as a percentage of exports from 1970 to 1989 was 42.8%. It began at 30% in 1970 and rose to 84% in 1974. This level then dropped to under 40% after 1979. In fact, the average total debt as a percentage of exports dropped in the period of 1990–2000 to 24.7% (unlike other countries examined in these cases). As a percentage of GDP, Botswana had relatively low levels of debt, with the 1970–1989 average of 26.9%. Here too debt peaked at around 40% from 1972 to 1977, and then declined to an average of 20%. From 1990 to 2000, the average was 13.8%, which was lower than during the Cold War period.

Looking at levels of debt, we see the MSO countries had higher level of debts by either measure, and we also see that the non-MSO countries had lower levels by either measure. Zambia was clearly the most indebted by these numbers, with highest levels of debt from 1970 to 1989, even if the DRC would surpass it from 1990 to 2000 for levels of debt weighted by exports.[212] The country with the least levels of debt by any measure was a non-MSO country, Botswana. Niger's numbers from 1990 to 2000 were not great, even if they were lower than those of Zambia and the DRC. Niger's numbers were also much better relative to these two MSO countries in the years 1970–1989. Therefore, high levels of debt were either missing or less bad in the non-MSO countries compared to the two MSO cases.

Inflation

As will be discussed in Chapter 6, inflation had empirically been linked with MSO in prior studies, so we will look to see if this relationship holds for minerals. Moreover, inflation should be expected for exporters of minerals, but unlike oil, prices for each country's major export would not be steady across our cases.

Inflation numbers for Zambia are hard to find before 1986, though for the years from 1986 to 1989, the average level of inflation was 69.3%. The average from 1986 to 2000 was 71%, so average from 1990 to 2000 was 71.6%, just slightly higher than the combined average. These are relatively high levels of inflation, even if they do not reflect hyperinflation.

Inflation in the DRC has shown to be quite volatile and quite high at times. From 1966 to 1989, it averaged 45% per year. For the years 1990–2000, inflation became more problematic for the DRC, with an average inflation rate of 1,007.7% per year. From 1991 to 1994, it was in the thousands of percent each year, and from 1995 to 2000, it was measured in the hundreds, aside from 1998. These data reflect clear hyperinflation for several years.

Botswana's inflation numbers were much tamer by comparison. During the Cold War, from 1976 to 1989, the average level of inflation was 11% (the Pula was introduced in 1974). From 1990 to 2000, the numbers were similar, but slightly lower, at 10.6%, with the overall average from 1975 to 2000 to be 10.8%. These were not high by African standards.

In Niger, from 1966 to 1989, the average level of inflation was relatively low, at 6.6%. From 1990 to 2000, it was even lower at 4.2%. The overall average from 1966 to 2000 was 5.8%. We need to keep in mind that Niger had a relatively independent bank as well as a currency backed by the French treasury – and the French had a majority vote on monetary policy.

Here we see clearly that inflation was much lower in the non-MSO countries, and it was hyperinflation in the case of the DRC post–Cold War. Even Zambia's inflation was high, just not extraordinarily so.

Levels of Democracy/Freedom

Another issue raised by resource curse literature, especially with oil, is the link of mining and oil to authoritarian regimes. During the Cold War, most countries in sub-Saharan Africa had either military regimes or one-party regimes, as discussed before, despite some variance in levels of authoritarianism. In fact, only three countries maintained multiparty regimes a decade after independence – one of which was Botswana.

Zambia emerged from independence as a one-party dominant system; however, it became a de facto one-party state with the banning of the main opposition party in 1972. The main ruling party, the United National Independence Party (UNIP), held approximately two-thirds of the seats until 1972, when it held a 100% through 1991.[213] During most of this period, Zambia was rated as partially free until 1980 when it edged into the not free category until 1983, whereupon it was rated as partly free until 1990. From 1980 until the return of multiparty elections, it was rated as either a 5 or a 5.5 for all those years (with 5 as partly free and 5.5 as not free). So, during the Cold War period, it was rated as a 5.2. With the start of its transition to multiparty rule, from 1991 to 1992, it was rated as free – though it soon returned to partly free through 2000.

The DRC did not come into independence with a single or dominant party, and it soon fell into a civil war.[214] By 1972, it became a de jure single party state under Mobutu. This party was named the Mouvement Populaire de la Révolution (MPR).[215] During the Cold War, the DRC's average level of freedom was 6.4, with this measure alternating between 7, 6.5, and 6. Of course, this means that the DRC was considered "not free" for the whole period. Unlike other countries in sub-Saharan Africa, the DRC did not have a transition to multiparty electoral competition – rather they had a blocked transition.[216] Following the Cold War, the ratings did not improve much, and Mobutu never allowed a transition to multiparty rule to emerge, and its first multiparty elections were not until after our period, in 2006.[217] It took a civil war and his overthrow to remove him from power. Nonetheless, the DRC has been rated as not free from 1972 to 2000.

Botswana has been of course, one of the primary exceptions to single party rule or military rule in sub-Saharan Africa, along with the Gambia and Mauritius. Nonetheless, Botswana did emerge following independence with a one-party dominant state: the Botswana Democratic Party (BDP) has won every election since and usually by wide majorities. Nonetheless, the country has been considered a multiparty democracy for nearly the whole time by most scholars.[218] In 1972, it scored 3.5, which is partially free. From then onwards, it has scored 2.5 or lower (which is considered to be free). Its Cold War average was 2.4, and from 1990 to 2000, it obtained a rating of 1.95. Overall, it scored 2.27 for political and civil rights from 1972 to 2000, which puts it into the free category unlike most of our other countries.

Niger, like most Francophone West Africa states, became a single party regime right after independence. As a result of economic distress following droughts, it experienced a coup in 1974.[219] Niger would not hold multiparty elections from then until 1993. From 1972 to 1989, Niger averaged 6.4, which was not free. Like other Francophone countries, during the period of transition, it too had a national conference in 1991 and held founding elections in 1993.[220] From 1993 through 1995, it was rated as partially free. However, a coup d'état in 1996 reversed the transition and led to military rule. The new regime, under Maïnassara, wrote a new constitution, and then held elections widely seen as not free or fair. In 1999, another military coup led to the death of Maïnassara, and a new regime emerged. From the end of the Cold War to 2000, its average level of freedom was 4.9, which is partially free, though two coups took place, with a "not free" interregnum between the two coups.

In our mining countries, we see the worst performer vis-à-vis political and civil liberties was a country with MSO of mining: the DRC. Also, we see that the best performer had less than majority ownership of its mining sector: Botswana. The rank order was not maintained for MSO and non-MSO because Niger was ranked as not free for the Cold War period, while Zambia was partly free. Both nations came to have partly free polities in the Cold War period. Niger had a three-year reversal period and Zambia only had a two-year period rated as free.

Violence and MSO

Zambia did not have much violence surrounding its postindependence society, either before or after it nationalized its mining sector. The Zambians did not fight a war for independence against the British, and no civil wars ensued during the period of study. In fact, only one incident of communal violence was recorded for 1964.[221]

Soon after the DRC began its independence, it experienced civil war from 1960 to 1965. It again experienced civil conflict in 1977 and 1978, 1996–97, and from 1998 to 2004 and beyond. So it experienced 13 years of civil war from 1960 to 2000.[222] Moreover, the civil war that began in 1996 consumed over 1,500,000 lives (through 2004), and over 149,000 battle deaths.[223] Moreover, between 1998 and 2007 over 5.4 million deaths have been estimated to have occurred, meaning that likely over 6 million lives have been lost since 1996.[224] Although this civil war became internationalized, the consequences have been clearly catastrophic for the DRC and its citizens.

Finally, of our two non-MSO countries, neither Botswana nor Niger experienced civil war. Additionally, neither country has had recorded levels of intercommunal violence during the Cold War period. Botswana, in particular, has been considered an island of stability for sub-Saharan Africa. Niger has not had any recorded years of civil war, but it has had seven years of recorded ethnic violence between 1990 and 1997, which was associated with 1,000 deaths and 500 battle deaths.

Conclusions

We can see that nearly every variable strongly linked to negative resource curse outcomes were stronger in the MSO mining countries than for the non-MSO countries, but not for all. However, even when the rank order was not perfectly maintained, the worst performer by that variable was nearly always an MSO country and the best performer was a non-MSO country – though usually both MSO countries were worse off than both the non-MSO countries for these variables.

Looking at the primary variable of growth, the two oil countries with MSO of this sector (the DRC and Zambia) featured *negative* per capita economic growth during this period. Low or negative economic growth was the most important negative consequence outlined by resource curse theory. Interestingly, we also had one non-MSO mining country which featured negative growth: Niger. This puts it in contrast with other non-MSO mining countries which had average positive growth for the period (see Table 2.3). This makes it the only one of our four non-MSO countries to have negative growth (please see prior chapters). Botswana, by contrast, had quite strong growth levels and has become one of the wealthier nations in sub-Saharan Africa.

Looking at the second variable of interest, wealth, the rank order was not maintained, as Niger's per capita incomes began and remained low until 2000, when it finally became the second highest of these four. For the first time, we see a non-MSO country have the worst outcome on one of these variables, at least for a while. As a landlocked, Sahelian nation with few resources, Niger began as the poorest and remained among the poorest. Botswana also started as one of the poorest nations in sub-Saharan Africa. However, with its non-MSO diamond industry, it grew to be one of the wealthier nations in the region – not the expected result of the resource curse. By contrast, both Zambia and the DRC started out with more wealth in terms of income than either Niger or Botswana, but both declined in wealth over time. Botswana was the best performer in terms of rising incomes, even if it started at lower incomes than did either Zambia or the DRC. Of the two non-MSO countries, Niger seems closer to the natural resource curse. Although Zambia, DRC, and Niger all had declining incomes, Zambia and DRC's fell the furthest, despite later rebounds. Niger started out among the poorest, and, like the MSO states, it also saw incomes decline. However, these declines only began in the early 1980s.

As discussed in Chapter 3, one potentially surprising finding is the lack of high levels of currency appreciation, on average, for the cases for most of the period. Currency appreciation is often considered to be the key mechanism producing much of the resource curse problem: the Dutch disease. Again, we find that none of the four have had average appreciation – in fact, all have had an average *depreciation* throughout our period, whether nominal or real. However, we do find the MSO countries had higher levels of nominal currency depreciation.

In fact, as discussed in prior chapters, the more likely culprit for the withering of alternative export sectors is currency overvaluation, and it has been shown that MSO countries have featured much higher currency overvaluation. The DRC/Zaire had by far the highest levels of currency overvaluation though 2000, with some years needing scientific notation to write levels. Zambia also had high levels of currency overvaluation for most of this period. By contrast, the two non-MSO countries had lower levels of overvaluation. Botswana had one of the lowest levels compared to most other African countries (and outside of the CFA zones). For Niger, only minor difference existed between the black market rates and official rates for its currency, the CFA. This is because the CFA, was freely convertibility, pegged to French currency, and guaranteed by France. Thus, it had no currency overvaluation by our measure.

Another primary predictor of the resource curse, and related to the above point, is the decline over time of alternative export sectors. Manufacturing and agriculture are often identified as the most likely alternative sources for exports or value added in sub-Saharan Africa. During the Cold War, manufacturing as a percentage of exports was low in all these countries. Nonetheless, some variance is apparent – the non-MSO countries had a slight lead in exports of manufactured items. With the end of the Cold War, manufacturing seemed to rise across the board, though it is still hard to disentangle ores and diamonds processing from non-mineral exports. Nonetheless, the evidence does indicate a slight correlation between low manufactured exports and MSO.

The MSO countries, which had more and better land than the non-MSO countries, saw a clear decline in the exports from agriculture over time. Zambia saw clear declines in the volume of agricultural exports during its independence period through the end of the Cold War. In fact, in 1981, Zambia's levels of agricultural exports were among the lowest in the region. The DRC also saw significant declines in agricultural productivity and its ability to export agricultural products. The overall direction of agricultural exports in both volume and value was negative for most recorded years. In the late 1990s with the civil war, these numbers would be even worse.

In the non-MSO countries, we see a slightly better performance in agricultural exports, despite their inherently more difficult environments. The percent change in the value of agricultural exports in Botswana was normally positive for most years – usually over 5%. In terms of export volumes, they sometimes contracted, and sometime rose. Botswana's agricultural outcomes are also highly dependent upon weather shocks, such as droughts. Nonetheless, given the rising value of exports through these years, the economy has not suffered from an apparent Dutch disease in the agricultural sector, even if it has underperformed due to climate. Not unlike Botswana, Niger also faces difficulties with drought and soil. Even so, the value of agricultural exports grew for a decade from 1975 to 1984, but it experienced a contraction from 1985 to 1989 – linked with drought events.

We also saw that the non-MSO countries had higher levels of investment. Given the argument that nationalization was a cure for keeping MNCs from draining away profits, the reverse should have been true. The non-MSO country of Botswana had the highest levels of savings for the most years of these countries. Niger and the DRC had quite similar numbers for percentage of GNI and per capita for investment, though Niger was one of the poorest countries in sub-Saharan Africa. Also, Niger had slightly better numbers for investment as a percentage of GNI relative to the DRC, even if the differences were not great. Zambia was unique in that it started with very high levels; nevertheless it had the steepest fall in per capita incomes – falling from second highest at nearly $500 per person down to $34 per person in 1989. So, one non-MSO country did not seem to have resource curse impacts in investment (Botswana), and one MSO country started strong, but its numbers dropped amazingly during the Cold War period (Zambia) as per the resource curse prediction.

Looking at levels of debt, as either a percentage of exports or of the GDP, we see the rank order of MSO countries having higher level of debt by either measure, and the non-MSO countries had lower levels by either measure. The country with the least levels of debt by any measure was a non-MSO country, Botswana. Although

Niger's numbers were relatively high, they were still lower than those of Zambia and the DRC, by either measure.

Next, with an examination of inflation, the non-MSO countries tended to have lower levels than the MSO countries, often by several orders of magnitude. The non-MSO countries had low two-digit levels or lower, while Zambia and the DRC had high two digits or higher, with the DRC registering hyperinflation.

In the case of our mining countries, and within this subsample of four countries, the rank order for levels of political and civil rights was not kept for all MSO and non-MSO since Zambia had better numbers than Niger. What is also clear is that the most authoritarian country was MSO, and the freest country was non-MSO. Moreover, Botswana, a non-MSO mining country, was ranked as free for nearly the whole period, which is exceptional for any African nation.

Finally, the country with the most domestic violence was an MSO country: the DRC. It experienced a bloody civil war associated with significant chaos during its early independence period. It also experienced civil war in the post–Cold War period. Moreover, like Angola, it has had alluvial diamonds which can be captured by small groups to fund conflict. By contrast, the other MSO country, Zambia, had little violence associated with its state-owners sector. Some might suggest that since the copper mines were deep mines, which were not lootable in the same way as alluvial diamonds are. Nonetheless, neither of the two non-MSO countries experienced civil war or significant periods of civil violence.

Notes

1 Mining (2017). Also see ReporterLink (2023). https://finance.yahoo.com/news/mining-global-market-report-2023-123400878.html#:~:text=The%20global%20mining%20market%20grew,(CAGR)%20of%206.1%25.
2 In 2016. See Ericsson and Löf (2019, 230).
3 Zimnisky (2017).
4 Business Research Company (n.d.).
5 Thus, coal is excluded from this statistic.
6 Ericsson and Löf (2019, 231).
7 Adu and Dramani (2018, 3).
8 Lange and Reggio (2013).
9 Unless stated otherwise, data in this section comes from World Bank (2002c), this data, appendix B.
10 *Economist* (2013)
11 Ibid.
12 Hilson, Hilson, and Pardie (2007).
13 United Nations (2009).
14 Ahoule et al (2015, 302).
15 Adomako, Deacon, and Meharg (2010).
16 South African Human Rights Commission (2016).
17 Bosson and Varon (1977, 19).
18 World Bank (2002b).
19 Unless stated otherwise, issues involving uranium mining come from Spoon (n.d.); for more details, see National Research Council (2012).

20 Dudar, Zakrytnyi, and Bugera (2015, 70).
21 Meyns (1984, 17).
22 Ibid., 18.
23 Cobbe (1979, 30).
24 World Bank (2011).
25 Makgetla, Levin, and Mtanga (2019).
26 Mfula, Kumwenda-Mtambo, and Evans (2018). Other bulk shippers were included in this mandate.
27 Much of this section comes from CIA (1986).
28 Morgan et al. (1985, 27).
29 By 1987, most copper and cobalt were exported through South Africa and not through the domestic rail-river system. Brooke (1987, 6).
30 CIA (1986).
31 Ibid., 5.
32 Foreign exchange/hard currency.
33 Though it reopened in 2018. See International Mining (2018).
34 *Africa South of the Sahara* (2011).
35 Unless stated otherwise, information in this section comes from Lionjanga and Raman (1990).
36 *Africa South of the Sahara* (2011). A rail line from Niamey to Parakou is planned, and one phase was opened in 2014. Reuters (2015). Also Africa News (2019).
37 Unless specified otherwise, information in this section comes from Manou (2003).
38 Clapham (1996), Krasner (1978, 1985), Quinn (2016).
39 Krasner (1978, 1985).
40 Krasner (1978, 1985), also Rood (1976); Quinn (2002).
41 United Nations Secretary General (1974).
42 Rood (1976, 431). British spelling has an s.
43 Raw Materials Group (2011).
44 Rood (1976), Quinn (2002), Shafer (1983).
45 The chapter will not examine negative externalities associated with mining exploration because it will be nearly impossible to draw inferences here: both MSO mining countries are copper exporters, and the two non-MSO countries export diamond and uranium. Any semblance of control through a quasi-experimental design will be lost as the types of pollution and externalities will be so significantly different given the variance in mineral produced. For case study design and issues, see King, Keohane, and Verba (1994); Collier (1993). For variation on most similar design, see Quinn (2009).
46 Quinn (2016, esp. chapter 8).
47 van de Walle (2001).
48 Unless stated otherwise, data from this section comes from Sklar (1975), this data p. 52.
49 The decline in prices was more inflation-adjusted than nominal. Copper did decline from 1974 to 1974 (from $2,059 to $1,237 MT in 1975). However, this price in 1975 was higher in nominal terms than all prices from 1950 to 1972. Also, 1973 was the first OPEC oil hike, with 1979 another significant hike. It can be argued that oil prices drown down relative copper prices as much as anything else did. For prices, see World Bank (1986).
50 Since cobalt is found in the same ore with copper, it is often included in the figures. This is because the extraction of cobalt – in addition to copper – does not increase the fixed cost of mining. Thus, it is much like heating oil is to gasoline.
51 *Africa South of the Sahara* (1990).
52 *Africa South of the Sahara* (various years).

53 Sikamo, Mwanza, and Mweemba (2016, 494).
54 Ibid.
55 Sklar (1975).
56 Craig (2001).
57 Ibid., 392.
58 Sikamo, Mwanza, and Mweemba (2016, 493); see also Shafer (1983).
59 *Economist* (1999); Craig (2001), Sikamo, Mwanza, and Mweemba (2016).
60 Shafer (1983, 94).
61 Sklar and Bergen (1990, table 1).
62 Vanderlinden (2000, 210).
63 Young and Turner (1985, 307).
64 Coakley and Szczesniak (1999).
65 Young and Turner (1985, 288).
66 Ibid., 289.
67 For details see ibid., 288–296, also Schatzberg (1984).
68 *Africa South of the Sahara* (1996).
69 *Africa South of the Sahara* (2004).
70 Carter Center (2017, 16–20). Mobutu was considered less valuable after the end of the Cold War. See Quinn (2004).
71 It was known as Shaba from 1972 to 1997. Although it is now broken into four new regions.
72 *Africa South of the Sahara* (2004).
73 Coakley (1999).
74 *Africa South of the Sahara* (2004).
75 Ibid.
76 *Africa South of the Sahara* (2004).
77 NS Energy (2020).
78 *Africa South of the Sahara* (2004).
79 African South of the Sahara (1996).
80 World Bank (2002c).
81 Quinn (2002, 100).
82 Young (1982).
83 For more on this, see Kaunda (1999, 259).
84 *Africa South of the Sahara* (2011).
85 World Bank (n.d.), ores and metals exports (% of merchandise exports). Uranium was their major export. Later Niger would find cassiterite, iron ore, calcium phosphates, salt, and coal; these were not exported in significant numbers. By 2015, they had reserves of gypsum, limestone, salt, silver, tin, and gold. In fact, in 1988, uranium constituted 98% of its inedible crude exports. *Africa South of the Sahara* (1996, 2015).
86 *Africa South of the Sahara* (1990).
87 Grancea et al. (2020, 65, table 1.21).
88 See, for example, Martin (1989). So, it was majority state-owned by the French government. Unless stated otherwise, this section draws information from *Africa South of the Sahara* (1996).
89 World Nuclear Association, "Uranium in Niger." https://world-nuclear.org/information-library/country-profiles/countries-g-n/niger. Also Grancea et al. (2020, 63, table 1.18).
90 Shafer (1983).
91 Although one could argue that poor economic management was partially behind the discontent that led to Mobutu's overthrow, see Quinn (2004, 2014).

92 Unless stated otherwise, per capita income comes fromFeenstra, Inklaar, and Timmer (2015). [Penn World Tables 9.1], real GDP expenditure side chained PPPs per capita 2011 US$.
93 See, for example, Shafer (1990).
94 Bank of Zambia (n.d.).
95 All data about official exchange rates, unless otherwise attributed, come from World Bank (n.d.), official exchange rate (LCU per US$, period average). So, a depreciation means that more local currency is needed to purchase the same amount of the hard currency, which in this case is the dollar.
96 Bank of Zambia (n.d.).
97 Real exchange rates taken from Darvas (2021). World Bank numbers were missing for some countries and more years.
98 When I was a Peace Corps volunteer in the early to mid-1980s, the joke/saying was this: "A zaire saved is a zaire lost." This was because the inflation rate was always higher than savings rate. Moreover, the real exchange rate was so different (and so much lower) from the black market rate that it did not make sense to exchange dollars at the bank if you could avoid it. Many did not, I have heard.
99 This leaves out the year of revaluation at it would be an outlier number.
100 Real exchange rates taken from Darvas (2021).
101 Cowitt (n.d.), Botswana; Callings (1978).
102 From 1977 onwards, it was only the Pula. The data for 1976 was left out given the change that year from one currency to another.
103 See, for example, *Africa South of the Sahara* (1996), regional organizations, the Franc Zone. See also Cowitt (n.d.), CFA Franc. It was slated to face significant changes in structure in 2020.
104 For background, see Central African Economic and Monetary Community: International Democracy Watch (n.d.) and Hadjimichael Galy (1997).
105 Grimm (1999).
106 World Bank (n.d.), official exchange rate (LCU per US$, period average), though that meant a 40% increase in value against the dollar over this time. See also Grimm (1999, 19). Over time it was mostly depreciating.
107 At least in official terms and compared to the dollar, the main international hard currency in which oil has nearly always been denominated.
108 Pick (various years) and Cowitt (various years).
109 World Bank (2000, 3–8). It was 1.69. A ratio of one is no overvaluation, and under one is currency undervaluation. Anything over one is currency overvaluation, at least by this measure.
110 Quinn (2002, 111).
111 World Bank (1992, table 3-8).
112 Ibid.
113 Ibid.
114 Calculated from ibid.
115 Quinn (2002, 111).
116 World Bank (2000, table 3-8).
117 Gulde (2016).
118 Ibid. The way overvaluation is measured, we capture only differences between official and parallel market rates.
119 Meyns (1984, 14).
120 Quinn (2002, 70); for impulses for ISI, see Hirshman (1968).

121 Meyns (1984, 14).
122 Unless stated otherwise, data from this section comes from World Bank (n.d.).
123 Makgetla (1994, 107).
124 Simson (1985, 53).
125 Unless stated otherwise, all data on manufactured exports comes from World Bank (n.d.), manufactures exports (% of merchandise exports), various countries.
126 World Bank (2002).
127 *Africa South of the Sahara* (1996). For other descriptions of industry, see Kaplan (1979, 182) and Young and Turner (1985, 305). For Peace Corps training, the regional representatives actually visited an auto assembly plant in Kinshasa during 1985.
128 Gran (1979), *Africa South of the Sahara* (1996).
129 Kaplan (1979).
130 World Bank (2002), manufacturing as share of GDP (%).
131 Hesselbein (2007, 35). Per capita value-added numbers were not available for the DRC.
132 World Bank (n.d.).
133 World Bank (2002).
134 Ibid.
135 Between 2008 and 2014. World Trade Organization (2016), table A1.1 (author's calculation). www.wto.org/english/tratop_e/tpr_e/s339_e.pdf
136 Calculated from *Africa South of the Sahara* (2004).
137 World Bank (2002a). Most other years are missing for this particular variable.
138 *Africa South of the Sahara* (various years).
139 World Bank (n.d.), manufactures exports (% of merchandise exports), Niger.
140 Though the years 1982–1994 were not in the database. World Bank (2002a).
141 *Africa South of the Sahara* (2004).
142 World Bank (1989, 279).
143 *Africa South of the Sahara* (1996).
144 Ibid.
145 World Bank (2000, table 11-4).
146 World Bank (n.d.), Zambia, employment in agriculture (% of total employment).
147 Ibid., WDI: agriculture, forestry, and fishing, value added (% of GDP).
148 World Bank (2002), value added (constant 1999) and population.
149 FAO (n.d.), Zambia: Tobacco.
150 African Development Indicators (1992, 8–9).
151 WDI, agricultural raw materials exports (% of merchandise exports).
152 WDI, employment in agriculture (% of total employment) (modeled ILO estimate).
153 WDI, value added Agriculture % GDP.
154 *Africa South of the Sahara* (2004).
155 Calculated by dividing agricultural exports (current $) from World Bank (2002a) by merchandise exports (current $) from World Bank (n.d.)..
156 *Africa South of the Sahara* (1996, 2004).
157 World Bank (2000, table 8-7).
158 World Bank (1992).
159 *Africa South of the Sahara* (1996), World Bank (1989, 279).
160 Colclough, and McCarthy (1980, 110).
161 "The Rural Income Distribution Survey," cited in Colclough and McCarthy (1980, 112).
162 Colclough and McCarthy (1980, 128).
163 WDI, agriculture, forestry, and fishing, value added (% of GDP).

164 WDI (n.d.).
165 World Bank (2002a), agricultural exports.
166 World Bank (2000, table 8-7).
167 World Bank (2000, 8–14), also World Bank (1992, table 8-16).
168 *Africa South of the Sahara* (1996).
169 *Africa South of the Sahara* (2015).
170 *Africa South of the Sahara* (1996).
171 World Bank (2000, 11–14).
172 Ibid., 8-7.
173 Ibid., 8–14.
174 *Africa South of the Sahara* (1990).
175 Two others would follow in 2003–5 and 2012. The locust invasions devastating Niger, See UNDRR, (2017).
176 *Africa South of the Sahara* (1990).
177 WNB (1992, 8–9).
178 *Africa South of the Sahara* (2015).
179 www.shalinaresources.com/copper-cobalt-facts.html.
180 Ibid.
181 *Africa South of the Sahara* (2013).
182 Mineral Commodity Survey (1988, 41), cobalt,
183 *Africa South of the Sahara* (2004), Zambia.
184 Ibid, 35.
185 Mining in Zambia (n.d.) This number includes a fourth one which was built in.
186 World Bank (2011, ii).
187 Ibid.
188 Ibid., 26.
189 *Africa South of the Sahara* (1996, 2004).
190 *Africa South of the Sahara* (1996), Zaire.
191 *Africa South of the Sahara* (1990), Zaire.
192 Young and Turner (1985, 296–298).
193 Kaplan (1979, 154).
194 Ibid., 155
195 Colclough and McCarthy (1980, 61).
196 Ibid., 149.
197 *Africa South of the Sahara* (1990), Botswana.
198 Bamangwato Concessions Limited (BCL) later changed to BCL Limited tout court.
199 *Africa South of the Sahara* (1990).
200 Murray (1991).
201 *Africa South of the Sahara* (1990).
202 Brook (2012, 3)..
203 Brook (2018)., .
204 Fasih (2014). After 2005, Botswana used the leverage of renewing its diamond lease with DeBeers to push for their support for more value-added sectors within the country (p. 3).
205 About this, see Sample (2003).
206 For a list of ownership and uranium mills, see EJOLT (2015).
207 Larsen and Mamosso (2013, 18).
208 *Africa South of the Sahara* (2000).
209 Ibid.

210 EIU (1992: I9), Smith New Court (1994: I7), cited in Craig (2001, 392), also see Sikamo, Mwanza, and Mweemba (2016).
211 Heff (2004, figure 1).
212 Even leaving out 1997 to 2000.
213 See Sklar (1974), *Africa South of the Sahara* (various years), Gertzel, Baylies, and Szeftel (1984).
214 Young and Turner (1985).
215 A few people in my village said MPR stood for *Mourir Pour Rien* (die for nothing). Personal conversations with locals. Peace Corps, Wamba, Zaire, 1985.
216 Bratton and van de Walle (1997).
217 Gettleman (2006).
218 Though it would not make Huntington's two turnover threshold (1993, 267). For Botswana democracy at that time, see Holm (1988).
219 McGowan (2003).
220 For links of these conference to French national assembly, see Robinson (1994); for conference in Togo and Benin, with an emphasis on associational groups, see Heilbrunn (1993).
221 Marshall (2006, annex 1a) and Sarkees and Wayman (2010) . Unless specified otherwise, data on conflict in this section comes from these two sources.
222 Though Marshall's data (2006) also includes 1984 and 1992–1996.
223 Its most recent civil war diffused and became a larger regional war, though with a continued civil war element; Lemarchand (2001), Prunier (2008), Quinn (2014).
224 International Rescue Committee (n.d.).

References

Adomako, Eureka E., Claire Deacon, and Andrew A. Meharg. 2010. "Variations in Concentrations of Arsenic and Other Potentially Toxic Elements in Mine and Paddy Soils and Irrigation Waters from Southern Ghana." *Water Quality, Exposure, and Health* 2: 115–124. https://doi.org/10.1007/s12403-010-0029-0.

Adu, George and John Bosco Dramani. 2018. *Africa's Mineral Economies: Breaking Their Dependence on Mining*. Uppsala: The Nordic Africa Institute.

Africa News. 2019. "Niger: Railway Section Inauguration." January 30. www.africanews.com/2016/01/30/niger-railway-section-inauguration

Africa South of the Sahara. Various Years. Various Countries. New York: Europa Publications.

Ahoulé, Dompé Ghislain, Franck Lalanne, Julie Mendret, Stephan Brosillon, and Amadou Hama Maïga. 2015. "Arsenic in African Waters: A Review." *Water, Air, & Soil Pollution* 226(9): 1–13.

Bank of Zambia. n.d. "Currency History." www.boz.zm/currency-history.htm#:~:text=History%20of%20Zambian%20Currency&text=Before%20Zambia'%20s%20independence%20in,banknotes%20and%20the%20ngwee%20coins

Bosson, Rex and Bension Varon. 1977. *The Mining Industry and the Developing Countries*. Oxford: Oxford University Press.

Bratton, Michael and Nicholas Van de Walle. 1997. *Democratic Experiments in Africa: Regime Transitions in Comparative Perspective*. Cambridge: Cambridge University Press.

Brook, Michael C. 2012. *The Journey of Botswana's Diamonds*. Gaborone: DTC Botswana.

Brook, Michael C. 2018. "The Botswana Diamond Pipeline: 'Prospecting to Jewellery.'" *Botswana Journal of Earth Sciences* 7: 43–57. https://minedocs.com/21/Debswana-Prospect-2018.pdf

Brooke, James. 1987. "Zaire: Hostage to a Railroad, Seeks to Cut South Africa Tie." *New York Times*, February 12.

Business Research Company. n.d. "Mining/Global/Coal Market." www.thebusinessresearchcompany.com/report/coal-market

Callings, Francis d'A. 1978. "The Rand and the Monetary Systems of Botswana, Lesotho, and Swaziland." *Journal of Modern African Studies* 16(1): 97–121.

Carter Center. 2017. *A State Affair: Privatizing Congo's Copper Sector*. Atlanta: Carter Center.

Central African Economic and Monetary Community: International Democracy Watch. n.d. http://webarchive-2009-2022.internationaldemocracywatch.org/index.php/monitored-igos/africa/551-central-african-economic-and-monetary-community.html

CIA. 1986. "Zaire's National Route: A Northern Option?" Washington, DC: Directorate of Intelligence. www.cia.gov/readingroom/docs/DOC_0000865339.pdf

Clapham, Christopher S. 1996. *Africa and the International System: The Politics of State Survival*. Cambridge: Cambridge University Press.

Coakley, George J. 1999. "The Mineral Industry of Congo (Kinshasa 1997)." *US Geological Survey*. https://d9-wret.s3.us-west-2.amazonaws.com/assets/palladium/production/mineral-pubs/country/1997/9244097.pdf

Coakley, George J. and Philip A. Szczesniak. 1999. "The Mineral Industry of Congo (Kinshasa)." https://d9-wret.s3.us-west-2.amazonaws.com/assets/palladium/production/mineral-pubs/country/1999/cg99.pdf.

Cobbe, James H. 1979. *Governments and Mining Companies in Developing Countries*. Boulder: Westview Press.

Colclough, Christopher and Stephen McCarthy. 1980. *The Political Economy of Botswana: A Study of Growth and Distribution*. Oxford: Oxford University Press.

Collier, David. 1993. "The Comparative Method." In Ada Finifter, ed., *Political Science: The State of the Discipline II*. Washington, DC: American Political Science Association.

Cowitt, Philip P. ed. Various Years. *World Currency Yearbook*. New York: International Currency Analysis.

Craig, John. 2001. "Putting Privatisation into Practice: The Case of Zambia Consolidated Copper Mines Limited." *Journal of Modern African Studies* 39(3): 389–410.

Darvas, Zsolt. 2021. "Timely Measurement of Real Effective Exchange Rates." Working Paper 2021/15, 23 December.

Dudar, Tamara, Ye Zakrytnyi, and Mihail Bugera. 2015. "Uranium Mining and Associated Environmental Problems in Ukraine." *Наукоємні технології* 1: 68–73.

Economist. 1999. "Selling the Family Copper." November 4.

Economist. 2013. "Africa and China: More Than Minerals." March 23. www.economist.com/middle-east-and-africa/2013/03/23/more-than-minerals

Ericsson, Magnus and Olof Löf. 2019. "Mining's Contribution to National Economies between 1996 and 2016." *Mineral Economics* 32(2): 223–250.

Fasih, Tazeen. 2014. *Skills Implications of Botswana's Diamond Beneficiation Strategy*. Washington, DC: World Bank.

Feenstra, Robert C., Robert Inklaar and Marcel P. Timmer. 2015. "The Next Generation of the Penn World Table." *American Economic Review*, 105(10), 3150–3182.

Food and Agricultural Organization. n.d. "Production Tables, Zambia: Tobacco." www.fao.org/faostat/en/#data/QV

Gertzel, Cherry, Carolyn Baylies, and Morris Szeftel, eds. 1984. *The Dynamics of the One-Party State in Zambia*. Manchester: Manchester University Press.

Gettleman, Jeffrey. 2006. "Congo Holds First Multiparty Election in 46 Years." New York Times, July 31.

Gran, Guy. 1979. "An Introduction to Zaire's Permanent Development Crisis." In Guy Gran, ed., *Zaire: The Political Economy of Underdevelopment*. New York: Praeger, 1–25.

Grancea, Luminita, Mark Mihalasky, Martin Fairclough, Jean Rene Blaise, Alexander Boytsov, Adrienne Hanly, Luis Lopez, James Marlatt, Gabi Schneider, and Robert Vance. 2020. *Uranium Resources, Production and Demand 2020*. No. NEA--7551. Organisation for Economic Co-Operation and Development.

Grimm, Sven. 1999. "Institutional Change in the West African Economic and Monetary Union (WAEMU) since 1994: A Fresh Start after the Devaluation Shock?" *Africa Spectrum* 34(1): 5–32. www.jstor.org/stable/40174785

Gulde, Anne-Marie. 2016. "Overview." In Anne-Marie Gulde and Charalambos G. Tsangarides, eds., *The CFA Franc Zone: Common Currency, Uncommon Challenges*. Washington, DC: International Monetary Fund, 1–24.

Hadjimichael, Michael T. and Michel Galy, 1997. "The CFA Franc Zone and the EMU." IMF Working Paper No. 97/156. Washington, DC: International Monetary Fund.

Heff, T. L. 2004. "History as a Prelude: The Outlook for Uranium." *Nuclear Energy Institute International Uranium Fuel Seminar*.

Heilbrunn, John R. 1993. "Social Origins of National Conferences in Benin and Togo." *Journal of Modern African Studies* 31(2): 277–299.

Hesselbein, Gabi. 2007. "The Rise and Decline of the Congolese State: An Analytical Narrative on State-Making." Crisis States Research Centre Working Paper No. 21. London: LSE/Destin Development Studies Institute. www.lse.ac.uk/international-development/Assets/Documents/PDFs/csrc-working-papers-phase-two/wp21.2-rise-and-decline-of-the-congolese-state.pdf

Hilson, Gavin, Christopher J. Hilson, and Sandra Pardie. 2007. "Improving Awareness of Mercury Pollution in Small-Scale Gold Mining Communities: Challenges and Ways Forward in Rural Ghana." *Environmental Research* 103(2): 275–287.

Hirshman, Albert O. 1968. *The Political Economy of Import-Substituting Industrialization in Latin America*. Boston: MIT Press.

Holm, John. 1988. "Botswana: A Paternalistic Democracy." In Larry Diamond, Juan J. Linz, and Seymore Martin Lipset, eds., *Democracy in Developing Countries*, vol. 2. Boulder: Lynne Rienner, 179–216.

Huntington, Samuel P. 1993. *The Third Wave: Democratization in the Late Twentieth Century*, vol. 4. Norman: University of Oklahoma Press.

International Mining. 2018. "Opening Up Historic Transport Route from DRC Mines." September 26. https://im-mining.com/2018/09/26/opening-historic-transport-route-drc-mines.

International Rescue Committee. n.d. www.rescue.org/report/mortality-democratic-republic-congo-ongoing-crisis

Kaplan, Irving, ed. 1979. *Zaire: A Country Study*. Washington, DC: The American University.

Kaunda, Jonathan M. 1999. "The Botswana Development Corporation: Divestiture Policy and Citizen Participation in the Private Sector." *Development Southern Africa* 16(2). https://doi.org/10.1080/03768359908440076.

King, Gary, Robert O. Keohane, and Sidney Verba. 1994. *Designing Social Inquiry: Scientific Inference in Qualitative Research*. Princeton: Princeton University Press.

Krasner, Stephen D. 1978. *Defending the National Interest: Raw Materials Investments and U.S. Foreign Policy*. Princeton: Princeton University Press.

Krasner, Stephen D. 1985. *Structural Conflict: The Third World against Global Liberalism.* Berkeley: University of California Press.

Lange, Andrew and Riccardo Reggio. 2013. "Mining in Africa: How Inclusive Solutions Can Mitigate Risk." *Monitor Deloitte* 2013: 1–12. www2.deloitte.com/content/dam/Deloitte/us/Documents/strategy/us-consulting-mining-in-africa.pdf

Larsen, Rasmus Kløcker and Christiane Alzouma Mamosso. 2013. "Environmental Governance of Uranium Mining in Niger: A Blind Spot for Development Cooperation?" *Danish Institute for International Studies*. www.jstor.org/stable/resrep13351

Lemarchand, René. 2001. *Exclusion, Marginalization and Political Mobilization: The Road to Hell in the Great Lakes*. Copenhagen: Centre of African Studies, University of Copenhagen.

Lionjanga, A. V. and V. Raman. 1990. "Transportation and Economic Development in Botswana: A Case Study." *Transportation Research Record* 1274. http://onlinepubs.trb.org/Onlinepubs/trr/1990/1274/1274-023.pdf.

Makgetla, Neva, Saul Levin, and Sithembiso Mtanga. 2019. "Moving Up the Copper Value Chain in Southern Africa." WIDER Working Paper 2019/52. www.wider.unu.edu/sites/default/files/Publications/Working-paper/PDF/wp-2019-52.pdf

Makgetla, Neva Seidman. 1994. "Control in the Parastatal Sector in Zambia: 1976–1986." In *State-Owned Enterprises in Africa*. Boulder: Lynne Rienner, 107–124.

Manou, B. 2003. *Niger Uranium Concentrates Transport (IAEA-CN-101)*. Geneva: International Atomic Energy Agency. https://inis.iaea.org/collection/NCLCollectionStore/_Public/34/055/34055997.pdf?r=1

Marshall, Monty G. 2006. "Conflict Trends in Africa, 1946–2004: A Macro-comparative Perspective." Africa Conflict Prevention Pool, Government of the United Kingdom.

Martin, Guy. 1989. "Uranium: A Case-Study in Franco-African Relations." *Journal of Modern African Studies* 27(4): 625–640.

McGowan, Patrick J. 2003. "African Military Coups d'état, 1956–2001: Frequency, Trends and Distribution." *Journal of Modern African Studies* 41(3): 339–370.

Meyns, Peter. 1984. "The Political Economy of Zambia." In Klans Woldring, ed., *Beyond Political Independence: Zambia's Development Predicament in the 1980's*. New York: Mouton, 7–22.

Mfula, Chris, Olivia Kumwenda-Mtambo, and David Evans. 2018. "Zambia's Chamber of Mines Says Rail Transport Law 'Inappropriate and Unworkable.'" *Reuters*, January 30.

Mining.com. 2017. "Just How Big Is the Oil Market?" https://oilprice.com/Energy/Crude-Oil/The-Oil-Market-Is-Bigger-Than-All-Metal-Markets-Combined.html

Mining in Zambia. n.d. https://miningforzambia.com/five-things-you-didnt-know-about-smelting

Morgan, George A., Ben A. Kornhauser, and Kevin Connor. 1985. *Zaire*. Washington, DC: US Dept. of the Interior, Bureau of Mines.

Murray, Roger. 1991. "Botswana." *Mining Magazine*. https://link.gale.com/apps/doc/A11283704/AONE?u=north1010&sid=ebsco&xid=089a8ed3

National Research Council. 2012. *Uranium Mining in Virginia: Scientific, Technical, Environmental, Human Health and Safety, and Regulatory Aspects of Uranium Mining and Processing in Virginia*. Washington, DC: The National Academies Press. https://doi.org/10.17226/13266.

NS Energy. 2020. "Top Five Diamond Mining Countries of Africa Profiled." March 9. www.nsenergybusiness.com/news/top-five-diamond-mining-africa

Pick, Franz. Various Years. *Pick's Currency Yearbook*. New York: Pick Publishing.

Prunier, Gérard. 2008. *Africa's World War: Congo, the Rwandan Genocide, and the Making of a Continental Catastrophe*. Oxford: Oxford University Press.

Quinn, John James. 2002. *The Road Oft Traveled: Development Policies and Majority State Ownership of Industry in Africa.* Westport: Praeger.

Quinn, John James. 2004. "Diffusion and Escalation in the Great Lakes Region: The Rwandan Genocide, the Rebellion in Zaire, and Mobutu's Overthrow." In S. E. Lobell and P. Mauceri, eds., *Ethnic Conflict and International Politics: Explaining Diffusion and Escalation*. New York: Palgrave Macmillan, 111–132.

Quinn, John James. 2009. "When You Cannot Find the Perfect Match: Using the Accumulated Most Similar Design Case Study." *Journal of Political Science Education* 5(3): 250–267.

Quinn, John James. 2014. "The Nexus of the Domestic and Regional within an International Context: The Rwandan Genocide and Mobutu's Ouster." In Amy L. Freedman, ed., *Threatening the State: The Internationalization of Internal Conflicts*. Oxford: Routledge, 39–74.

Quinn, John James. 2016. *Global Geopolitical Power and African Political and Economic Institutions: When Elephants Fight*. Lanham: Lexington Books.

Raw Materials Group. 2011. *Overview of State Ownership in the Global Minerals Industry*. Washington, DC: The World Bank.

Reuters. 2015. "Benin, Niger Finalise Terms of Bollore's One Billion Euro Rail Link." 8 April. www.reuters.com/article/idUSKBN0MY27Z/

ReporterLink. 2023. "Mining Global Market Report 2023." (April 21). https://finance.yahoo.com/news/mining-global-market-report-2023-123400878.html?guccounter=1

Robinson, Pearl T. 1994. "The National Conference Phenomenon in Francophone Africa." *Comparative Studies in Society and History* 36(3): 575–610.

Rood, Leslie L. 1976. "Nationalisation and Indigenisation in Africa." *Journal of Modern African Studies* 14(2): 427–447.

Sample, Ian. 2003. "Is Niger a Good Source of Uranium?" *The Guardian*, July 17. www.theguardian.com/science/2003/jul/17/thisweekssciencequestions2

Sarkees, Meredith R. and Frank Wayman. 2010. *Resort to War: 1816–2007*. Washington DC: CQ Press.

Schatzberg, Michael. 1984. "Zaire." In Timothy Shaw and Olajide Aluko, eds., *The Political Economy of African Foreign Policy*. Aldershot: Gower, 283–318.

Shafer, D. Michael. 1983. "Capturing the Mineral Multinationals: Advantage or Disadvantage." *International Organization* 37(1): 93–119.

Shafer, D. Michael. 1990. "Sectors, States, and Social Forces: Korea and Zambia Confront Economic Restructuring." *Comparative Politics* 22(2): 127–150.

Shalina Resources. n.d. "About US/Copper and Colbalt Facts." www.shalinaresources.com/copper-cobalt-facts.html

Sikamo, Jackson, Alex Mwanza, and Cade Mweemba. 2016. "Copper Mining in Zambia: History and Future." *Journal of the Southern African Institute of Mining and Metallurgy* 116(6): 491–496.

Simson, Howard. 1985. *Zambia: A Country Study*. Uppsala: Scandinavian Institute of African Studies.

Sklar, Richard L. 1975. *Corporate Power in an African State: The Political Impact of Multinational Mining Companies in Zambia*. Boulder: Westview Press.

Sklar, Richard L. and Geoffrey Bergen. 1990. "Mineral Industries and Development in Sub-Saharan Africa." In Anatoly A. Gromyko and C. S. Whitaker, eds., *Agenda for Action: African-Soviet-U.S. Cooperation*. Boulder: Lynne Rienner, 111–120.

South African Human Rights Commission. 2016. "National Hearing on the Underlying Socio-economic Challenges of Mining-Affected Communities in South Africa." www.sahrc.org.za/home/21/files/SAHRC%20Mining%20communities%20report%20FINAL.pdf

Spoon, Marianne. n.d. "How Uranium Mining Works." *How Stuff Works*. https://science.howstuffworks.com/uranium-mining5.htm.

UN Secretary General. 1974. "Permanent Sovereignty over Natural Resource." A/9716 (Supplement to E/5425), September 20.

UNDRR. 2017. "The Locust Invasions Devastating Niger." *PreventionWeb*. www.preventionweb.net/news/view/51992

United Nations. Economic Commission for Africa; African Union Commission (2009-02). *Africa Mining Vision*. Addis Ababa. © UN. ECA. https://hdl.handle.net/10855/23743

US Geological Survey. 2010. *Mineral Commodity Survey 1988*. Washington, DC: US Geological Survey.

van de Walle, Nicolas. 2001. *African Economies and the Politics of Permanent Crisis, 1979–1999*. Bruxelles: Centre de Recherche et d'Information Socio-Politiques.

Vanderlinden, Jacques, ed. 2000. *Du Congo au Zaïre: 1960–1980: Essai de Bilan.*

World Bank. 1986. *Commodity Trade and Price Trends*. Washington, DC: The World Bank.

World Bank. 1989. *Sub-Saharan Africa: From Crisis to Sustainable Growth*. Washington, DC: The World Bank.

World Bank. 1992. *Africa Development Indicators*. Washington, DC: The World Bank.

World Bank. 2000. *Africa Development Indicators*. Washington, DC: The World Bank.

World Bank. 2002a. *African Database* CDROM. Washington D.C.: World Bank.

World Bank. 2002b. *It's Not Over When It's Over: Mine Closure around the World*. Washington, DC: The World Bank.

World Bank. 2002c. *Treasure of Trouble: Mining in Developing Countries*. Washington, DC: The World Bank.

World Bank. 2011. "What Is the Potential for More Copper Fabrication in Zambia?" Finance & Private Sector Development Unit, June. http://documents1.worldbank.org/curated/en/464461468178438692/pdf/623790ESW0P1070sclosed0Dec027020110.pdf.

World Bank. n.d. "World Development Indicators." https://databank.worldbank.org/source/world-development-indicators.

World Nuclear Association. n.d. "Uranium in Niger." https://world-nuclear.org/information-library/country-profiles/countries-g-n/niger.

World Trade Organization. 2016. "Trade Policy Review." Democratic Republic of the Congo. WT/TPR/S/339. www.wto.org/english/tratop_e/tpr_e/s339_e.pdf

Young, Crawford. 1982. *Ideology and development in Africa*. New Haven: Yale University Press.

Young, Crawford and Thomas Turner. 1985. *The Rise and Decline of the Zairian* State. Madison, WI: University of Wisconsin Press.

Zimnisky, Paul. 2017. "Global Natural Diamond Production Forecasted at 142M Carats Worth $15.6B." www.mining.com/web/2017-global-natural-diamond-production-forecasted-142m-carats-worth-15-6b

5 Updating Post-2000 Trends

Status of Ownership, New Mineral- or Oil-Exporting Nations, Economic and Political Liberalization, and International Changes Impacting Mineral- or Oil-Exporting Nations

Changes or Continuation of Ownership of Mining or Oil Sectors

A worldwide trend in privatization emerged first in Europe in the 1970s, which then began to spread to the developing world near the end of the Cold War. With over 8,000 acts of privatization worldwide, over a trillion dollars was raised with the privatization of state-owned firms.[1] Thus, the movement toward privatization in sub-Saharan Africa was part of a larger workwide trend, though it also took the form of the partial fragmentation of both economic and political power with the end of the Cold War.[2]

Prior to 1990, only 15 African countries had significant experience with privatization, though these countries' largest and most lucrative sectors usually remained in state hands.[3] This process of privatization in Africa really began with smaller scale industries and then spread to larger and larger sectors, especially for countries which came under strong structural adjust programs.[4] As more acts of privatization were pursued, larger industries were privatized later, and the mining or oil sectors were often the last to go – if at all. Many privatizations were seen in the region between 1991 and 2002, when around 2,300 acts of privatization were recorded in Africa, with sales of nearly \$9 billion.[5] This number would climb to over \$12.5 billion from 2000 to 2008.[6] Throughout sub-Saharan Africa important movements toward privatization were seen in most countries by 2001.[7]

Although the largest firms and large export sectors were usually the last to be privatized, if at all, some regional privatization in the mining sector was evident. Ethiopia, Tanzania, and Ghana sold important portions of their mining sectors. The Ashanti gold mines in Ghana were privatized successfully in 1993/4, representing 47% of all Ghanaian divestiture revenue from 1989 to 1998.[8] Importantly, none of these countries had more than 30% of its exports coming from these sectors. Nonetheless, many other governments retained majority state ownership (MSO) of natural resource sectors, especially in the petroleum sector.

In terms of our case studies, we see significant privatization taking place in mining. We also see continued MSO in oil as well as continued less-than-majority state ownership among what had been the non-MSO countries. Zambia was one of the first to privatize such a large mineral sector and so completely. In fact, its government finished reducing its ownership in mining to less than a majority share by

DOI: 10.4324/9780429423390-5

2000 when it privatized its main mining parastatal, ZCCM-IH (which had replaced ZCCM [Zambia Consolidated Copper Mines]). The context of their privatization has much to do with the strong, albeit partial, political and economic liberalization process that began to unfold near the end of the Cold War as well as the losses that were being accumulated by its mining sector.[9] In fact, Zambia had been so reluctant to privatize that it passed on a more lucrative privatization deal a few years before, obtaining $40 million less in price, and missing out on $75 million in debt assumption, and $500 million in rehabilitation and expansion.[10] Even with privatization, the government still retains a share of ownership in all mining companies, usually between 10% and 20%. As such, this lower threshold means that Zambian copper is no longer MSO.

The Democratic Republic of the Congo (DRC) also experienced the privatization of its copper mining sector, but in the context of what can be seen as an unpredictable hodgepodge of events associated with extreme political instability. The privatization of the copper sector has occurred in the circumstance of several regime changes, shifting international alliances, and a civil war. In the wake of the Rwandan genocide, the diffusion of refugees into the DRC helped spark a civil war.[11] The Alliance des forces démocratique pour la liberation du Congo-Zaire (AFDL), led by Laurence Kabila, emerged victoriously, and overthrew Mobutu by 1997. In the early phase of the war, the AFDL had obtained effective control of Gécamines in Katanga. Before he controlled Kinshasa, Kabila signed an agreement with American Mineral Fields International (AMFI), which gave it exclusive rights to rehabilitate key Gécamines mines.[12] Kabila later signed other agreements for mines that came under his control as he marched toward the capital. After gaining control of the capital, however, Kabila cancelled many of these earlier contracts arguing that investment in the mines by these companies had been inadequate.[13]

With the second rebellion in the east, this time against Kabila, Kabila turned to the Southern Africa Development Community (SADC) for support, and Zimbabwe provided early and significant military support.[14] Soon thereafter, Gécamines signed an agreement with Ridgepoint, a Zimbabwean company, which had 80% of the Central Mining Group transferred to it. Ties with Zimbabwe became even closer when Zimbabwean Billy Rautenback was appointed Managing Director of Gécamines. The signed contracts were often honored more in breach than in law. Nonetheless, despite Gécamines continued strong control over many aspects of the mining sector, such joint ventures beginning in 1998 meant that its MSO of the sector was in decline.

The mining code of 2002 was another important change for the DRC.[15] It was meant for the opening and regulation of mining in Congo.[16] Nonetheless, private companies were allowed to mine copper beginning in 2001, starting with Kababankola Mining Company, with 80% private ownership.[17] Also, Kamoto Copper Company became 75% owned by Glencoe.[18] In addition, the Manono lithium-tin project was awarded to an Australian company with 75% private ownership.[19]

While the mining code was meant for the opening and regulation of mining in Congo, Gécamines has used it to continue to collect revenues through its control of mining permits.[20] According to the Carter Center, "Gécamines' privileged position as the state-owned trader of mining permits allows it to decide who will operate in the copper belt and receive direct payments from its partners that are not destined for the state treasury."[21] Even though privatization was legally in place, the state-owned enterprise (SOE) continued its control over the sector indirectly. Nonetheless, DRC can now be coded as having non-MSO of its copper-exporting sector.

Niger continues to have majority *private* ownership in its mining sector, but the government does demand 10% ownership with issuance of any permit. It also reserves the right to purchase additional shares in private mining companies up to the level of 33%.[22] Its structure remains almost the same as during the Cold War period, with the partial exception that more non-French firms are participating in this sector.

Niger would also later discover and exploit other natural resources, that is, petroleum and gold. Even with the relative decline of uranium, it plus petroleum and gold would keep Niger listed as having natural resources driving exports.[23] Large oil deposits were discovered near Lake Chad, and extraction began in earnest in 2012. Fuel exports in that year represented about 18% of exports, which rose to 31% in 2013.[24] By 2020, oil would add more to the GDP than uranium.[25] Niger also began exporting gold as well. Despite having some exploitation since the 1980s, production spiked significantly in 2005, going from 1,531 kg in 2004 to 5,000 kg the next year.[26] Its gold exports fluctuated between 2000 and 2021. In 2014, it represented about 9% of exports, rising to 17% in 2015. In 2019, it constituted 31.7% of all exports. In 2020, 63.7%, and in 2021, 71.4%.[27] Thus, Niger is still a natural resource exporter, but it is no longer so reliant upon the sole source of uranium exports for funding.

Botswana retains its coding as a country with less than MSO, in line with its continuing 50% ownership of BEBSWANA. In 2008, the Diamond Trading Company (DTC) was created, and it became the world's largest rough diamond sorting and valuing operation. This company is also 50% owned by the government of Botswana in conjunction with the Diamond Trading Company.[28] Botswana has also moved up the sales chain in the post–Cold War period. For example, in 2009, the government began a strategy to develop diamond cutting, polishing and jewelry making skills so this process could be completed within the country.[29] A very recent deal has also changed the sharing of diamonds between Debswana and De Beers. Traditionally, Botswana obtained 25% of the rough stones, but a new agreement will increase this to 30%, rising to 50% by the end of a decade.[30]

In the case of the oil-exporting nations in the case study, we see more government ownership and domination of the sector, though with a few cracks emerging. Looking first at Angola, we see that it formally abandoned Marxism-Leninism right at the end of the Cold War.[31] Even with this change, clear limits exist as to how far Angola can privatize its oil sector: Angola has state ownership of oil written into its 2010 constitution, and all concessionaires must maintain an association with Sonangol.[32] The government is the owner of all natural resources in the nation, and foreign participation in the oil and gas sector is limited to 49%.[33] A slight move toward privatization of the sector began in 1992 when one part of the offshore parcel, CABGOC fields, experienced a decline in government ownership to 41%.[34] Since that time, more offshore blocs have become less-than-majority state-owned, some with only 20%, some with none.[35] However, Sonangol continues to own 51% or more of all onshore joint ventures. Even where the state has MSO, private sector and foreign investors have experienced more managerial and operational control through joint ventures or with production-sharing agreements (PSAs).[36] A reform in 2004 standardized PSAs was passed to draw in even more private and foreign investment.[37]

Despite limits on privatization, Sonangol has begun to sell off its stock in some privately owned companies. Some suggest that could eventually lead even to privatization of Sonangol itself.[38] For example, the Angolan Finance Minister announced that shares of Sonangol and Endiama would be floated on the stock market in 2022.[39] There were rumors that Sonangol may privatize up to 30% of the petroleum parastatal itself, but this would not change its coding to less-than-majority state-owned at that stage.[40] Currently, plans are to start this privatization process for Sonangol and Endiama in 2024.[41] In another development, Angola finally joined OPEC in 2007.[42] In sum, Angolan petroleum should still be thought of as MSO, though it is more a preponderance of ownership, rather than a monopoly.

In Nigeria, the oil sector has been mostly governed by the 1969 Petroleum Act, which vests MSO of oil and natural minerals in the hands of the federal government. In 2021, however, the Nigerian government passed the Petroleum Industry Act, which amended the 1969 act, with the intent of reforming and making the petroleum sector more commercially viable.[43] The main intent of this reform was to make the NNPC operate on a commercial basis (i.e., without as much government funding/subsidies). Nonetheless, the government remains the sole owner of shares of the new NNPC Limited, even if the selling shares is now possible.[44] Also, the terms of joint ventures have been changed even as the NNPC retained the right to hold up to 60% of carried interest participation.[45] However, by 1993, the NNPC's share of Shell fell to 55%. Nonetheless, MSO remains the case in Nigeria despite talk of privatization.[46]

One new development for Gabon's petroleum sector is that a national oil parastatal, the Gabon Oil Company (GOC), was created in 2010 to increase the government's participation in oil production along with gaining greater equity in future awards.[47] Nonetheless, its level of state ownership is such that the government takes a minimum 10% equity, while the GOC is entitled to purchase an additional 15% share at market prices.[48] As such, Gabon remains a not majority state-owned country, even with it now featuring a state-owned national oil company. Gabon also rejoined OPEC in 2016, which it had left in 1995, citing high fees and low production at the time of leaving.[49] One main norm of participation in OPEC is that their government have a national oil company.[50]

A bit of change came to Cameroon when it passed a new petroleum code in 2019, holding that all petrochemicals within Cameroon belong to the state. Even so, the Société Nationale des Hydrocarbures (SNH), which manages petroleum extraction in Cameroon, only holds ownership of 20% in Total, Pecten and Perenco.[51] Thus, most production is still conducted by companies with less than MSO.

Examining the case study countries, the oil-exporting countries that had had MSO during the Cold War continue to do so, for the most part – with a bit of privatization for Angolan offshore oil. The non-MSO countries, as expected, continue not to have MSO. By contrast, looking at the mining cases, both MSO mining countries have experienced significant or full privatization of mining, and all the non-MSO countries continue to have less than MSO. This represents a meaningful change from the first period.

Countries New to Oil or Mineral Exporting

Petroleum

Several countries in sub-Saharan Africa became important oil exporters after the end of our period of study. Chad and Equatorial Guinea, for example, now have oil representing more than 30% of their exports.[52] Equatorial Guinea became a major oil exporter in the mid-1990s. By 2002, petroleum comprised over 90% of its exports, and this remained so through 2019.[53] The size of the discovery of oil in Equatorial Guinea was large enough for it to become the fifth most important exporter in sub-Saharan Africa, only after Nigeria, Angola, Sudan, and the Republic of Congo. As Equatorial Guinea had previously been one of the poorest African nations before this discovery, the development of this sector led to an increase in its GDP of over 38 times its pre-oil size.[54] On a per capita basis, Equatorial Guinea has become one of the richest countries in the region. Unfortunately, the wealth is not widely shared within the nation, and over 70% of its population continues to live in poverty.[55]

Importantly, Equatorial Guinea did not adopt MSO of this sector; the government only demands between 15% and 30% ownership from companies exploiting newer fields.[56] Most such oil explorations have been led by joint venture companies, including such partners as Marathon, Hess, and Exxon-Mobil. Nonetheless, the sector in Equatorial Guinea is far from free of political interference from the political elites as several employment agencies owned by the president's relatives have made sure that only friends, relatives, or patrons of the party and other elites can work in the oil sector. In fact, "the Nguema family seems to maintain tight … control of the political and economic mechanisms of the country."[57]

Chad began large scale extraction of its oil in 2003, and production levels would grow until 2005. From 2005 onwards, oil has represented at least 77% of Chad's annual exports.[58] Chad cannot be coded as MSO, as private companies have been involved in exploration and exploitation of its oil. The companies that extract oil are mostly MNCs, led by Exxon-Mobil.[59]

Chad's oil position was quite different from other nations for a while, as it is landlocked and had no uncomplicated way to bring its oil to market. Given that it had been one of the poorest nations on the planet before this, Chad borrowed money from the World Bank to build an oil pipeline to reach the Atlantic Ocean, though this required passage through Cameroon. In return for the loan, the World Bank required that money paid to Chad by the consortium of producers (led by Exxon-Mobil) had to be paid to an offshore account – with the World Bank getting a veto on how much of the money was spent.[60] Once its loans were paid off, Chadian political elites no longer had this check on their spending power.[61]

Ghana later discovered oil as well, but petroleum exports have not consistently represented 30% or more of its exports. Beginning in 2011, petroleum represented 27% of exports from 2011 to 2019.[62] Given Ghana's other exports in cocoa and gold, it does not fit as a traditional oil-exporting nation, though it is a natural resource–exporting nation. Although its petroleum sector is managed by the Ghana National Petroleum Corporation (GNPC), which is an SOE, the Ghanaian oil sector cannot be coded as MSO because international oil companies (IOCs) exported petroleum independently of the GNPC, which means the GNPC does not have a monopoly of these exports.[63] For example, in 2019, the IOCs exported 58,242,307 barrels of crude oil during the year 2019 while GNPC exported 12,743,158 barrels (the latter representing less than 18% of total oil exports).[64]

Minerals

Since 2000, mining has become even more important to Africa.[65] There has also been a spate of mines opening since 2000, and this number has risen even more quickly after 2012 (going from an average of under 10 per year to nearly 60 in that year).[66] For example, Burkina Faso, Ghana, and Mali became major exporters of gold after 2000.[67] In 2010, gold represented nearly 30% of merchandise exports from Ghana.[68] From 2012 onwards, Ghanaian exports of gold were worth more than 30% of all exports. From 2016 to 2021, it was an average of 38%. Given the data on oil from above, oil and mineral exports became 50% or more of merchandise exports from 2011 onwards. As discussed above, the gold producing sector had been privatized decades before. Mali also became a major gold exporter by 2001.[69] By 2014, gold exports had grown to represent over 75% of all exports, by value.[70] In Burkina Faso, gold went from being around 10% of exports from 1995 to 1996 to 45% from 2012 to 2013.[71]

Relative Change in Openness of African Nations

Although many of these trends began during the late Cold War, they seem to have really coalesced and deepened in the post-2000 years. As discussed elsewhere, we saw in sub-Saharan Africa regional economic trends moving toward more open economies, including (1) a move away from inward-oriented economic policies, (2) greater flows in international trade, (3) a regionwide increase in the number and importance of acts of privatization of formerly majority state-owned industries, and (4) a rise in levels of foreign direct investment (FDI). Moreover, the region has also seen (5) increased African membership in intergovernmental organizations established to lower trade barriers, increase trade flows, and/or increase economic regional integration, and (6) an attendant rise in bilateral investment treaties.[72] The region also has experienced much debt relief through the Heavily Indebted Poor Countries (HIPC) program and the Multilateral Debt Relief Initiative (MDRI), which have improved African countries financial bases, though debt increases seem to be on the rise again.[73]

In terms of increased economic globalization (which is an indirect measure of openness that includes protection as well as financial openness), Africa scored 31 in 1970, and scored this continued to rise to 36.9 by 1989.[74] This level rose even further, to 42.45 in 2000 and continued to increase until it plateaued around 44 from 2010 to 2020. This trend line seems to nearly match, in a parallel fashion, that of world economic globalization – though the world levels have always been higher. With trade openness (one of two components of the above measure), a similar pattern emerges, even if it is at lower levels. It starts at about 32 in 1970 and rises to a peak of 43.62 in 2011, where it plateaus or slightly declines, especially after 2018.

Increase in Political and Civil Rights

Nearly all countries in sub-Saharan Africa have moved from one- and no-party states to countries with de jure multiparty competition for elections. Many countries in sub-Saharan African also saw a commensurate increase in the levels of political and civil rights. Between 1975 and 1985, during the Cold War, the average level of political and civil rights for the region was 5.6, which Freedom House rates as not free.[75] At this time, only three countries (6.7%) were ranked "free," 15 countries (33.3%) were considered "partly free," and 27 countries (57.4%) were considered "not free." After the Cold War and the transitions to multiparty rule, between 1995 and 2005, the regional average became 4.5, which is rated as "partly free." And during the second period, six countries (12.8%) were ranked "free," 27 (57.4%) were considered "partly free," and 12 countries (25.5%) were considered "not free." This indicates a small movement toward more free countries, but a much larger movement of countries from the "not free" to the partly free category.

Despite regional gains, this movement toward higher levels of freedom post–Cold War has not spread strongly to the oil- or mineral-exporting countries, even if all have adopted de jure multiparty regimes. Among such countries from our mineral- and oil-exporting sample, we see only an average of 0.54 increase in rights occurred between the 1975–1985 and 1995–2005 period. Looking at countries by category of freedoms and between 1975 and 1985, we see that one country was listed as free, five were partly free, and nine were not free. In the second period, one country was listed as free, six were partly free, and eight were not free. So, in aggregate, we only saw a net gain of one major mineral- or oil-exporting country going from "not free" to partly free. This is consistent with prior findings: countries that were significant exporters of mineral or petroleum did not see a significant gain in political or civil rights between these two periods.[76]

Of our case studies from the sample, most countries saw no or little change in levels of rights or the rankings of these countries, on average. Botswana was listed as free for both periods; Nigeria was partly free for both periods as was

Zambia. Angola, Cameroon, and the DRC all averaged a listing of "not free" for both periods. Only Gabon and Niger changed from not free to partly free. So only two non-MSO countries saw a change in rating through 2000. Moving to the present, we see that Botswana remains listed as free, Nigeria, Zambia, and Niger have remained partly free, and Angola, Cameroon, and the DRC remain not free. Gabon has moved to not free, and Niger has suffered a recent coup which will lower their scores. Thus, minor change has emerged for these cases since 2000.[77]

Economic Growth

For the region long known for low or negative growth during the Cold War period, sub-Saharan Africa performed much better in the post 2000 period until quite recently.[78] Between 2000 and 2022 most of Africa experienced an average growth level of 1.22% annual per capita growth and GDP growth of 3.97%.[79] However, if we calculate only the first 15 years 2000–2015, the average per capita growth was nearly 2%, and GDP growth was 4.79%.[80]

These levels of growth have been much heralded as symbolizing a new economic era for Africa. In fact, *The Economist* reported that over a dozen African countries had growth rates of 6% or higher between 2007 and 2011.[81] With this growth, incomes have climbed, and over 60 million Africans came to have incomes above $3,000 per year. In addition, from 2000 to 2011, six of the top ten growing countries in the world were in Africa, a feat that would have been quite unthinkable in the 1980s. Examples of African nations above or near 4% growth from 2000 to 2018 were Equatorial Guinea (8%), Ethiopia (6%), Djibouti (5.6%), Rwanda (5.1%), Chad (4.6%), Sudan (4.6), Mozambique (4.4%), Nigeria (4.1%), and Cape Verde (3.6%).[82] The few countries with negative growth rates during this period were Burundi, Central African Republic (CAR), Eritrea, Gabon, the Gambia, Liberia, South Sudan, and Zimbabwe.[83] All the rest experienced positive growth rates. Although the causes of this growth are debated, many see international movements toward reform, increased globalization, more political liberalization, inflation being kept under control, more international investment, and better commodity prices as being helpful for growth.[84] Growth in India and China, along with their increased demands for commodities, was clearly important as well.

Of the oil countries in our case sample, all experienced positive growth rates from 2000 to 2022: Nigeria (5.1%), Angola (4.7%), Cameroon (3.96%), and Gabon (2.13%). These numbers are quite dissimilar to Cold War averages. The economic growth for Nigeria and Angola indicates a significant turnaround of the fortunes of these oil-exporting countries from the prior period.

Another important change which has likely impacted growth is the change in capacity to produce (and export) oil. Both Gabon and Cameroon have seen decreases in production, while Nigeria and Angola have seen increases. Gabonese petroleum production peaked in 1997 at 370,000 barrels a day (Mb/d) and fell to 220 Mb/d by 2014.[85] This amount fell to 195 Mb/d by 2022. Similarly, Cameroon has experienced a decline in petroleum production from 122 Mb/d in 1998 to 60

Mb/d in 2022. By contrast, Nigeria and Angola saw an initial increase on production followed by a decline. Nigeria increased production from 2,136 Mb/d in 2000 to 2,405 in 2014. Starting in 2015, however, production declined to under 2,000 for most years, falling to 1,426 Mb/d by 2022. Angola increased production from 746 Mb/d in 2000 to 1,756 by 2014, though this would decline to about 1,235 by 2022 – though this represented a higher level of production than 2000.

The average level of growth for the mineral case study countries from 2000 to 2022 was 5.4% for Zambia, 5.12% for Niger, 4.9% for the DRC, and 3.46% for Botswana.[86] All three Zambia, Niger, and the DRC outperformed Botswana in this post–Cold War. But we must remember that for Zambia and the DRC, the former's ownership structure had already changed to "non-MSO" by 2000.

In terms of availability and production levels for the mineral case study countries, we see some variance, but none seems in long-term decline like oil in Gabon or Cameroon. Interestingly, Zambia had seen continued falling production levels until 2000. However, after elevated levels of reinvestment associated with privatization, production later increased to the point of rivaling prenationalization levels. In 2000, the level of production was 25,000 tons, but by 2013, it had increased to 763,000 tons.[87] The years 2015 and 2016 saw declines in production, but only falling to around 400,000 tons. By 2020, Zambian production was well in excess of 760,000 tons.[88]

Diamond exports from Botswana grew in the post-2000 period from 24,600 carats in 2000 to between 30,000 and 34,000 carats between 2003 and 2008.[89] Then in 2009 (following the near collapse of banking in 2008), it fell to 17.7 in 2009. From here it rose to 24,400 carats in 2014. Then it declined to 20,000 carats in 2016. It has plans to have production of around 21,000 carats in the near term. Botswana saw major decreases in diamond sales from 2018 to 2020, associated with COVID-19: its sales fell from 60 million in 2018 to 42.5 million pulas in 2020.

The production levels of copper from the DRC nearly collapsed with the civil war, falling from above 500,000 metric tons in 1988 to below 50,000 metric tons between 1992 and 2000.[90] From 2000 onwards, the DRC has seen a steady increase in copper output, rising to just under 300,000 metric tons in 2008. By 2020, DRC output achieved the level of 1.59 megatons.[91] So the post-2000 years saw a dramatic increase in copper output.

Niger has seen a major decrease in production of uranium, but the most important reason for this occurred in 2015 with the closing of the Somina mine. Within five years of its closure, production fell from 4,116 to 2,816 tons in 2021.[92] However, with an increase in prices since 2002, along with increased interest in nuclear power as a response to global warming, more countries became interested in investing in Niger. This included major investments in this sector from China. However, prices fell with the 2008 banking crisis, though they would rebound in 2010. Nonetheless, volatility in uranium prices has clearly impacted production levels.[93]

For the Cold War to 2000 period, we saw low or negative growth in the two MSO mineral countries, but one non-MSO country also had low or negative growth. In the post-2000, and with the high commodity prices, this trend is no longer apparent, though we no longer have clear differences in ownership structure for these mineral-exporting nations anymore vis-à-vis MSO. Moreover, examining this reversal of levels of growth for both the mineral- and oil-exporting countries, regression to the mean could be a partial answer.[94]

Extractive Industries Transparency Initiative

One post-2000 development that could clearly affect both mining and oil countries was the emergence of the Extractive Industries Transparency Initiative (EITI), launched by Tony Blair, the then Prime Minister of the UK in 2002. The EITI was formed in 2003 as "an international organization through which governments, private citizens, and corporations seek to reduce the rampant pilfering of wealth in the oil, gas, mineral, and other extractive industries."[95] Its webpage says its main goal is "promoting the open and accountable management of oil, gas and mineral resources."[96] It was created to address many of the problems associated with the resource curse.

The EITI is a voluntary transnational public–private partnership, and it is comprised of countries, politicians, nongovernmental organizations (NGOs), civil society groups, and companies – especially MNCs involved in exploiting oil or mineral sectors in other countries.[97] It began as a movement to have companies "publish what they pay" to oil or mineral developing nations in order to increase transparency and accountability for these notoriously corrupt sectors. The IMF and World Bank also participated in its establishment, and many other international entities, such as the European Union, African Union, G8 and G20, and the UN, have endorsed it.[98] The IMF even required an African oil-exporting nation, Equatorial Guinea, to adopt measures to increase transparency and accountability, one of which was to join EITI.[99] Over 50 countries have joined, counting 28 from Africa, though the level of compliance of each country differs.[100]

The primary purpose of the EITI was to make publicly available basic information about the actions of companies and governments involved in natural resources. This is intended to increase accountability, or increase "governance by disclosure."[101] To increase such information, companies and countries are expected to meet several benchmarks: one of these is for companies to publish what they pay policymakers for the right to extract or explore for resources.[102] Similarly, government officials are to record the amounts they have received and to create an independent administrator to compare these sales and revenues. Within resource rich partner countries, governments are to establish a "multi-stakeholder group" comprised of civil society partners who can oversee these matters and to make an independent assessment of the validity of receipts from business and government. Finally, outside organizations are to validate EITI implementation in consultation with stakeholders.

Despite the clear goals of EITI, implementation has been uneven. For example, by 2007, only 14 of 23 countries required firms to publish what they actually paid, what they received, or if they had actually set up the multi-stakeholder group.[103] EITI divides countries into the categories of candidate and compliant, with those meeting minimum qualification put into the former, and those meeting more into the latter. By 2015, 31 countries were considered compliant.[104] Candidate countries were to have become compliant within two years. Despite more countries becoming "compliant," many suggest that EITI is not as effective in reducing corruption or meeting all of its goals as was originally hoped.[105] In an evaluation of EITI, it was found to be most effective in meeting institutional goals, such as establishing its brand, increasing membership and partners, and raising anticorruption as a norm. Less successful were operational and developmental goals, even if implementing countries did seem to obtain more FDI and Official Development Assistance (ODA).[106]

All the countries in the oil case studies are members. Angola had only recently expressed its intent to join in September of 2020, and it officially joined in June 2022.[107] It has taken some steps toward EITI implementation, but it has yet to be assessed. Ironically, issues with Angolan oil were part of the motivation for the formation of EITI. Nigeria joined in 2007, and it had its last validation in 2019, from which it was determined that Nigeria was in good standing – making "satisfactory progress." Cameroon also joined in 2007 and had its latest validation in 2021. Its listed status is "meaningful progress." Gabon had joined in 2007, but it was later delisted in 2013 for failure to submit its validation report in a timely fashion.[108] It later rejoined in October 2021, and it has yet to be assessed as of this writing.

Of the mineral case-study countries, only Botswana is not a member. Part of this may have to do with unique aspects of the diamond trade. The government of Botswana suggested that its not joining had to do with "the historical secrecy of the diamond industry, the confidentiality of the revenue-sharing agreements with De Beers and Debswana, and a desire not to give away confidential commercial information to competitors."[109] Perhaps most importantly, a large portion of the agreements between the government and De Beers is not in public domain.[110] Nonetheless, Botswana has had a history of publishing much of what EITI would require.[111]

The DRC joined EITI in 2007. Its last evaluation was in 2022, and it was listed as having "high" status. Zambia joined two years after the DRC in 2009. Its last validation was also in 2021, and it also was listed as having "high" status. Interestingly, like Gabon, Niger had been a member before, joining in 2007. After ten years of compliance and drafting reports, it withdrew in 2017 after having been found "not in compliance" with the 2016 standards. It would likely have been found to be "inadequate" in making progress. Niger applied again and was readmitted in 2020, but it has yet to be evaluated by the standard since rejoining. Its validation will be within two and a half years after becoming a candidate.

It is unclear if EITI, or other similar NGOs, will exert the type of normative force necessary to change the way minerals are produced. Nonetheless, the fact that countries and companies are appearing to comply with EITI's mandates may bode well for more transparent and meaningful reform in the mineral and oil resource sectors in the medium to long term.[112]

Natural Gas and Flaring

One substantial difference in the post-2000 period for oil-exporting nations is that most of them have begun to produce natural gas and/or limit how much natural gas they flare. Africa may become a new and important source of natural gas, especially in the wake of the Russian invasion of Ukraine and the sanctions placed upon Russia. Africa has 13% of the world's known reserves of natural gas, and many new plants for making liquefied natural gas (LNG) are in the pipeline.[113] According to *The Economist*, proposed gas projects in sub-Saharan Africa may result in an additional 90 billion cubic meters (bcm) in annual LNG capacity by 2030. Some estimate that natural gas production from the continent could reach over 450 bcm by 2037 if all plans are invested in and properly executed.

Angola announced in 1998 plans to build a liquid natural gas plant to produce for both domestic markets as well as export markets. Prior to this time, Angola had not felt it was economically viable to capture natural gas. Chevron and Sonangol first discussed creating a liquefied natural gas plant, and other companies soon came onboard.[114] Envisioned to start production in 2012, the plant was commissioned in 2013, and Angola began exporting natural gas in mid-2013.[115]

When the plant gets to full production, it could produce over 5 million tons per year (250 billion cubic feet) of LNG.[116] The main plant is owned by a consortium, including Sonangol (22.8%), Chevron (36.4%), Total (13.6%), BP (13.6%), and Eni (13.6%), so it is not majority state-owned.[117] According to this consortium, the LNG project was the largest investment project in Angola's history. Angola started producing liquid natural gas in 2004, at 3 TBPD, rising to 65,000 barrels per day in 2019. The average level of production for these years was 22.5 TBPD. The modal output between 2004 and 2010 was 10 TBPD. By 2022, Angola was producing 70 Mb/d.[118]

Nigeria currently has one operating LNG plant on Bonny Island, which is managed by Nigeria LNG. It has several trains, with a new one expected, which should raise its production from 22 tons per year to 30 tons per year. It is owned jointly by NNPC (49%), Shell (25.6%), Total (15%) and Eni (10.4%), and therefore, it is not majority state-owned, even if the government has the largest share.[119] From 2010 to 2019, it averaged a production of 50,000 barrels a day.[120] Another plant at Escravos is managed by Chevron and was opened in 2014. Several other projects for natural gas are underway and had proposed realizations for 2017 and beyond.[121] Nigeria also helped build a regional pipeline to carry LNG to other West African nations, and it began operating in 2011. This West African Gas Pipeline (WAGP) pipeline has usually run at about 30% capacity.[122] In addition, Algeria and Nigeria are in talks to build another pipeline envisioned to cross the Sahara through Algeria and get to a Mediterranean port. As of 2020, Nigerian production provided for 40% of domestic LPG gas needs, and it has limited gas flaring from 65% to below 25%.[123]

In Cameroon, in 2002, nine companies were invited to bid for spots in the Sanaga Dus gas field, and then a PSA was signed later with Perenco. Cameroon opened an electricity plant that runs on natural gas at Kiribi in 2012 which can be used to contribute up to 20–30% of electricity needs.[124] Up to this point, hydroelectric power had been supplying over 98% of the electrical needs of the country.[125] No LNG plants exist on Cameroonian soil, but Cameroon can process natural gas at a plant in Equatorial Guinea, owned by Marathon. This plant would like Cameroon to pipe its gas there.[126] By 2016, Cameroon started producing natural gas, but at very low levels according to EITI.[127] Cameroon began exporting natural gas in 2018 following the completion of an offshore floating platform used to turn gas into LNG, producing approximately 1.2 million ton per year.[128] The use of the floating platform allows economies of scale given the volume of gas and the cost of onshore plants. It is the first floating LNG conversion plant in Africa.

Gabon was listed at zero for production of natural gas through 2018, despite having between 3 and 5 trillion cubic feet (tcf) of gas reserves.[129] Most of it has been reinjected underground, remains underground, or has been flared during production; only small amounts are used for energy production for the capital.[130] Gabon is not seeking to create a large LNG plant for export, but it is trying to capture what is being flared and reroute it for domestic energy production.

The increased capture and production of natural gas also has impacts on flaring, as many developing and oil-producing countries routinely flair natural gas instead of trying to capture it. Gas flaring is associated with oil exploration, especially in less developed countries, and it is a major source of local air pollution as well as carbon emissions.[131] This flaring amounts to a tremendous loss of potential energy and profit. According to one source:

> Globally, some 143 billion cubic meters (bcm) were flared in 2021, roughly equivalent to the total volume of natural gas imported into Germany, France, and the Netherlands. At a price of $10 per thousand British thermal units (Mbtu), this represents $55 billion of lost sales revenue.[132]

Over 40 bcm flared each year are from Africa, and 35 bcm come from sub-Saharan Africa.[133]

Many environmental and developmental activists have tried to raise awareness of this potentially unnecessary contributor to global warming. In fact, in 2015, the World Bank launched the zero-flaring initiative with the ambition to get all countries to end flaring by 2030.[134] Like EITI, it is voluntary, but it helps to publish data and help countries reduce emission if they wish to do so. Data taken from satellites indicate that Nigeria accounted for about 5.4% of world flaring in 2017. Russia was the worst that year, but Nigeria was ahead of every other African country.[135] Recently, some progress has been made: Nigeria reduced its average flaring of 22.68 bcm during 1995 to 2010, down to an average of 8.06 bcm during the period of 2013–2017. Angola went from an average of 4.8 bcm from 1995 to 2010, to 3.84 bcm from 2013 to 2017. Gabon's average went from 3.18 to 1.52, and Cameroon's went from 1.06 to 0.98 during the same periods.

China and Africa

China's involvement in Africa is part of its larger international foreign policy seeking to rise as an economic player and to secure access to resources needed to advance politically, economically, and militarily. In the post–Cold War period, and especially after 2000, China has become more and more important to Africa, politically and economically.[136] Some have even suggested that Chinese involvement in Africa is the most important foreign policy development for the region in decades.[137] China is now counted as Africa's largest trading partner and most important bilateral creditor as well as being a key source of infrastructure investment.[138] This renewed interest by China in Africa undermines the view that Africa is marginalized from the world stage.

Chinese economic involvement with the region solves several economic issues facing the management of Chinese development and economic policies. First, China often suffers from domestic overproduction with so many state-owned firms often producing excess product, given the often competing economic and social goals pursued by many of these MSO firms.[139] By exporting and moving production overseas, it reduces the problems associated with domestic oversupply. It also keeps employment high as so many of these Chinese firms operating abroad bring along Chinese labor for their projects. Second, in view of China's trade surpluses vis-à-vis so much of the rest of the world, it has too much foreign currency to be absorbed into its domestic market. Lending money denominated in hard currency abroad reduces the pressures on inflation, currency readjustment, or other instabilities resulting from this trade imbalance. Third, China needs access to increasingly higher levels of natural resources to feed its industrial machine and keep its economy running. Although China has abundant natural resources of its own, the domestic demand easily outstrips the domestic supply. To solve all three of these problems, China tasked their banks "to support overseas projects focused on industrial production, infrastructure, and natural resource acquisition and to facilitate the participation of Chinese firms in these projects."[140]

FOCAC

In 2000, China launched the triannual Forum on China-Africa Cooperation (FOCAC). It was a partnership platform between China and nearly all African states, except those that maintained diplomatic relations with Taiwan.[141] It was created to build, harmonize, and centralize relationships between African nations and China. Some have suggested that it was part of China's Belt and Road Initiative, especially where it concerned Africa.[142] It has resulted in several meetings, and it helps coordinate trade and investment between China and Africa. The launching of this forum would deepen already emerging strong ties between African nations and China in terms of trade, investment, aid, and diplomacy. It is a multilateral institution which helps coordinate planning and development projects between China and African nations. It also is a venue for China to express its official foreign policy goals in a developing world setting. It is through FOCAC that China has arranged aid and debt forgiveness. So far, there have been eight meetings or summits for FOCAC, each with China announcing aid, debt forgiveness, or plans for more infrastructure. However, after the last meeting in Dakar, some suggest China is pulling back a bit, as the amount of aid announced was less than prior levels and no mention of infrastructure was made at all.

Trade with Africa

Although trade with China was low during the Cold War, it has grown exponentially since 1990. In terms of value, Chinese-African trade increased by 430% between 1989 and 1997. In volume of trade, it has more than quintupled again through 2006.[143] In overall trade terms, China became sub-Saharan Africa's largest import partner in 2006 as well as its largest export partner in 2012.[144] To put this in context, in 1989, Chinese trade with Africa was not even worth $1 billion, but by 2000, it was worth $50 billion, and by 2010, $100 billion.[145] This grew to greater than $160 billion in 2011, and to $200 billion by 2022.[146] However large this trade is relative to Africa, it only represents a small portion of the Chinese trade portfolio, only constituting approximately 4% of global Chinese trade in 2021. Thus, many scholars argue that China is more important to Africa than Africa is to China.[147]

But for the imports China cares most deeply about, many of these come from Africa. For example, energy security is a driving issue for China, and it was the third largest importer of oil in 2004, as well as the second largest consumer of oil in 2003.[148] Quite a bit of early Chinese trade in Africa (in the 1990s) was initially based on the extraction of oil, strategic minerals, and raw materials in exchange for manufactured goods. Chinese imports from Africa have mainly included "minerals, metals, agricultural products, crude oil, and agricultural products."[149] In 1997, African oil accounted for around 17% of Chinese imports and this rose to 28.7% in 2004.[150] By 2004, African oil came to represent about 28% of all oil imports to China.[151] The value of this trade had already exceeded $160 billion by 2011.[152] Minerals and oil comprised almost 80% of African exports to China through 2013.[153] China also became the largest consumer of base metals around 2000. This demand has even helped the increase in commodity prices that so benefited SSA post-2000.

Belt and Road Initiative

As part of China's economic foreign policy, with an emphasis on creating more trade and growth opportunities, China deepened such commitments through its 2013 Belt and Road Initiative (BRI). This undertaking has sought to link China to other economies worldwide through building trade routes and infrastructure for this trade route to ensure Chinese access to strategic imports for its economy. This investment in other counties' infrastructures helped accelerate levels of trade as well as redirect much of it toward China. Originally called "One Belt, One Road," this program sought to reduce the costs of Chinese companies that shifted production to cheaper labor markets. It also sought to integrate other nations' economies more closely to the Chinese economy, especially as a way to offload surplus domestic production.

The "Belt" part of the name refers to the Silk Road Economic Belt (on land), and the "Road" part of the name to the 21st Century Maritime Silk Road (so by sea).[154] These were proposed by President Jinping Xi of China during trips to Central and Southeast Asia in 2013. At its core, it involves "China underwriting billions of dollars of infrastructure investment in countries along the old Silk Road linking it with Europe."[155] The costs to China in the short term have been quite high, as it has financed much of this project: China was spending about $150 billion a year in 68 countries by 2017.[156] Moreover, Chinese overseas investment and construction since 2005 is estimated to have amounted to around $2.2 trillion.[157] Consequently, along with other initiatives, China has become the largest creditor in the world, though it has not joined the Paris Club, which is a group of creditor nations which try to make debt repayment sustainable.[158] This project, or sets of projects, is ultimately about creating a trading zone in Eurasia to rival the transatlantic trade zone.

Investment, Aid, and Belt and Road

With the end of the Cold War, and increasing with the BRI, China has become one of the largest sources for lending, aid, and investment for the region. In fact, from 2000 to 2014 Chinese aid and loans would make China the second largest source for development finance, and a majority of Chinese aid projects would be in Africa.[159] However, since most loans did not contain the 25% grant element necessary to be considered ODA, they were closer to commercial loans than ODA. Brautigan calls these flows other official flows (OOF).[160]

Loan commitments to Africa from China have risen quite a bit from 2000 onwards, when they went from representing less than 2% of sub-Saharan African external public debt to 17% by 2021.[161] The commitments of loans as a percentage of GDP rose from around 0.1% of GDP to 1.7% in 2016. However, this level declined from 2017 onwards to around 0.1% again in 2021. Despite the decline in new promised loans, China remains the largest bilateral official lender to African countries – even if the total debt owed to it remains at less than 6%. Interestingly, most of this debt is held by only five countries – Angola, Cameroon, Kenya, Nigeria, and Zambia – three of which are among our case studies of oil exporters, and one of which is among our mineral exporters.

China has led in a new trend of resource-backed loans, beginning when China lent money to Angola in the mid-1990s.[162] These loans can be repaid in natural resources. Within Africa, Angola had the highest value of such loans (at $24 billion). Next in order were the Republic of the Congo (at $5.1 billion) and then the DRC (at $3.5 billion). Over half of these types of loans came from one of two Chinese Banks: China Eximbank and China Development Bank (CDB). Niger, Ghana, Zimbabwe, and Sudan have received resource-backed loans from China Eximbank. The main potential problem for these loans is their lack of transparency, though they may be a cheaper form of getting loans for countries with natural resources as collateral.

Nonetheless, these new loans to African countries from China are clearly having an impact on development and construction in the region. They have also changed which companies are obtaining contracts to build within Africa. Before 1990, American and European companies obtained more than 85% of construction contracts in Africa.[163] However, by 2020, Chinese firms were obtaining around a third of such contracts worth $50 million or more.

China has also become a more important source of FDI for the region. Chinese FDI increased from $2.7 billion in 2002 to $123.1 billion in 2014, though most of this was in transportation, mining, and energy.[164] The largest recipients in the region of Chinese FDI between 2006 and 2018 were Nigeria, Ethiopia, Angola, Kenya, the DRC, Zambia, Republic of the Congo, and South Africa. It is interesting to note that Nigeria, Angola, and the Republic of the Congo were major oil exporters, while the DRC and Zambia were major mineral exporters. South Africa is also a major exporter of minerals. Only Kenya and Ethiopia were not major exporters of oil or minerals (in either absolute or relative terms).[165]

Chinese investment has also led to a great increase in the number of Chinese firms in Africa. One source suggests that over 10,000 Chinese firms are active on the continent.[166] About half of all construction contacts are awarded to Chinese companies. Also, about a third of Chinese firms in Africa are engaged in manufacturing. Some suggest that these firms account for about 12% of Africa's industrial production. Many of these are private, though the largest Chinese firms are MSO.

This leads to another quite interesting aspect of Chinese investments in Africa, and elsewhere: many of these investments involve majority state-owned companies – from China. Despite the larger movement toward the privatization of industries and oil companies worldwide, the (still) communist country of China continues to have state-owned companies dominate many aspects of its economy. This could lead analysts to suspect that such Chinese overseas investment reflects Chinese foreign policy more than being merely a market response.

The lending and investment in Africa, and elsewhere, were expanded with China's BRI. From 2007 to 2020, development banks from China lent $23 billion for infrastructure, with all other development banks, contributing $9.1 billion.[167] However, beginning in 2016, Chinese investment to Africa has begun to decline.[168] Nonetheless, as part of its investment, China has built a large amount of infrastructure for countries in the region.[169] According to one source, little of Belt and Road was about aid, but it was mostly about investment and trade, often with wealthier countries.[170] It is meant to increase Chinese influence and power.

Many critics of the BRI see this program as offering an alternative development model that moves away from democracy and the West.[171] Others suggest that the lending associated with the building of infrastructure can lead to a debt trap in developing countries as most credit was given on commercial terms.[172] Some of the deals, as in Angola and Congo, required linkage between repayment and the extraction of natural resources.[173] Also, countries in deep debt to China might be subject to more pressure from China in connection with things like voting at the UN. Importantly, many of the entities making loans are state-owned companies, diminishing the firewalls between the Chinese government and its enterprises abroad. Given early Chinese investment into natural resources, especially mining and oil resources, along with investing in infrastructure for promoting bilateral trade between China and the rest of the world, the idea of China following a mercantilist foreign policy is reinforced.

However, these actions for lending and FDI are also consistent with solving domestic Chinese economic and political issues, which is still pursing national self-interests. As discussed above, Chinese trade surpluses with the rest of the world have created dilemmas and opportunities for China: having too much foreign currency brought into the domestic market could be quite inflationary as well as potentially destabilizing – creating a type of resource curse which would undermine its own ability to export in the medium to long term. Moreover, by issuing loans in hard currency, a return is made on monies that are not being invested domestically. Also, these very same state-owned companies can continue to produce, even should they have saturated the domestic market. It also allows for more employment, as so many Chinese firms bring along Chinese labor for their projects. In many ways, they are acting in a manner like those described as what the MNCs from America were doing in the developing world during the Cold War period. Nonetheless, they are providing needed infrastructure and an economic stimulus to many African nations.

The close ties between African and China could also be a two-edged sword for many. A recent report by the IMF suggests African growth rates could decline should China's economy begin to slow down or reverse.[174] Since China is the region's largest single country trading partner, and largest source of bilateral loans, Africa can be quite sensitive as well as vulnerable to economic contractions in China. In fact, China purchases around 20% of region's exports of metals, minerals, and fuel. It also sells much of the machinery and manufactured goods and machinery purchased by African countries. The authors suggest that for every point of growth decline China experiences, Africa may also have a 0.25% growth decline within a year. Also, as discussed above, lending to Africa has decreased in recent years which may also be a drag on African growth rates.

Military Ties

Africa may also be part of the Chinese plan to project power outside of its immediate region. China has a naval base in Djibouti, which is its first military base overseas.[175] However, China says it is for logistical purposes more than military. Interestingly, four other countries have military bases there, including the US, France, Italy, and Japan. Given Djibouti's position near the mouth of the Red Sea and the start of the Indian Ocean, it is a quite strategic location on the Bab-el Mendeb Strait, a choke point for the Suez Canal, and a strategic one for the Horn of Africa, the Middle East, and the Indian Ocean. The Bab-el Mendeb Strait is the busiest maritime lane in the world. According to the EIA, over 6 million barrels per day of oil, condensate, and refined petroleum products pass through this strait on the way to the US and Asia.[176] The strait connects the Indian Ocean via the Gulf of

Aden to the Red Sea, and then through the Suez Canal, the Mediterranean Sea, thus serving as a main conduit for goods between Asia and Europe.

China wanted this location ostensibly to help police the piracy of the area (as did other nations as well). They had been involved in antipiracy in the area since 2008.[177] According to one source, China is also in talks with Equatorial Guinea as well as Tanzania for access to other ports or bases.[178] Even if these countries only allow access to bases, and not the bases themselves, they could greatly increase Chinese ability to project power in the region. The investment side could matter as well. According to a source, China is funding 61 ports in 30 countries, increasing its chances of gaining such access.[179] Clearly these ports can be thought as dual use: to promote and facilitate trade with China as well as one day serving for military purposes.

Chinese Influence in Case Studies

Angola

Angolan exports to China mostly revolve around oil. Angolan exports to China represented an average of 61% of all Angolan exports for the years 2018–2020.[180] By value, around 80% of this was oil. Angolan oil was also a large share of Chinese oil imports: in 2010, Angolan oil represented about 18% of all such Chinese imports, making it close to Saudi Arabia and Iran as a source of oil. In terms of imports, China was the source of approximately 15% of all imports for these same years. Angola also bought arms from China, though it only represented about 5% of all Angola's arms purchases.[181]

China provided Angola with loans when western nations were more reluctant, though China was operating out of self-interest. In fact, China became a significant financial player from 2004 onwards when it began to secure offshore oil blocks from Angola from 2004 to 2005.[182] Moreover, Chinese loans to Angola were usually not very concessional and were more based upon ability to pay.[183] And many of these loans were oil backed.[184] Loans and investment to Angola from China reached around $10 billion by 2003.[185] Between 2005 and 2023, loans to Angola reached approximately $27 billion for construction projects or investment.[186]

Through these investments, China has also acquired ownership shares of Angolan oil. For example, SINOPEC obtained shares in association with a line of credit from the Chinese Export and Import Bank in March 2004.[187] China also obtained partial ownership of some offshore oil blocks: they bought a 50% share of bloc 18, which had been managed by BP.[188] A Chinese state-owned company, SINOPEC (China Petroleum & Chemical Corporation), also invested around $2.2 billion, first $740 million in 2006, and $1.5 billion in 2013. According to another source, China holds a 70% or 75% share of two oil investments made in 2006 and 2011.[189] China is also involved in two port projects, including Cabina and Lobito, with one more under consideration.[190] Chinese loans were backed by oil guarantees and the money was put into the building of infrastructure. China would often let countries repay their debts in resources.[191] China did forgive some of Angola's debt, despite it being above the HIPC poverty line.[192]

Nigeria

Trade between Nigeria and China is of increasing importance, though clearly this trade is a larger percentage of trade for Nigeria than for China. Overall, Nigeria was the second largest African trading partner with China in 2021 (after South Africa) and the largest export market for the Chinese.[193] In fact, imports from China to Nigeria represented about 16% of all exports to Africa, but Nigeria was not even in the top five of major sources of imports for China. Nigeria has also bought a fair number of arms from China in the post-2000 period. From 2014 to 2019, it purchased 20% of its total arms from China, though that was behind Russia at 36% of its arms imported for those years.[194]

In terms of investment, from 2005 to 2023, Chinese investment and construction projects were valued at approximately $35.6 billion.[195] During this time, in 2018, Nigeria joined the BRI.[196] Several of the major investments were of course in oil. For example, China National Petroleum Corp (CNPC) invested around $840 million in 2020; a group of four investors (including CNPC and Sinopec) invested $5.79 billion in 2019; Sinopec invested $2.5 billion in 2012, and China National Offshore Oil (CNOOC) invested around $2.3 billion in 2006 as well as $170 million in 2017. Other investments were in transportation, such as the China Civil Engineering Construction Company building a rail line between Kano and Ibadan.[197] Another agreement was signed with the China Railway Construction, which was to connect the capital of Abuja to Itakpe, which would then link to the recently opened Abujea-Warri line, which runs from Abuja to the port of Warri.[198]

Cameroon

Trade between Cameroon and China was less than several of these other nations, but China was the largest source of imports for Cameroon by value, averaging about 19% of total imports between 2016 and 2018.[199] Cameroon also imported many of its arms from China. In fact, between 2014 and 2019, approximately 48% of Cameroon's arms were supplied by China.[200] Exports to China grew steadily, rising from the fourth largest market for Cameroonian exports to the largest, going from $150 million to $944 million. This early trade represented an average of 15% of Cameroon's exports, though it came to comprise nearly a quarter by 2018.

China invested about $10.88 billion in Cameroon between 2005 and 2023.[201] Of this, $540 million was invested by China Petroleum and Chemical (Sinopec), for 80% ownership of an oil sector investment. Most other investments were in construction, though investments in the hydroelectric sector were also made. Cameroon joined the BRI in 2015.[202]

Gabon

China became Gabon's largest trading partner from 2013 onwards.[203] China was Gabon's third largest source of imports between 2016 and 2018.[204] This trade was around $400 million and Chinese imports accounted for about 8% of all Gabonese imports. Gabonese exports to China increased at this time, from $950 million to $1.8 billion. China became Gabon's largest export market in 2017, replacing Congo. On a percentage basis, it went from about 9% to around 20%. Total trade represented $2.7 billion in 2018. By 2020, the value of trade was $4.55 billion.[205]

Between 2005 and 2023, China had loans for construction projects valued at about $1.96 billion in Gabon. Gabon joined the BRI in 2018.[206] In 2005, Gabon had signed an agreement with a Chinese consortium to exploit iron ore deposits, which included the construction of a 560 kilometer rail line and a deepwater port.[207] After disputes between the two governments, the Chinese partner withdrew, and no one has assumed this project.

Congo DRC

Chinese trade with Congo represented over $15 billion in 2021. This represented about 6% of all Chinese-African trade, making the DRC the fifth largest trading partner for China in Africa, behind Nigeria and Angola, each of which was closer to 10%.[208] This rose to $930 million in 2019, making Congo the top recipient of Chinese investment that year.[209]

China has also invested heavily in the DRC. From 2005 to 2023, Chinese investment in the DRC was estimated at $21.8 billion.[210] And this is even though the DRC only joined the BRI in 2021. Quite a substantial amount of this investment was in mining. In 2007, the DRC signed an agreement with China Railway Engineering Corporation (CREC) that was a "resource for infrastructure" (RFI) agreement.[211] This gave CREC export licenses in Kolwezi in exchange for raising money for public infrastructure deals. The deal was worth an estimated $9 billion. In return, CREC was to obtain $3 billion worth of financing for public goods infrastructure projects, including roads and hospitals, as well as another $3 billion for the mining project itself. The government of DRC (and Gécamines) holds a 32% stake as part of the deal.

Many other Chinese companies have invested in DRC mining. For example, China Nonferrous Metal Mining invested $1.4 billion, Zijin Mining invested around $690 million, China Molybdenum invested around $550 million, and Zhejiang Huayou Cobalt invested around $500 million during this period.[212] Chinese companies control between 40% and 50% of cobalt produced in the DRC.[213] A deal in 2007 worth around $6 billion, called "minerals for infrastructure" resulted in China securing mining rights in a major cobalt mine by building roads, highways and hospitals."[214] China was also granted access to rights for major quantities of copper and cobalt as a result of 68% ownership in a joint venture with Gécamines and China Railway Engineering Company and Sinohydro Corporation.[215]

Beyond mining, some Chinese companies hold investment in smelting. For example, the Lualaba copper smelter in the DRC opened in 2020, and it is the largest smelter in the country. It is owned by two Chinese companies: 60% is owned by China Nonferrous Mining Corp (CNMC) and 40% by Chinese SOE, Yunnan Copper.[216] This plant should have an annual capacity of 400,000 tons of blister copper.[217] It is estimated that China refines about two-thirds of the world's cobalt.[218] In fact, in Congo, China has a stranglehold over Congolese production, with Chinese firms owning or having a stake in 15 of Congo's 19 cobalt-producing mines in 2020.[219]

Zambia

Zambian trade with China is quite high, with China representing the largest export market and the second or third largest source of imports between 2018 and 2020.[220] In 2020, trade with China amounted to $2.35 billion. This also represented almost 19% of its export trade and almost 17% of its sources of imports. Arms were also a part of this trade: Zambia bought most of its imported arms from China from 2014 to 2019, representing nearly half of all arms, at 47%.[221] The next two highest sources were Italy and Russia.

China also had major investments in Zambia, especially in its copper industry. Its first big investment in Zambia occurred in 1998 when CNMC bought a mine that had been closed for ten years.[222] This purchase was for 85% ownership and CNMC paid $20 million and agreed to invest an additional $130 million to return it to profitability. By 2005, over 160 Chinese companies had invested in Zambia. Despite, or perhaps because of, the size of the investments in the country, the relations in Zambia between Chinese firms and Zambians have not always been cordial.[223] In 2005, many Zambian workers were killed in an explosion in a Chinese-owned mine, which took place in an explosive plant on mining grounds. These events soured perceptions of Chinese investments, and they even became an issue in the subsequent presidential election – with the opposition candidate using an anti-Chinese populist message. Nonetheless, under Hu Jintao, Zambia was promised an economic and cooperation zone funded by China.

Subsequent to this, between 2005 and 2021, Chinese entities invested approximately $16.97 billion in a variety of areas in Zambia.[224] As discussed above, mining was one of the key areas. In fact, between 2006 and 2018, China Nonferrous Metal Mining (which is state-owned in China), invested over $2 billion.[225] Not only did China invest in Zambia, but it also lent quite a bit of money to it. In fact, by 2022, Zambia owed approximately $5.5 billion to Chinese entities.[226] Zambia joined the BRI in 2018.[227]

Botswana

China is not a major export destination for Botswana. In 2021, it only received 3.44% of all Botswanan exports.[228] Nor was China among the top five sources of imports for Botswana in that year, only accounting for 2.85% of imports. South

Africa dominates the source of imports, accounting for about 60%, though in the years 2000 to the present, this level rose to the high 70s/low 80s in percentage. Of the exports that did go to China, most were diamonds and copper, representing about 99.3% of this trade.[229]

Botswana only joined the BRI quite recently. In January 2021, it signed a memorandum of understanding, becoming the 46th African country to sign.[230] Chinese companies invested approximately $1.64 billion into Botswana between 2005 and 2021.[231] Most of this was in construction, with some recent investment by China Petroleum and Chemical Corporation (Sinopec). This involved the purchase of Chevron's petroleum business in both South Africa and Botswana, though in Botswana, Sinopec attempted to acquire 100% ownership of the former Chevron petroleum business.[232] Later sources suggest that the deal fell through, and that the deal went to a Swiss company.[233]

Niger

China was also an important trading partner with Niger, especially for imports. It was second to France, but only by a bit. These imports were valued at $1,649.7 million between 2018 and 2020, compared to imports from France at $1,764.2 million. Chinese goods represented about 20% of all Nigerien imports for these years. In terms of exports to China, the latter was not even listed as a major export market by one source.[234] Another source places exports to China at around 9% for 2020 and 2021.[235]

Interestingly, Niger found oil and began to exploit it at significant levels in 2011, and this has proved to be an entrée for Chinese companies. Oil exploration is being pursued by the CNPC.[236] Moreover, a pipeline is being constructed to carry the oil from Niger to Benin at a deepwater port by CNPC, and it will be the longest oil pipeline in Africa.[237] CNPC made investments worth $4.99 billion in 2010 and $1.31 billion in 2019. Operations were scheduled to begin in 2022, but oil was first loaded onto a ship in May 2024.[238] CNPC is government-owned from mainland China. It is estimated that the pipeline could carry 90,000 barrels per day.[239] Overall, from 2005 to 2021, Niger obtained $7.46 billion in investments from Chinese sources.[240]

Importantly, China National Nuclear Corporation (CNNC) invested in Niger, with the Société des Mines des Azelik SOMINA.[241] This broke 40 years of French control over uranium through its company Areva (Afane).[242] Production began in 2010. The company is owned by two Chinese companies: China Nuclear International Uranium Corporation (Sino-Uranium) (37.2%), and ZXJOY Invest (ZXJOY) (24.8%). Most of the rest is owned by the Société de Patrimoine des Mines du Niger (SOPAMIN) (33%) and the rest by Korea Resources Corporation (KORES).[243] Arvena and a Korean company (Kepco) have expressed interest in more investing in Niger with a bid to invest in a joint venture with 66.7% going to these two firms, and the rest to the Nigerien country through SPOAMIN. Interest in investing in uranium in Niger seems to rise and fall with the price of uranium, however, and production was halted in several mines by 2019 due to low prices in conjunction with depleted mines.[244] Overall, Chinese investments in Niger's uranium sector have become quite important. In 2018, Niger announced new Chinese investment into exploration of uranium in the Agadez region.[245] It also had investments from the American company Orana, which could lead Niger to move from the fourth largest exporter of uranium to the second.[246] In 2019, Niger received the sixth highest level of investment from China destined to sub-Saharan Africa, at $178 million from all types of investment.[247]

Conclusions

Several post–Cold War and post-2000 developments and changes may lead to a diminishing of conditions which helped lead to outcomes attributed to the natural resource curse. First several countries have partially or fully privatized their mineral-exporting sectors. For example, Ghana, Zambia, and the DRC all privatized their mineral-exporting sectors in the 1990s or early 2000s. Others, such as Togo, maintain majority government ownership. Since MSO of oil or mineral export was shown to increase the severity of the resource curse, then as more countries privatize these sectors, we should expect to see fewer, or less severe versions, of these negative outcomes. Also, most of the new countries to oil or mineral exporting have less than MSO of these sectors. By contrast, little progress in privatization was reflected among the oil-exporting countries which had been MSO. Although there are rumors of Angola privatizing 30% of Sonangol, this sector would still be considered MSO.[248] Also, Nigeria's NNPC is to become more autonomous, though it remains majority state-owned.

Second, much of Africa has experienced an increase in political and civil rights associated with a regionwide adoption of de jure multiparty electoral systems. In many countries in the region, significant increases in political and civil rights did emerge, with as many as nine countries becoming rated as "free," and more countries became rated as "partly free" rather than "not free." However, among our oil and mineral exporters, few countries have had significant increases in these political and civil rights. Most of our countries that were partly free remain so after the Cold War, and most countries that had been not free remain so. This finding is supported by prior work as these countries were less dependent upon aid or less vulnerable to international pressure to democratize given the available exports of mineral or oil.[249] This lack of a strong movement toward political liberalization would argue for continued poor economic policies associated with mineral- or oil-exporting sectors.

Third, with the end of the Cold War, most countries in sub-Saharan African nations have become more open to international trade and investment, reflecting a move away from inward-oriented development strategies and more moves toward market based economic policies.[250] The KOF index of globalization shows a steady increase in trade and an openness of the region. Moreover, clearly linked to the rise of privatizations, a rise of increased FDI flowed into the region. Although much was from China, as discussed above, companies form around the world were the most likely source of money for the privatization of formerly majority state-owned assets – as opposed to domestic or regional investors. This more open trading environment would likely weaken resource curse tendencies.

Fourth, and related to the above issues, many sub-Saharan Africans have experienced an amazing period of economic growth (with speed bumps around 2008 and 2019).[251] As discussed above, most countries, especially those exporting commodities to India and China saw robust growth post-2000–2018. Thus, one of the predictions of the resource curse would be less likely to prevail in the region for this period. This could beg the question of whether there was a resource curse, or if the condition which had led to it had changed and its impact would be less severe. Growth would clearly move away from the worst prediction of the resource curse, though commodity price are likely to remain volatile.

Fifth, an international attempt to target several negative aspects of the resource curse resulted in the emergence of EITI. Although many debate about its efficacy, it is aimed specifically at stemming much of the corruption often associated with mineral resource exploitation. This may slightly reduce some of the worst aspects of what is discussed in the resource curse agenda. However, the jury is still out to what degree EITI can reduce some of these outcomes.

Sixth, more oil-exporting nations in the region have attempted to create a natural gas market associated with what had been mostly the flaring of natural gas. This trend could create and deepen the horizontal and vertical linkages between oil exploration and other sources of exports linked to it. This move could also draw in more FDI and technology associated with this highly technological sector. MSO oil companies, especially, did not have either the resources or the technology to capture the natural gas, and so much was wasted. This movement may also help countries meet any Paris Agreement commitments as flaring natural gas directly into the environment is a major source of greenhouse gas emissions.

Finally, in this later period, China has risen as an economic powerhouse and has increased its economic, diplomatic ties with the region, with important consequences for development. Its interests in the region were especially strong with oil- or mineral-exporting nations. To the degree that a Washington-led coalition is weakening as a more multipolar system emerges, African leaders might obtain more policy autonomy, leading to incentive which may bring back prior policies associated with lower growth. Moreover, should closer economic ties with China creates more debt for African nations, then this new trend may have both positive and negative implication for the return of a natural resource curse. Chinese demand for oil and mineral resources could keep commodity prices high, with two effects. On the one hand, this could offset negative growth patterns. On the other hand, this same increase in demand could push countries deeper into their natural resource export specialization. Moreover, loans, aid and FDI from China without any political or economic conditionality could mean that the resource curse outcomes could more easily return if African leaders can walk away from economic and political conditionality and purse the types of policies which had led to lower growth. Also, FDI from China (and elsewhere) could help African nations grow their economies as so much Chinese investment has gone into infrastructure and transportation which could open other venues for opportunities in these countries.

Nonetheless, given then changes in the international system, as well within African domestic economies, we should expect to see less of the natural resource curse outcome following 2000 than we saw during the period of study. This should be especially so in countries where the sector is, or has become, less than MSO. African economies have seen more growth in recently years, their economies are more open to investment and trade, and their political systems are slightly more liberal. Also, EITI may help reduce resource curse outcomes, and the movement of oil-exporting countries into natural gas capture and production can lead to more diversification of their economies and less waste of resources. Finally, the rise of China may keep commodity prices at higher rates as well as provide much needed investment into infrastructure.

Notes

1 Brune, Garrett, and Kogut (2004).
2 Quinn (2016, esp. chapters 6 and 7); also Tangri (1999).
3 White and Bhatia (1998, appendix 1, pp. 138–139); see also Bennell (1997).
4 Bennell (1997), Brune, Garrett, and Kogut (2004), Buchs (2003), Craig (2002), Quinn (2016), Tangri (1999), White and Bhatia (1998).
5 Buchs (2003).
6 Calculated from World Bank Group Privatization Database, 2000–2007. And there might be some double counting, but the numbers are suggestive.
7 Craig (2002).
8 Appiah-Kubi (2001, 209).
9 For an overview of this regional trend, see Quinn (2016); for an overview of worldwide privatization trends, see World Bank Group Privatization Database, Young (1987), Megginson (2000), Brune, Garrett, and Kogut (2004).
10 *Economist* (1998, 46); also *Economist* (1999).
11 For Rwandan genocide and regional impacts, see Adelman and Suhrke (1999), Emizet (2000), Gnamo (1999), Hintjens (1999), Lemarchand (1999), McNulty (1999), Prunier (1995), and Quinn (2004).
12 *Africa South of the Sahara* (2004).
13 Coakley (1997).
14 Unless stated otherwise, details from this section come from *Africa South of the Sahara* (2004).
15 Carter Center (2002). A later code was passed in 2018, but this had more to do with royalties and taxes than ownership. *Africa South of the Sahara* (2022). It also dealt with environmental and health and safety regulations. See "Spotlight: Mining Law in Democratic Republic of Congo," *Lexology*, October 12, 2022. www.lexology.com/library/detail.aspx?g=11d3b5dc-9361-4490-8440-55de51cc8cde#:~:text=18%2D001%20of%209%20March,in%20the%202002%20Mining%20Code.
16 Carter Center (2002).
17 For a longer list of private and public companies, see Democratic Republic of Congo, Ministry of Mines (2003).
18 *Africa South of the Sahara* (2002).
19 Mining Technology (2022).
20 Ibid.

21 Ibid., 6.
22 Mining Code of the Republic of Niger. www.howwemadeitinafrica.com/wp-content/uploads/2010/05/Niger_-Mining-Code.pdf.
23 Unless stated otherwise, data in this section comes from Observatory of Economic Complexity (n.d.).
24 World Bank (n.d.c).
25 *Africa South of the Sahara* (2020), though in 2018 and 2019, gold contributed almost the same as petroleum and both contributed twice the value to the GNP compared to uranium.
26 *Africa South of the Sahara* (2020).
27 Observatory of Economic Complexity (n.d.).
28 DTC Botswana (n.d.,).
29 Brook (2012a, 2012b).
30 Eligon (2023). The agreement also includes investment of over $800 million in Botswana over a decade.
31 Schraeder (2004, 132–134). Afro-Marxism was dropped by Mozambique in 1989, Cape Verde and Sao Tome and Principe in 1990, Benin, Congo, Angola, Ethiopia in 1991, and Madagascar in 1993.
32 Energy Information Administration (2014).
33 *Africa South of the Sahara* (2022).
34 *Africa South of the Sahara* (various years); despite these changes over time, Jones-Luong and Weinthal (2010) have also listed Angola from 1970 to 2010 as majority state-owned; see appendix B.
35 See, for example, IEA (2006).
36 Jones Luong and Weinthal (2010).
37 IEA (2006, 19).
38 Falcão and Nadorff (2020).
39 Qekeleshe (2020). So far, no reports of oil privatization have been confirmed as of July 2023 at least nothing close to Sonangol becoming less than majority state owned.
40 Almeida (2021).
41 Simões (2023).
42 OPEC (n.d.).
43 Nwuku (2021).
44 Clowes (2022); see also Petroleum Industry Act (2021).
45 Nwuku (2021).
46 Nigeria has been a member of OPEC since 1971, at the beginning of its strong oil sector.
47 EIA (n.d.).
48 Privacy Shield (n.d.); see also US Department of State (2021). The government ownership was lowered from 20% to 10% in 2019. See also USEIA (n.d.).
49 For Gabon leaving, Bloomberg Business News (1995); for rejoining see OPEC (n.d.).
50 Ross (2012)
51 USAID (n.d.).
52 Unless said otherwise, data on exports from 2013 to 2017 comes from UCTAD (2019).
53 Data from Frynas (2004) and Cherif and Matsumoto (2021, table 2).
54 Frynas (2004, 540).
55 The most recent available data showing this was 2009. See United Nations Population Fund, "UNFPA Equatorial Guinea." www.unfpa.org/data/transparency-portal/unfpa-equatorial-guinea.

56 Unless stated otherwise, material in this section comes from Colom-Jaén and Campos-Serrano (2013, 4–8).
57 Colom-Jaén and Campos-Serrano (2013, 8).
58 Cherif and Matsumoto (2021, table 2). These were averages of 5 years.
59 Colom-Jaen and Campos-Serrano (2013, 4).
60 *Economist* (2002).
61 *Economist* (2008).
62 World Bank (n.d.c).
63 EITI (n.d.a).
64 EITI (2019).
65 As extractive industries have come to account for two-thirds of African exports from 2001 to 2014. For example, see Chuhan-Pole et al. (2017, xvii).
66 Chuhan-Pole et al. (2017, table 2.1, p. 2).
67 For Mali and Burkina Faso, see UNCTAD (2016).
68 This section comes from UNCTAD data. https://unctadstat.unctad.org/wds/TableViewer/tableView.aspx; gold SITC 971; fuel SITC 3.
69 Calculated from UCTAD; ores, metals, precious stones, and nonmonetary gold (SITC 27 + 28 + 68 + 667 + 971) divided by total exports. https://unctadstat.unctad.org/wds/TableViewer/tableView.aspx; see also *Africa South of the Sahara* (2011).
70 Bastagli, Toulmin (2014, 4).
71 UNCTAD (2016, table 10, p. 27).
72 Quinn (2016, chapter 7), van de Walle (2001).
73 Coulibaly, Gandhi, and Senbet (2019). For an overview of debt relief, see Callaghy (2010).
74 Data for this section comes from KOF Globalization Index. https://kof.ethz.ch/en/forecasts-and-indicators/indicators/kof-globalisation-index.html.
75 Unless stated otherwise, data comes from Freedom House (2024).
76 Quinn (2016, chapter 8).
77 However, Gabon and Niger experienced coups in 2023, which has not yet shown up in the data.
78 For early low growth, see, for example, Ravenhill (1986), and Easterly and Levine (1997). For recent stronger growth, see, for example, Devarajan and Fengler (2013).
79 Calculated from World Bank (n.d.c).
80 2020 was a bad year for growth, following from COVID-19.
81 Data for this section comes from *Economist* (2011). For views of African growth in prior decades, see, for example, Callaghy and Ravenhill (1993), Ravenhill (1986).
82 Unless stated otherwise, growth comes from World Bank (n.d.c).
83 COVID-19 clearly impacted the world economy, and Africa's growth rate from 2016 to 2020 was –1.2. World Bank (n.d.).
84 Archibong, Coulibaly, and Okonjo-Iweala (2021).
85 Data in this part, unless stated otherwise, comes from EIA, "Refined Petroleum Products Production."
86 World Bank (n.d.c).
87 Sikamo et al. (2016, 494).
88 https://tradingeconomics.com/zambia/exports/copper#:~:text=Zambia%20Exports%20of%20copper%20was,updated%20on%20November%20of%202023.
89 Unless specified otherwise, data comes from UNCTAD (2017) or *Africa South of the Sahara* (2022).

90 Metorex, "Mining Analyst Visit to the DRC." May 26, 2010. https://web.archive.org/web/20120425142404/http://www.metorexgroup.com/downloads/presentations/2010/Analysts_visit_26-28_Mayfinal.pdf.
91 *Africa South of the Sahara* (2022).
92 World Nuclear Association (2023).
93 *Africa South of the Sahara* (2022).
94 Regression to the mean suggests that data which reflects very high or very low averages compared to other similar units, once the cause of deviation is lifted, the mean quickly returns to the larger average.
95 Davison (2017).
96 EITI. https://eiti.org/our-mission.
97 For an overview and test of effectiveness of EITI, see Sovacool et al. (2016: 179–192).
98 Ibid.
99 *Economist* (2021a); Equatorial Guinea did apply in 2019, but it was rejected in 2020. See EITI (n.d.a). The country had joined in 2007, but it was delisted in 2010 over concerns of repressing civil society groups. See, for example, Human Rights Watch (2019).
100 See EITI (n.d.b).
101 Sovacool et al. (2016).
102 Unless stated otherwise, material in this section comes from Aaronson (2011) or EITI (n.d.a).
103 Aaronson (2011).
104 Sovacool et al. (2016, 179).
105 Aaronson (2011), Sovacool et al. (2016).
106 Lujala, Rustad, and Le Billon (2017).
107 Reuters (2020); also EITI (n.d.).
108 Lujala (2018, 371).
109 Ibid., 77.
110 Chatham House (2015).
111 Jefferis (2009).
112 See, for example, van den Brink et al. (2019); also Goodland (2012).
113 Unless stated otherwise, information in this section comes from *Economist* (2023a).
114 Reed (2021, 90).
115 EIA (2014).
116 EIA (n.d.).
117 Ibid.
118 Ibid.
119 NNPC (n.d.).
120 EIA (2016).
121 Ibid.
122 *Africa South of the Sahara* (2011).
123 Ibid.; also Nigeria LNG Limited (n.d.).
124 Business in Cameroon (2020).
125 *Africa South of the Sahara* (2004). Low water levels can disrupt service and its reliability.
126 New Africa (2020).
127 EITI. https://eiti.org/cameroon#oil-and-gas-production.
128 Société Nationale des Hydrocarbures (n.d.).
129 Hawilti (2021).

130 Ibid.
131 Ngene et al. (2016).
132 Andrew Reid and Arjun Flora, "UK Offshore Flaring and Venting." *Institute for Energy Economics and Financial Analysis*, March 30, 2023. https://ieefa.org/resources/uk-offshore-flaring-and-venting#:~:text=Globally%2C%20some%20143%20billion%20cubic,billion%20of%20lost%20sales%20revenue.
133 Okafor and Aniche (2016).
134 World Bank (n.d.b).
135 World Bank (n.d.a).
136 For good sources of China's role in Africa and development, see Brautigam (2009), Dreher et al. (2022), Large (2021), and Tull (2006).
137 Tull (2006).
138 *Economist* (2022b).
139 For these points, see Dreher et al. (2022, 4–9).
140 Dreher et al. (2022, 4).
141 Taylor (2011), Omolo (2022).
142 Taylor (2011).
143 Tull (2006, 463).
144 Mudronova (2018).
145 Ghazvinian (2007, 276–277).
146 For 2011, see Alden (2012, 11); for 2022, see Foreign Affair Committee, "China Regional Snapshot: Sub-Saharan Africa." https://foreignaffairs.house.gov/china-regional-snapshot-sub-saharan-africa.
147 *Economist* (2022b).
148 Alden (2012, 12).
149 Mureithi (2022).
150 Ghazvinian (2007, 276).
151 Tull (2006, 466).
152 Alden (2012, 11).
153 *Economist* (2013).
154 Liu and Dunford (2016).
155 *Economist* (2017).
156 Ibid.
157 China Global Investment Tracker (n.d.).
158 Dreher et al. (2022, 299). Unless mentioned otherwise, information from here.
159 Dreher et al. (2022), *Economist* (2022c).
160 Brautigam (2009).
161 Unless stated otherwise, information in this section comes from Abdel-Latif et al. (2023).
162 Unless specified otherwise, most data in this section comes from Mihalyi, Adam, and Hwang (2020).
163 *Economist* (2022a).
164 Unless stated otherwise, most information in this section comes from Mudronova (2018).
165 Some have suggested China is very involved in African mining. See Ericsson Ericsson, Löf, and Löf. (2002).
166 Unless stated otherwise, information for this section comes from *Economist* (2022d).
167 *Economist* (2022a).

168 *Economist* (2023b). Unless stated otherwise, much of this section draws from this source.
169 Ghazvinian (2007, 277).
170 *Economist* (2023b).
171 For a discussion of Chinese model, see Boone (2009), Taylor (2011), and Ishiyama (2023).
172 "China's Debt-Trap Diplomacy." January 23, 2017. www.project-syndicate.org/commentary/china-one-belt-one-road-loans-debt-by-brahma-chellaney-2017-01.
173 *Economist* (2022c).
174 Abdel-Latif et al. (2023).
175 Reuters (2017).
176 EIA. www.eia.gov/todayinenergy/detail.php?id=41073.
177 Masuda (2023).
178 *Economist* (2022e).
179 Ibid
180 *Africa South of the Sahara* (2020).
181 Large (2021, table 7).
182 Weiner and Vines (2012, 85); see also *Africa South of the Sahara* (2022).
183 Thus, not qualifying as ODA, but as Other Official Flows (OOFs). See Brautigam (2009, 185).
184 *Africa South of the Sahara* (2022).
185 Weiner and Vines (2012, 86).
186 China Global Investment Tracker (n.d.).
187 Alves (2012, 106).
188 Weiner and Vines (2012, 88).
189 China Global Investment Tracker (n.d.).
190 "(In)Roads and Outposts: Critical Infrastructure in China's Africa Strategy." www.nbr.org/wp-content/uploads/pdfs/publications/sr98_inroadsandoutposts_may2022.pdf; see also Taylor (2011).
191 Brautigam (2009, 56).
192 Ibid., 130.
193 Mureithi (2022).
194 Large (2021, table 7, p. 181).
195 China Global Investment Tracker (n.d.).
196 Sacks (2021).
197 *Africa South of the Sahara* (2022).
198 Ibid.
199 Ibid.
200 Large (2021, table 7, p. 181).
201 China Global Investment Tracker (n.d.).
202 Sacks (2021).
203 Xinhua (2023).
204 *Africa South of the Sahara* (2022).
205 Xinhua (2023).
206 For investment data, see China Global Investment Tracker (n.d.); for Belt and Road joining, see Sacks (2021).
207 *Africa South of the Sahara* (2022).
208 Mureithi (2022).
209 Large (2021, table 4, p. 87).

210 China Global Investment Tracker (n.d.); for Belt and Road, see Sacks (2021).
211 Much of the following comes from Landry (2018).
212 China Global Investment Tracker (n.d.). These are added across the period.
213 Savage (2020).
214 Ibid.; see also *Economist* (2002c).
215 Africa South of the Sarah (2022).
216 Fastmarkets (2018).
217 "Refining Copper DRC." www.mining-technology.com/projects/kamoa-copper-project-katanga.
218 Ibid. Many see cobalt as key to electric car market and their control of this sector has been seen as reflecting long-term Chinese economic foreign policy goals. See *Economist* (2021b).
219 *Economist* (2022d).
220 *Africa South of the Sahara* (2020).
221 Large (2021, table 7, p. 181).
222 Much of this first part comes from Brautigam (2009, 5).
223 Brautigam (2009, 5).
224 China Global Investment Tracker (n.d.).
225 Ibid.
226 *Economist* (2022c).
227 Sacks (2021).
228 Unless stated otherwise, data in this section comes from https://oec.world/en/profile/country/bwa?yearSelector1=2021.
229 https://oec.world/en/profile/bilateral-country/chn/partner/bwa.
230 Devonshire-Ellis (2021).
231 China Global Investment Tracker (n.d.).
232 China Business Law Journal (2017).
233 Glencore (2017).
234 Data for this section comes from *Africa South of the Sahara* (2020).
235 OEC. https://oec.world/en/profile/country/ner?yearSelector1=2020
236 African Business (2021).
237 Offshore Technology (2021).
238 Maritime Executive (2024).
239 Reed (2021).
240 Large (2021, 87); Also China Global Investment Tracker (n.d.).
241 *Africa South of the Sahara* (2022) suggests it was in 2002, but China Global Investment Tracker (n.d.) has 2008, and Environmental Justice Atlas (n.d.) places the investment in 2007. All agree production had begun by 2010.
242 https://ejatlas.org/conflict/chinese-uranium-mine-invades-nigers-traditional-pastoral-territory.
243 Environmental Justice Atlas (n.d.).
244 *Africa South of the Sahara* (2022).
245 Tzinieris (2018).
246 Ibid.
247 Large (2021, table 4, p. 87).
248 *Africa South of the Sahara* (various years), Almeida (2021), Falcão and Nadorff (2020), Qekeleshe (2020), Simões (2023). So far, no reports of oil privatization have been confirmed at the time of submission for publication.

249 See Quinn (2016) for logic of why patrimonial systems with oil or mining (MSO or not) would continue to be able to fund their patronage systems, even if at lower levels.
250 Archibong, Coulibaly, and Okonjo-Iweala (2021), Quinn (2016), van de Walle (2001).
251 Archibong, Coulibaly, and Okonjo-Iweala (2021), Devarajan and Fengler (2013), *Economist* (2011).

References

Aaronson, Susan Ariel. 2011. "Limited Partnership: Business, Government, Civil Society, and the Public in the Extractive Industries Transparency Initiative (EITI)." *Public Administration and Development* 31(1): 50–63.

Abdel-Latif, Hany, Wenjie Chen, Michele Fornino, and Henry Rawlings. 2023. "China's Slowing Economy Will Hit Sub-Saharan Africa's Growth." *IMF*, November 9. www.imf.org/en/News/Articles/2023/11/09/cf-chinas-slowing-economy-will-hit-sub-saharan-africas-growth.

Adelman, Howard and Astri Suhrke, eds. 1999. *The Path of a Genocide: The Rwanda Crisis from Uganda to Zaire*. New Brunswick: Transaction.

Africa South of the Sahara. Various Years. Various Countries. London: Europa Publications.

African Business. 2021. "Niger: An Attractive Nation with an Emerging Oil Industry." November 8.

Alden, Chris. 2012. "China and Africa: From Engagement to Partnership." In Marcus Power and Ana Cristina Alves, eds., *China and Angola: A Marriage of Convenience?* Oxford: Pambazuka Press, 10–26.

Almeida, Henrique. 2021. "Angola Tests Market for Stake in State Oil Giant with Bank Sale." *Bloomberg/Quint*, April 20. www.bloombergquint.com/politics/angola-begins-sale-of-state-bank-as-test-for-oil-privatization.

Alves, Ana Cristina. 2012. "Taming the Dragon: China's Oil Interests in Angola." In Marcus Power and Ana Cristina Alves, eds., *China and Angola: A Marriage of Convenience*. Oxford: Pambazuka Press, 105–123.

Appiah-Kubi, Kojo. 2001. "State-Owned Enterprises and Privatisation in Ghana." *Journal of Modern African Studies* 39(2): 197–229.

Archibong, Belinda, Brahima Coulibaly, and Ngozi Okonjo-Iweala. 2021. "Washington Consensus Reforms and Lessons for Economic Performance in Sub-Saharan Africa." *Journal of Economic Perspectives* 35(3): 133–156.

Bastagli, F. and C. Toulmin. 2014. "Mali: Economic Factors behind the Crisis." European Parliament, Directorate-General for External Policies of the Union, Directorate B, Policy Department.

Bennell, Paul. 1997. "Privatizing in Sub-Saharan Africa: Progress and Prospects during the 1990." *World Development* 25(11): 1785–1803.

Bloomberg Business News. 1995. "Gabon Plans to Quit OPEC." *New York Times*, 9 January, D10.

Boone, Catherine. 2009. "The 'China Model' in Africa: A New Brand of Developmentalism." In R. Springborg, ed., *Development Models in Muslim Contexts: Chinese, "Islamic" and Neo-Liberal Alternatives*. Edinburgh: Edinburgh University Press, 47–83.

Brautigam, Deborah. 2009. *The Dragon's Gift: The Real Story of China in Africa*. Oxford: Oxford University Press.

Brook, M. C. 2012a. "Botswana's Diamond Pipeline: Prospecting to Jewellery." https://minedocs.com/21/Debswana-Prospect-2018.pdf

Brook, M. C. 2012b. "The Journey of Botswana's Diamonds." www.dtcbotswana.com/publications/

Brune, Nancy, Geoffrey Garrett, and Bruce Kogut. 2004. "The International Monetary Fund and the Global Spread of Privatization." *IMF Staff Papers* 51(2): 195–219.

Buchs, Thierry D. 2003. "Privatization in Sub-Saharan Africa: Some Lessons from Experiences to Date." *International Finance Corporation.* www.researchgate.net/publication/23748571_Privatization_in_Sub-Saharan_Africa_Some_Lessons_from_Experiences_to_Date

Business in Cameroon. 2020 "Cameroon: Natural Gas Can Contribute 20–30% of the Energy Mix, SNH says." May. www.businessincameroon.com/energy/2911-9729-cameroon-natural-gas-can-contribute-20-30-of-the-energy-mix-snh-says.

Callaghy, Thomas. 2010. "The Paris Club, Debt and Poverty Reduction: Evolving Patterns of Governance." In Jennifer Clapp and Rorden Wilkinson, eds., *Global Governance, Poverty and Inequality*. London: Routledge, 162–184.

Callaghy, Thomas M. and John Ravenhill, eds. 1993. *Hemmed In: Responses to Africa's Economic* Decline. New York: Columbia University Press.

Carter Center. 2002. *A State Affair: Privatizing Congo's Copper Sector*. Atlanta: Carter Center.

Central Intelligence Agency. n.d. "World Factbook, Natural Gas."

Chatham House. 2015. "Connecting Resources and Society in Botswana Africa Programme Conference Summary." November23–24. www.chathamhouse.org/sites/default/files/events/2016-11-23-connecting-resources%20and-society-botswana-meeting-summary.pdf.

Cherif, Reda and Akito Matsumoto. 2021. *Sub-Saharan African Oil Exporters: The Future of Oil and the Imperative of Diversification.* Washington, DC: International Monetary Fund, African Department.

China Business Law Journal. 2017. "Sinopec Enters Downstream Oil Industries in Africa." April 26.

China Global Investment Tracker. n.d. "American Enterprise Institute." www.aei.org/china-global-investment-tracker.

Chuhan-Pole, Punam, Andrew L. Dabalen, and Bryan Christopher Land. 2017. *Mining in Africa Are Local Communities Better Off?* Washington, DC: The World Bank.

Clowes, William. 2022. "Nigeria's State-Owned Energy Firm Starts Commercial Operations." *Bloomberg*, July 19.

Coakley, George J. 1997. "The Mineral Industry of Congo (Kinshasa 1997)."https://d9-wret.s3.us-west-2.amazonaws.com/assets/palladium/production/mineral-pubs/country/1997/9244097.pdf

Colom-Jaén, Artur and Alicia Campos-Serrano. 2013. "Oil in Chad and Equatorial Guinea: Widening the Focus of the Resource Curse." *European Journal of Development Research* 25(4): 584–599.

Coulibaly, Brahima S., Dhruv Gandhi, and Lemma W. Senbet. 2019. "Is Sub-Saharan Africa Facing Another Systemic Sovereign Debt Crisis?" *Africa Growth Initiative Policy Brief.* Washington, DC: Brookings.

Craig, John. 2002. "Privatisation and Indigenous Ownership: Evidence from Africa." *Annals of Public and Cooperative Economics* 73(4): 559–576.

Davison, Adam. 2017. "How Trump Is Quietly Dismantling the Architecture of Global Governance." *New Yorker*, November 10. www.newyorker.com/news/news-desk/how-trump-is-quietly-dismantling-the-architecture-of-global-governance.

Democratic Republic of Congo, Ministry of Mines. 2003. "Guide of Mining Investor." June. www.miningcongo.cd/pdf_divers/guide_of_mining_investor.pdf.

Devarajan, Shantayanan and Wolfgang Fengler. 2013. "Africa's Economic Boom: Why the Pessimists and the Optimists Are Both Right." *Foreign Affairs* 92(3): 68–81.
Devonshire-Ellis, Chris. 2021. "China's 2021 Progress across the African Belt & Road Initiative." *Silk Road Briefings*. http://jiahoninternational.com/newsinfo/650567.html
DTC Botswana (n.d.) Sales Agreement. www.dtcbotswana.com/sales-agreement
Dreher, Axel, Andreas Fuchs, Bradley Parks, Austin Strange, and Michael J. Tierney. 2022. *Banking on Beijing: The Aims and Impacts of China's Overseas Development Program*. Cambridge: Cambridge University Press.
Easterly, William and Ross Levine. 1997. "Africa's Growth Tragedy: Policies and Ethnic Divisions." *Quarterly Journal of Economics* 112(4): 1203–1250.
Economist. 1998. "Overpricing Zambia's Family Silver." May 9.
Economist. 1999. "Selling the Family Copper." November 6.
Economist. 2002. "Oil in Chad: Useful Stuff, Maybe, for Once. A Novel Scheme to Extract Oil without Fueling Corruption or Bloodshed." September 12.
Economist. 2008. "Breaking the Bank: A Vaunted Model Development Project Goes Awry." September 25.
Economist. 2011. "The Sun Shines Bright: The Continent's Impressive Growth Looks Likely to Continue." December 3.
Economist. 2013. "Africa and China: More than Minerals." March 23.
Economist. 2017. "What Is China's Belt and Road Initiative? The Many Motivations behind Xi Jinping's Key Foreign Policy." May 17.
Economist. 2021a. "Equatorial Guinea Is Still Waiting for Its IMF Bail-Out." January 21.
Economist. 2021b. "The Electric-Car Boom Sets off a Scramble for Cobalt in Congo." March 31.
Economist. 2022a. "How Chinese Firms Have Dominated African Infrastructure." February 19.
Economist. 2022b. "The Chinese-African Relationship Is Important to Both Sides, but also Unbalanced." May 20.
Economist, 2022c. "Chinese Loans and Investment in Infrastructure Have Been Huge: An Era of Big Loans and Big Projects is Coming to an End. How Did It Change Africa?" May 20.
Economist. 2022d. "Zambia Wants to Be a Model for Resolving Africa's Debt Crises." May 14.
Economist. 2022e. "Ace of Bases." May 20.
Economist. 2023a. "Why Africa Is Poised to Become a Big Player in Energy Markets: It Has Plenty of Natural Gas, Sunshine and Wind." July 18.
Economist. 2023b. "The Path ahead for China's Belt and Road Initiative." September 6.
Eligon, John. 2023. "Botswana and De Beers Sign Deal to Continue Rich Diamond Partnership." *New York Times*, July 1.
Emizet, Kisangani. 2000. "The Massacre of Refugees in Congo." *Journal of Modern African Studies* 38(2): 163–202.
Energy Information Administration. 2014. "Angola." www.eia.gov/international/content/analysis/countries_long/angola/archive/pdf/angola_2014.pdf.
Energy Information Administration. 2016. "Country Analysis Brief: Nigeria." www.eia.gov/international/content/analysis/countries_long/Nigeria/nigeria.pdf.
Energy Information Administration. n.d. www.eia.gov.
Environmental Justice Atlas. n.d. "Chinese Azelik Uranium Mine in Ingall, Niger." https://ejatlas.org/conflict/chinese-uranium-mine-invades-nigers-traditional-pastoral-territory.

Ericsson, Magnus, Olof Löf, and Anton Löf. 2002. "Chinese Control over African and Global Mining: Past, Present and Future." *Mineral Economics* 33(1): 153–181.

Extractives Industries Transparency Initiative. n.d.a. https://eiti.org.

Extractives Industries Transparency Initiative. n.d.b. https://eiti.org/documents/eiti-africa#:~:text=The%20EITI%20has%2024%20member,half%20of%20the%20global%20total.

Falcão, Gonçalo and Norman Nadorff. 2020. "Angola's Back! Five Key 2020 Moves to Increase Oil and Gas Stakeholder Returns." *Mayer/Brown*, December 10. www.mayerbrown.com/en/perspectives-events/blogs/2020/12/angolas-back-five-key-2020-moves-to-increase-oil-and-gas-stakeholder-returns.

Fastmarkets. 2018. "CNMC's DRC Blister Copper Facility to Launch in 2020." May 2.

Freedom House. 2024. "Country and Territory Ratings and Statuses, 1973–2023."

Frynas, Jędrzej George. 2004. "The Oil Boom in Equatorial Guinea." *African Affairs* 103(413): 527–546.

Ghazvinian, John. 2007. *Untapped: The Scramble for Africa's Oil*. New York: Harcourt.

Glencore. 2017. "Proposed Acquisition of Shareholdings in Chevron South Africa and Chevron Botswana." October 6. www.glencore.com/media-and-insights/news/proposed-acquisition-of-shareholdings-in-chevron-south-africa-and-chevron-botswana.

Gnamo, Abbas H. 1999. "The Rwandan Genocide and the Collapse of Mobutu's Kleptocracy." In Howard Adelman and Astri Suhrke, eds., *The Path of a Genocide: The Rwanda Crisis from Uganda to Zaire*. New Brunswick: Transaction, 321–350.

Goodland, Robert. 2012. "Responsible Mining: The Key to Profitable Resource Development." *Sustainability* 4(9): 2099–2126.

Hawilti Desk. 2021. "Gabon Exposes Clear Vision on What to Do with Its Natural Gas." November 4. https://hawilti.com/energy/naturalgas/gabon-exposes-clear-vision-on-what-to-do-with-its-natural-gas.

Hintjens, Helen M. 1999. "Explaining the 1994 Genocide in Rwanda." *Journal of Modern African Studies* 37(2): 241–286.

Human Rights Watch. 2019a. "Equatorial Guinea: A Move to Rejoin Anti-Corruption Group: Repression at Odds with Extractive Industry Watchdog's Requirements." June 21. www.hrw.org/news/2019/06/21/equatorial-guinea-move-rejoin-anti-corruption-group.

Human Rights Watch. 2019b. "Repression at Odds with Extractive Industry Watchdog's Requirements." 21 June. www.hrw.org/news/2019/06/21/equatorial-guinea-move-rejoin-anti-corruption-group.

International Energy Agency. 2006. *Angola: Towards an Energy Strategy*. Paris: OECD/IEA.

International Energy Agency. n.d. "Data and Statistics." www.iea.org/data-and-statistics.

Ishiyama, John. 2023. "Who Is Attracted to the Chinese Model in Africa?" *Journal of Asian and African Studies*: 1–14.

Jefferis, Keith. 2009. "The Role of TNCs in the Extractive Industry of Botswana." *Transnational Corporations* 18(1): 61–92.

Jones Luong, Paula and Ericka Weinthal. 2010. *Oil Is Not a Curse: Ownership Structure and Institutions in Soviet Successor States*. Cambridge: Cambridge University Press.

KOF Globalization Index. n.d. https://kof.ethz.ch/en/forecasts-and-indicators/indicators/kof-globalisation-index.html Economic Globalization.

Landry, David G. 2018. "The Risks and Rewards of Resource-for-Infrastructure Deals: Lessons from the Congo's Sicomines Agreement." Working Paper No. 2018/16. Washington, DC: China-Africa Research Initiative, School of Advanced International Studies, Johns Hopkins University. www.sais-cari.org/publications.

Large, Daniel. 2021. *China and Africa: The New Era*. Boston: Polity.
Lemarchand, René. 1999. "The Crisis in the Great Lakes." In John W. Harbeson and Donald Rothchild, eds., *Africa in World Politics: The African States System in Flux*. Boulder: Westview Press, 324–352.
Liu, Weidong and Michael Dunford. 2016. "Inclusive Globalization: Unpacking China's Belt and Road Initiative." *Area Development and Policy* 1(3): 323–340.
Lujala, Päivi. 2018. "An Analysis of the Extractive Industry Transparency Initiative Implementation Process." *World Development* 107: 358–381.
Lujala, Päivi, Siri Aas Rustad, and Philippe Le Billon. 2017. "Has the EITI Been Successful? Reviewing Evaluations of the Extractive Industries Transparency Initiative." *U4 Brief*. www.u4.no/publications/has-the-eiti-been-successful-reviewing-evaluations-of-the-extractive-industries-transparency-initiative.pdf.
The Maritime Executive. 2024. "Landlocked Niger with China's Aid Starts Oil Exports with Pipeline to Benin." (May 19): Top Stories. https://maritime-executive.com/article/landlocked-niger-with-china-s-aid-starts-oil-exports-with-pipeline-to-benin
Masuda, Kanako. 2023. "Competition of Foreign Military Bases and the Survival Strategies of Djibouti." *Japanese JICA*. www.jica.go.jp/jica_ri/publication/knowledge/__icsFiles/afieldfile/2023/12/25/knowledge_report_08_2.pdf
McNulty, Mel. 1999. "The Collapse of Zaire: Implosion, Revolution, or External Sabotage?" *Journal of Modern African Studies* 37(1): 53–82.
Megginson, William. 2000. "Privatization." *Foreign Policy* 118(Spring): 14–27.
Mihalyi, David, Aisha Adam, and Jyhjong Hwang. 2020. *Resource Backed Loans: Pitfalls and Potential*. New York: Natural Resource Governance Institute.
Mining Technology. 2022. "DRC Issues Ministerial Decree for Manono Lithium-Tin Project." May. www.mining-technology.com/news/drc-decree-manono-lithium.
Mudronova, Jana. 2018. "How Can Africa Maximize Its Mineral Wealth? Development Strategies and Chinese Investment in Africa's Mining Sector." *South African Institute of International Affairs*, October.
Mureithi, Carlos. 2022. "Trade between Africa and China Reached an All-Time High in 2021." *Quartz Africa*, February 8.
New Africa. 2020. "Cameroon: A Balanced Economy." April 10. https://newafricanmagazine.com/22999.
Ngene, Stanley, Kiran Tota-Maharaj, Paul Eke, and Colin Hills. 2016. "Environmental Implications of Flaring and Venting in Crude Oil and Natural Gas Production." *International Journal of Environmental Monitoring and Analysis* 4(6): 154–159.
Nigeria LNG Limited. n.d. www.nlng.com/Our-Company/Pages/Profile.aspx.
NNPC Group. n.d. "Gas Operations." https://napims.nnpcgroup.com/our-services/Pages/Gas-Operations.aspx.
Nwuku, Kasirim. 2021. "Nigeria's Petroleum Industry Act: Addressing Old Problems, Creating New Ones." *Brookings Institute*, November 24. www.brookings.edu/blog/africa-in-focus/2021/11/24/nigerias-petroleum-industry-act-addressing-old-problems-creating-new-ones.
Observatory of Economic Complexity. n.d. "Country Profile, Cameroon." https://oec.world/en/profile/country/cmr.
Offshore Technology. 2021. "Niger–Benin, Niger." *Market Data*, October 29.
Okafor, Jude and Ernest Aniche. 2016. "Nigeria and World Bank Global Gas Flaring Reduction (GGFR) Partnership: The Tragedy of the Commons." *Developing Country Studies* 6(12): 44–57.

Omolo, Loreen Auma. 2022. "Assessing China–Africa Relations under the Forum for China–Africa Cooperation (FOCAC) (2000–2019)." *Africa Review* 15(1): 24–42.
Organization of Petroleum Exporting Countries. n.d. "About Us/Members." www.opec.org/opec_web/en/about_us/3520.htm.
Petroleum Industry Act. 2021. www.petroleumindustrybill.com/wp-content/uploads/2021/09/Official-Gazette-of-the-Petroleum-Industry-Act-2021.pdf.
Privacy Shield. n.d. www.privacyshield.gov/article?id=Gabon-Petroleum-and-Crude-Production.
Prunier, Gérard. 1995. *The Rwanda Crisis: History of a Genocide*. New York: Columbia University Press.
Qekeleshe, Sihle. 2020. "Angola's Sonangol and Endiama to be Privatized by 2022." *Energy, Capital and Power*, November 26. https://energycapitalpower.com/angolas-sonangol-and-endiama-to-be-privatized-by-2022.
Quinn, John James. 2016. *Global Geopolitical Power and African Political and Economic Institutions: When Elephants Fight*. Lanham: Lexington Books.
Quinn, John James. 2004. "Diffusion and Escalation in the Great Lakes Region: The Rwandan Genocide, the Rebellion in Zaire, and Mobutu's Overthrow." In: Lobell S.E., Mauceri P. (eds.), *Ethnic Conflict and International Politics: Explaining Diffusion and Escalation*. New York: Palgrave Macmillan.
Ravenhill, John, ed. 1986. *Africa in Economic Crisis*. New York: Columbia University Press.
Reed, Ed. 2021. "Niger-Benin Pipeline Ceremony Due May 20." *Energy Voice*, May 19.
Reuters. 2017. "China formally Opens First Overseas Military Base in Djibouti." August 1.
Reuters. 2020. "Angola to Join Oil and Extractives Transparency Group." August 29.
Ross, Michael L. 2012. *The Oil Curse: How Petroleum Wealth Shapes the Development of Nations*. Princeton: Princeton University Press.
Sacks, David. 2021. "Countries in China's Belt and Road Initiative: Who's In and Who's Out?" *Council on Foreign Relations*. www.cfr.org/blog/countries-chinas-belt-and-road-initiative-whos-and-whos-out
Savage, Luiza Ch. 2020. "How America Got Outmaneuvered in a Critical Mining Race." *Politico*, February 12.
Schraeder, Peter J. 2004. *African Politics and Society: A Mosaic in Transformation*, 2nd ed. Belmont: Thompson, Wadsworth.
Sikamo, Jackson, Alex Mwanza, and Cade Mweemba. 2016. "Copper Mining in Zambia: History and Future." *Journal of the Southern African Institute of Mining and Metallurgy* 116(6): 491–496.
Simões, Alberto Galhardo. 2023. "Angola's Privatisation Programme Forges Ahead." *African Business*, September 20.
Société Nationale des Hydrocarbures. n.d. "LNG Exports." www.snh.cm/index.php/en/gas-up/export-of-natural-gas.
Sovacool, Benjamin K., Walter Götz, Thijs Van de Graaf, and Nathan Andrews. 2016. "Energy Governance, Transnational Rules, and the Resource Curse: Exploring the Effectiveness of the Extractive Industries Transparency Initiative (EITI)." *World Development* 83: 179–192.
Tangri, Roger. 1999. *The Politics of Patronage in Africa: Parastatals, Privatization, and Private Enterprise*. Trenton: Africa World Press.
Taylor, Ian. 2011. *The Forum on China–Africa Cooperation (FOCAC)*. New York: Routledge.
Tull, Denis M. 2006. "China's Engagement in Africa: Scope, Significance and Consequences." *Journal of Modern African Studies* 44(3): 459–479.

Tzinieris, Sarah. 2018. "Niger's Yellow Cake Uranium: Resource Curse or Force for Change?" *Best of Africa*, October 22. www.researchgate.net/publication/368961556_Niger's_Yellow_Cake_Resource_Curse_or_Force_for_Change_The_Best_of_Africa

United Nations Conference on Trade and Development. 2016. *Special Unit on Commodities: Commodities at a Glance*. Geneva: UNCTAD.

United Nations Conference on Trade and Development. 2017. *Diamond Exports from Botswana and Sierra Leone: The Role of Institutions in Mitigating the Impact of Commodity Dependence on Human Development*. Geneva: UNCTAD.

United Nations Conference on Trade and Development. 2019. *State of Commodity Dependence 2019*. New York: United Nations.

US Department of State. 2021. "2021 Investment Climate Statements: Gabon." www.state.gov/reports/2021-investment-climate-statements/gabon.

US Energy Information Administration. n.d. www.eia.gov.

USAID. n.d. "Cameroon, Minerals." www.land-links.org/country-profile/cameroon/#minerals.

van de Walle, Nicolas. 2001. *African Economies and the Politics of Permanent Crisis: 1979–1999*. Cambridge: Cambridge University Press.

van den Brink, Susan, René Kleijn, Arnold Tukker, and Jaco Huisman. 2019. "Approaches to Responsible Sourcing in Mineral Supply Chains." *Resources, Conservation and Recycling* 145: 389–398.

Weiner, Marcus and Alex Vines. 2012. "China's Angolan Oil Deals, 2003–11." In Marcus Power and Ana Cristina Alves, eds., *China and Angola: A Marriage of Convenience?* Oxford: Pambazuka Press, 85–104.

White, Oliver Campbell and Anita Bhatia. 1998. *Privatization in Africa*. Washington, DC: The World Bank.

World Bank. n.d.a. "Global Gas Flaring Reduction Partnership (GGFR)." www.worldbank.org/en/programs/gasflaringreduction/global-flaring-data.

World Bank. n.d.b. "Zero Routine Flaring by 2030 (ZRF) Initiative." www.worldbank.org/en/programs/zero-routine-flaring-by-2030/about.

World Bank. n.d.c. "World Development Indicators, GDP Per Capita Growth (Annual %) – Sub-Saharan Africa." https://data.worldbank.org/indicator/NY.GDP.PCAP.KD.ZG?locations=ZG.

World Bank Group Privatization Database 1988–2007. n.d. Washington, D.C.: World Bank.

World Nuclear Association. 2023. "Uranium in Niger." https://world-nuclear.org/information-library/country-profiles/countries-g-n/niger.aspx.

Xinhua. 2023. "Gabonese President Hopes Accelerated Gabon-China Relations to Bring More Benefits." April 21. http://english.scio.gov.cn/internationalexchanges/2023-04/21/content_85243921.htm#:~:text=Enjoying%20friendly%20relations%20that%20go,hope%20that%20an%20accelerated%20bilateral

Young, Peter. 1987. "Privatization around the World." *Proceedings of the Academy of Political Science* 36(3): 190–206. https://doi.org/10.2307/1174108.

6 Conclusions and Implications

> A competitive party system can only survive if two conditions are met: opposition to the national government must be accepted as legitimate and there must be channels for acquiring wealth and status outside the patronage of government.
>
> —Richard Hodder-Williams

> When asked why he robbed banks, "Because that's where the money is."
>
> —Willie Sutton

The resource curse theory literature suggests that nations which export significant levels of mineral or oil commodities suffer from several common economic problems.[1] These include low or negative growth, lower incomes, higher levels of debt, declining alternative export sectors, and other negative outcomes. This book has shown that many key negative outcomes linked to the natural resource curse in mineral- or oil-exporting nations were worse in those African countries where these sectors were majority state-owned between the 1960s and 2000. However, instead of finding that these mineral- or oil-exporting countries exhibited high levels of currency appreciation, it was found that the majority state ownership (MSO) countries had very high levels of currency overvaluation – which was more the issue impacting alternative export sectors. Given the main finding of this work, effects of the structural variable of MSO need to be included to have a complete understanding of the resource curse.

Chapter 1 describes and overviews the literature on the resource curse as well as describing other developmental challenges associated with mining or mineral exporting. It also outlines a political and economic logic as to why this structural variable of MSO of minerals or petroleum (or most capital-intensive industries) can create incentives for these economic sectors to be managed to maximize political power rather than economic efficiency.[2] These incentives associated with ownership by a political class helped create more extractive (or predatory) economic (and political) institutions in the nations concerned.[3] It has been argued here and elsewhere that when the political elite owns a majority of their major economic sectors, they are managed with an eye to patronage politics, more than with

DOI: 10.4324/9780429423390-6

an eye to economic efficiency – or the long-term development of the state.[4] The "efficiency" of these policies is manifest in the political and the personal, not the economic.[5]

Chapter 2 examines a cross-section of mineral- or oil-exporting countries in sub-Saharan Africa from 1966 through 2000 to see if MSO of these sectors did indeed lead such countries to have more intense or extreme resource curse outcomes compared to other similar countries which did not feature MSO. Paired t-tests illustrated that countries with MSO of the major oil- or mineral-exporting sector (MSO-1) experienced worse resource curse outcomes on average.[6] Similar outcomes were associated with either MSO of their oil or mining exporting sector (MSO-1) or most of their industries with or without MSO of the mining or oil sector (MSO-2). As such, MSO countries (either MSO-1 or MSO-2) experienced similar or worse outcomes on nearly all the variables associated with the resource curse. On average, MSO countries experienced negative or lower levels of economic growth, lower per capita incomes, lower value added in agriculture or manufacturing, lower levels of investment, lower levels of political and civil rights, higher levels of currency overvaluation, higher levels of debt, and more years of civil conflict. One variable which did not seem to differ much by MSO/non-MSO for the combined case was level of real currency appreciation; however, this variable should have been positive and high for most of these countries as per the resource curse literature. It was only positive for the oil countries, and it did not seem especially high.

Dividing the sample into mineral-exporting countries or oil-exporting countries in case studies, the same general patterns emerge – with a few differences. The oil-exporting nations, as a category, had a few differences relative to the combined cases. First, the oil-exporting MSO-1 countries featured lower levels of debt as a percentage of GDP. In addition, the average debt servicing levels for MSO-1 oil countries were lower than for non-MSO, though the differences were not statistically significant. The MSO-2 oil-exporting countries, however, either had more debt, or were not statistically different – and were also more comparable to the larger sample. Third, no statistically significant differences were seen for the level of political and civil rights among the oil exporters (either MSO-1 or MSO-2). MSO, or lack thereof, did not seem to matter for levels of political and economic rights among oil exporters: all had relatively low levels of political and civil rights during this period, although this trend did not hold for debt.[7] This finding about oil and rights is consistent with Ross' findings.[8] Nonetheless, and most importantly, on average, the MSO countries had negative economic growth for the period under study, and the non-MSO countries had positive levels of economic growth.

The subset of mineral-exporting countries had almost identical differences between groups as the larger sample – exhibiting worse outcomes for the MSO countries. Chapter 2 shows that there are nearly identical outcomes as the combined category. One place where the findings were different was for levels of conflict for MSO-2, where the differences were no longer significant. Also, the differences for MSO-1 were only significant at the 90% level. Another place of difference was all mineral-exporting nations featured currency depreciation. None had any appreciation, on average, for this period. However, there was no statistically significant difference between MSO and non-MSO, even if MSO countries had lower levels of depreciation.

Returning to the issues of political and civil rights, we should point out a few things. First, although we did find the non-MSO countries had more political and civil rights than the MSO countries in the combined cases, we should remember that the non-MSO countries were rated as partly free on average, and the MSO countries as not free. The differences were significant for the combined and mineral cases, but each was close to the partly free/not free line of 5.5. In the mineral group, the differences were slightly larger, but the MSO countries averaged not free while the non-MSO countries were rated as partly free. The small differences in their levels, as well as the nonstatistical difference for oil are also consistent with a prior finding that countries that exported significant levels of oil or minerals did not show significant increases in political or civil rights in the post–Cold War period.[9] These patronage systems still had access to resources with which to fund their systems, even if at a lower level. Only if we had had non–oil-exporting or non–mineral-exporting nations would we see the greater differences in regimes in the post–Cold War period vis-à-vis political and civil rights.

Chapters 3 and 4 feature a deeper analysis of either four oil-exporting countries or four mineral-exporting countries, including some discussions concerning the developmental challenges and difficulties unique to mining or oil, MSO or not. In these chapters, only countries with significant levels of ownership of their mineral or oil export sector itself were included as MSO (so no MSO-2 countries).[10] On average, MSO countries were found to have experienced worse resource curse outcomes than non-MSO countries on most variables, even if this was not so for every single one. Notably, when a country performed *very* poorly on several of the measures, it was always one of the MSO countries. By contrast, when a country performed comparatively well on several of the variables, it was always one of the non-MSO countries. Nonetheless, every now and then an MSO country outperformed or tied a non-MSO country on an indicator or two, but never on most of the resource curse indicators – which is consistent with the aggregate statistics from Chapter 2.

Looking at the specific findings from Chapter 3, which examines the oil-exporting nations, and starting with the headline variable of economic growth, we see that the resource curse was stronger in the two MSO oil-exporting countries: Angola and Nigeria featured *negative* annual per capita economic growth. Negative economic growth was the most important negative consequence outlined by the resource curse theory. Both Cameroon (non-MSO) and Gabon had overall positive levels of growth, even if low.

In Chapter 4, which examines only mineral-exporting countries, we see that negative growth is associated with the two MSO countries, though one non-MSO country also featured average negative growth (Niger). Botswana, which did not have MSO of its mineral sector, had clearly positive and quite high levels of economic growth for the first period. In fact, few other countries in sub-Saharan Africa had such high growth levels during that time. Looking across the oil and mineral cases, three of the non-MSO countries experienced positive economic growth, while one non-MSO country did not – and all the MSO countries experienced negative economic growth during this period.

One surprising (non)finding, given the resource curse literature, was that the average level of real currency appreciation was negative for all the mineral-exporting nations (either MSO or non-MSO) as well as for the non-MSO oil-exporting nations. As outlined in Chapter 1, part of the resource curse explanation is that the export boom leads to currency appreciation, which then leads to a decline in alternative export sectors.[11] Against expectations, the averages showed that mineral exporters had an average depreciation of their real currency, not appreciation. This result seems like Holmes' dog that did not bark. Only the MSO oil-exporting countries experience an average appreciation of their real currencies, though these levels were quite low, on average. Moreover, for the mineral-exporting countries, all had real currency depreciation, on average, during the first period.

How can one square this circle of these countries experiencing low levels of real currency appreciation or actual real currency depreciation combined with the decline in the alternative export sectors of manufacturing or agriculture? Currency overvaluation was the culprit. Elevated levels of currency overvaluation arose in these countries without hard currencies, with fixed exchange rates, and high debts and/or inflation. The effects of currency overvaluation mimic the effects of currency appreciation and mirror the Dutch disease's mechanisms. Currency overvaluation acts like a tax on exports and a subsidy for importers – at least those lucky enough to gain access to the now-scarce foreign currency. All exporters experience this tax if they are paid in their local currency rather than the now subsidized hard currency. This creates incentives for investors to move out of exporting sectors into importing sectors or into protected producing sectors (which are not taxed by the effects of an overvalued currency).

In the larger sample, as well as in the case studies, it was clear that the mineral- or oil-exporting nations examined in this work all experienced some currency overvaluation. However, currency overvaluation was *much higher* in the MSO cases than in the non-MSO cases, and these differences were always statistically significant. Looking at a larger sample of countries from sub-Saharan Africa, including both non–resource-exporting and resource-exporting nations, MSO countries had much higher levels of currency overvaluation compared to the non-MSO countries: Leaving out the CFA nations, currency overvaluation for MSO countries was 210.6%, while it was 32.7% for non-MSO between 1966 and 1986.[12] This suggests that what is attributed to natural resources was also found in some countries without significant levels of such exports, but which also featured a version of MSO of industries. This policy functioned as a tax on all exports, including manufacturing and agriculture. Although non-MSO currency overvaluation may have been high relative to countries outside the region, the MSO countries had such elevated levels that we needed scientific notation to report it.

Another primary predictor of the resource curse, and related to the above points, is the decline over time of alternative export sectors. Manufacturing and agriculture are often identified as the alternative sources for exports for most sub-Saharan African countries. We see in the cross-section in Chapter 2 as well as in the case studies chapters that the MSO countries featured either lower or declining levels of manufacturing and/or agricultural exports during the period of study. To be fair, during the Cold War, manufacturing, as a percentage of exports, was low in all the mining and oil-exporting countries, though the MSO countries experienced a steeper decline. Also, MSO countries experienced a greater decline in agricultural exports. These outcomes are key as a decline in the levels of other export sectors represents one of the strongest predictions of the resource curse.

Among the mineral exporters, the percentage of exports of manufactured goods was highest in Botswana, then Niger, then the DRC, then Zambia – which indicates at least the rank order of non-MSO and MSO was found in the data. Among the oil exporters, Nigeria had the lowest levels of manufactured exports, and Angola saw declining levels for the whole time. Both Cameroon and Gabon had stable, but low levels of manufactured exports, with only small periods of decrease. None of these countries featured a booming (non-mineral) manufacturing export sector, however.

Moreover, the agriculture sectors of MSO nations saw significant declines in export levels over time, while the non-MSO countries had more years of increase (in non-drought years). Among the oil exporters, we see the volume of Angolan agricultural exports dropped each year.[13] Similarly, Nigeria saw declines in the volume of agricultural exports nearly every year. For Cameroon, it initially showed increases in agricultural volume exported from 1975 to 1989, unlike the other oil-exporting countries. Nonetheless, Cameroon had an average increase in value of agricultural exports. Gabon, too, experienced stronger agricultural exports than most other oil countries and even had a slight increase in the volume of agriculture during these years.

The mineral-exporting countries witnessed similar trends. In fact, Zambia, as an MSO mining country, went from having one of the most vibrant agricultural exporting sectors to having the third lowest level in sub-Saharan Africa (and this was without a war). The DRC too saw significant declines in the volume and value of agricultural exports over the period. By contrast, both Botswana and Niger saw periods of increases in volume and value of agricultural exports through parts of this period. Even though both saw some increases in volume and value over time, both countries have significant amounts of land categorized as desert, and they are associated with frequent droughts, which disrupts their agricultural sectors.

Let us turn to another predicted resource curse variable: investment. Within the oil economies, we see the oil-exporting countries that had the highest levels of investment were the non-MSO countries (by either measure). This was also found in the case studies, with the rank from highest to lowest from Gabon to Cameroon (both non-MSO), to Angola, and then Nigeria (MSO). An irony of this outcome is that one of the main arguments for the nationalization of oil or mining sectors in the early independence period was to capture more profits to re-invest domestically instead of the profit being drained away from the periphery to the core.[14] For the mineral-exporting countries, the rank order was not perfectly preserved as the ranking for investment was Botswana, Zambia, and then Niger and the DRC (which had similar levels and both were low). Thus, Zambia, which was MSO, outperformed Niger (non-MSO) by this average. However, Zambia had relatively high levels of investment initially, but these then declined over time, as per a resource curse prediction. As shown in Chapter 4, Zambia was the only nation to experience an average negative change in fixed investment as a percentage of GNI, and it also featured steep falls in its GNI. So, Zambia had a high average for investment in the cross-sectional data point, but over the time indicated we see a declining level of investments. This indicates a strong resource curse outcome.

In terms of debt, we see a significant divergence for the first time between oil and mineral exporters. The MSO mineral exporters, as we saw in Chapter 2, had higher levels of debt, measured as a percentage of GDP or as a percentage of exports, while the oil exporters had lower levels of debt by either measure in aggregate. For the case studies of oil, the rank order was mixed for debt as a percentage of exports, with Angola having the highest levels of debt, then followed by Cameroon, then by Nigeria, and then by Gabon. Thus, the MSO country Nigeria performed better by this measure than the non-MSO country Cameroon. However, when debt is measured from highest to lowest as a percentage of GDP, the rank order was Angola, Nigeria, Cameroon, and then Gabon (which indicated MSO countries experienced higher levels than non-MSO countries). Therefore, the country with the least amount of debt was always a non-MSO country, while the country with the highest levels of debt was an MSO country, though the order was not strictly followed for both measures.

In terms of conflict, states with MSO experience more frequent or more prolonged periods of civil war. This was seen in the t-tests from Chapter 2, and they were seen in the oil-exporting nations. Among these latter states, we see that Angola experienced near continuous civil wars. Nigeria had about 17% of its years to 2000 in civil war. Even if the main civil war in Nigeria occurred before the majority ownership of the oil sector, the oil sector had clearly been politicized. Cameroon and Gabon did not seem to have any negative effects vis-à-vis civil war or civil conflict during this period.[15] However, as Hodges suggests in the case of Angola, the existence of these resources may not have caused the conflict, but they prolonged it. This may be even more the case when the state owns or manages the sector, politicizing it even more.

For the mineral-exporting countries, the pattern is a bit different. For the DRC, it experienced many years of civil war. Several of these years were before nationalization, with additional later conflicts leading to a total of 13 years up to 2000. This was an average of 32% of its time in civil conflict from independence onwards. For the DRC, the first civil war was clearly associated with the immediate postcolonial (and prenationalization) period, even if control of the minerals were clearly on the mind of those declaring independence for the copper areas.[16] By contrast, neither Zambia nor the two non-MSO countries of Niger or Botswana had years of civil war recorded from decolonization through 2000.

For political and civil rights, the results were more mixed, especially comparing the oil-exporting nations to the mineral-exporting nations. To begin with, none of the oil-exporting nations had continuous experience with multiparty elections, nor did any of them score high on political and civil rights scores for this period, with one partial exception: Nigeria seesawed back and forth between periods of military rule and multiparty electoral systems. It experienced some years under free, partly free, and not free; but it ended in 2000 as partly free. Angola was "not free" the entire time. Cameroon was "partly free" in the early 1970s and "not free" through 2000. Gabon was "not free" until the end of the Cold War and then was listed as "partly free." Therefore, the most consistently authoritarian state was Angola, then Cameroon, then Gabon, and Nigeria was mixed. This is consistent with the findings in Chapter 2 (as there was no significant difference between the MSO and non-MSO groups).

Within the mineral exporters, we do see some divergence between MSO and non-MSO countries. The best performing country vis-à-vis political and civil rights was Botswana, with a ranking of free for the whole period. Niger was "not free" during the Cold War, but it alternated between "partly free" and "not free" between 1989 and 2000. The DRC was consistently rated as "not free," as it did not hold its first multiparty election until well past this period under review. Zambia was on the line between "partly free" and "not free" during most of the Cold War, and then it was rated as "free" for two years, and through 2000, it was rated as "partly free." So, the rank order is not maintained here in terms of freedom, but the country with the best outcome was non-MSO, and the country with the worst was MSO. Interestingly, Zambia, like Nigeria, had more periods of "partly free" than many other countries.

For most of the measures examined in Chapter 2, we see similar patterns in the case studies. Sometimes, however, an MSO country had better numbers compared to a non-MSO country, but only on one or two indicators. On most of the other indicators related to resource curse outcomes, we see that the MSO countries experience a more severe version of these outcomes – especially on the key indicators of negative economic growth and the decline of rival export sectors. It has been shown in the case studies, as well as in the cross-section, that countries that had over 30% of their exports in mining or oil exports, and which featured MSO of these same sectors, experienced lower levels of growth and saw their rival export sectors in more decline as predicted by the resource curse literature. By contrast, nearly all the countries in sub-Saharan African that did not have MSO of these sectors, on average, had (positive) economic growth and saw less of a decline in their manufacturing and agricultural export sectors. Niger was the only case of negative growth rates, though the decline of its agricultural sector was less severe than the MSO cases.

The unevenness of the difficulties of development in countries with mineral or oil-exporting sectors does call into question the existence of the resource curse that equally affects all mineral- or oil-exporting nations. We should better call it *the resource challenge*, which is even more serious in developing African nations that feature MSO of its resource sector. The resource challenge may be common for developing nations, but it is not a ubiquitous resource curse. Negative growth is associated with the political economy of MSO of these sectors within developing African nations.

Implications or the "So What?" Question

Some scholars and policymakers will now ask the "So what?" question, especially as more scholars have begun to question the underlying premise of the mineral or oil resource curse.[17] Ross and others have suggested that a true test of the resource curse would be to include countries that have significant oil production per capita and not just oil exports.[18] Such cases are not included as this would expand the sample normally used to test the resource curse. By keeping closer to the original measures of the resource curse literature, this analysis tests this theory in the hardest cases: countries that should have had the resource curse by prior arguments. As such, this analysis does not directly test the resource curse hypothesis per se; rather, it shows that countries with MSO have experienced more severe forms of the variables often associated with the resource curse – among the countries most likely to have suffered from it. The idea that the curse is only for those with such a sizable percentage of their exports is not spurious in this examination, as all included countries are those with significant levels of mineral or oil exports.

Some scholars have held that given the role of choice over domestic economic policy, the resource curse is far from inevitable and heterogeneity in outcome exists.[19] This author agrees. However, I argue that an underexplored variable can help predict which countries are likely to suffer from the worst forms associated with the resource cures: MSO of these sectors. Therefore, an understudied variable common commonly found among developing countries with significant mineral- or oil-exporting sectors seems to be a major contributor to this outcome, be it endogenous or not.[20] The developing nations that feature MSO of their resource sector have implicit incentives for particular actions – which are not predetermined – but they are certainly more likely under such conditions.

Importantly, MSO has previously been shown to be linked to more inward-oriented development policies in sub-Saharan Africa between 1966 and 1986 – for either most capital-intensive industries or mining- or oil-exporting sectors.[21] And these policies were linked to lower levels of wealth. Thus, it seems logical that what has been attributed to mineral or oil exporting can also be partially attributed to the structure of its ownership structure as well as the resulting inward-oriented development policies. The implication is that the resource curse, or its extreme manifestation, is not a necessary outcome for all developing countries with such high dependence upon such exports.

Another approach to understanding the resource curse can be seen in the literature on rent seeking that suggests that resource curse outcomes are the result of aggregated action seeking to gain access to the windfalls and revenues of the result of oil or mineral booms.[22] This general idea is fully consistent with the idea of MSO, and under the condition of MSO, politicians clearly have greater ability to raid or gain access to the revenues, management, and resources of the MSO economic sector. Shaffer discusses how the nationalization of copper in both Zaire (DRC) and Zambia eliminated "political insulation" between the sector and the greed and perfidy of many politicians.[23] MSO companies are more susceptible to political intrusion than other similar companies are – even in the same sector.[24] In a book looking at state-owned timber firms, Ross showed that politicians would raid the fund, or allow it to be raided when windfalls were large enough.[25] Here we see institutional breakdown as the political elite intrude into the resources they were to have been agents of. In another work, and using a principal–agent paradigm, corruption (one significant manifestation of rent seeking) was shown to be higher in states with MSO of either most capital-intensive industries OR major mining or oil-exporting sectors.[26] This sample was cross-regional and included countries from Africa, Europe, Latin American, North American, Australia, and Asia.[27]

Michael Ross, among others, suggested that the resource curse was most pronounced between the 1970s and the 1990s and that it may no longer be so strong.[28] With the rise of the Extractive Industries Transparency Initiative (EITI) and other such organizations, this could be true. Ross has also proposed that the nationalization of the oil sector quite clearly made things worse, especially concerning democracy and conflict. By his reckoning, the resource curse was most common when MSO of oil was more frequent. His arguments and findings are consistent with this analysis, even if it dates the resource curse and limits it to a mid-level theory (or middle range or mid-range). Importantly, he offers abundant logic as to why nationalization (AKA MSO) would worsen the oil curse, especially on the political side. Ross did not specifically test empirically the links with MSO/nationalization or set up an examination of differences between the two groups. This book seeks to fill an important empirical gap in the resource curse debate.

Given the relative autonomy of developing nations vis-à-vis the superpowers during the Cold War, it is easy to imagine that international conditions help lead to more of a resource curse. In fact, it could be argued that the worldwide trend of nationalizations that took place were due to a search for balance between the capitalist and socialist superpower at the time.[29] This policy autonomy of African leaders and access to resources not tied to economic efficiency could be a partial explanation for some negative policy outcomes associated with the resource curse as these policies were well outside those later recommended by the International Financial Institutions (IFIs).[30] Stronger external constraints imposed upon weaker oil- and mineral-exporting countries associated with the World Bank and IMF were clearly applied more forcefully post-2000, and they could partially explain a post-2000 reduction in policies associated with the resource curse. Should this be true, any decrease in external restraints on economic policy might later correlate with increased poor economic policy environments. The relative decline of the US, or the rise of China, or the decrease in funding by the IMF and World Bank may create conditions for a repeat of the conditions that led to the resource curse during this prior period. China has been giving aid and loans without conditionality (other than repayment), and this clearly reduces outside pressure that can be wielded by the IFIs. Any decrease in fragments of political accountability, agencies of restraint, or economic accountability could again lead to the policy agendas of the late 1970s and early 1980s.[31] This could lead to a reemergence of the worst of the resource curse outcomes.

Should the resource curse be limited by decades, and within subsets of countries, or types of countries, it is still an important structural consideration for understanding the developmental path of many poorer nations. Therefore, the resource challenge seems to have been most extreme among developing nations featuring MSO of their oil or mining sectors during the Cold War period. Countries in sub-Saharan Africa with MSO of most industries had similar developmental outcomes. With modification, the theory can be considered, at a minimum, a mid-level theory, or a theory that is useful depending on the larger regional or temporal context. Practitioners of comparative politics should be comfortable with mid-level theories that do well for a period, or in a particular region. The idea that a trend does not occur everywhere and always, and to different degrees, should not discourage us from looking for important trends that are bound by time and space. As comparative scholars now argue, mid-level (or mid-range) theories are probably where some of the best theories can be found.[32] As Gourevitch writes: "For social scientists who enjoy comparisons, happiness is finding a force or event which affects a number of societies at the same time."[33] This sentiment is necessarily at the heart of mid-level theories. This also would partly answer why some debate if the resource curse existed, as some show it is not everywhere and always. But this is an empirical question.

Moreover, even if the "resource curse" was most common during one historic period, understanding its pathology and origins makes it easier for scholars to predict when and where it might reemerge. It could well be that the combined effects of the rise of the Washington Consensus and the decrease in the relative autonomy of African leaders resulted in less policy variance in the developing regions for a period.[34] If true, this may have reduced the severity of inward-oriented policies associated with the resource curse (or mistaken for it), which reduced harm to alternative export sectors.[35] However, it could well be that this second period (with the ascension of the Washington Consensus) might itself be the true transitional period and the relative autonomy of African leaders (especially those with significant mining or oil-exporting sectors) in setting economic international foreign policy could prove a better description of longer-term trends.[36] On this point, the rise of China or the relative decline of America might mean that African leaders will have more access to lending without the conditionality placed on economic policy by the western IFIs. Should these resources flow from China or other BRIC members (Brazil, Russia, India, and China (and sometimes South Africa)), then their relative autonomy in establishing policies that led to poor growth could reemerge. Therefore, background conditions for the resource curse may become ascendant again.

Policy Prescriptions

One strong implication flowing from this analysis is that the developing nations that discover significant amounts of minerals or oil should consider less than majority ownership of this new sector.[37] Given Botswana's relative economic successes, we cannot infer that ownership must be below 50%. However, governments should keep enough ownership that they prosper from the extraction of their nations' natural resources – as well as have enough ownership to effectively monitor the private actors' actions. Unaccountable elites, be they political or economic, can make choices not in the best interest of the nation in which they operate. Nonetheless, governments clearly have a special fiduciary duty to their fellow citizens to counteract many of the challenges associated with mineral or oil exploitation. Also, government elites with less than MSO should have more incentives to monitor the many externalities associated with natural resource extraction if the main burden for the remediation of these issues falls on the company and its shareholders – and not the political elites and/or their taxpayers.

Another implication is that countries which currently have MSO of oil or mining should privatize their holdings down to 50% or lower. Although this monograph did not evaluate the effect of privatization, this seems implicit from the evidence. For example, the Zambian copper sector seems to have rebounded after its privatization. However, privatization could actually lead to more corruption and mismanagement in the short term – depending how it is carried out.[38] Arguments that privatization should be complete (down to 0% government ownership) are not supported from the empirics of this analysis.[39] The optimal level of privatization is far from clear, though theoretically having exactly 50% would mean that neither a coalition of private owners nor the government could force the hand of the other owners into policies or practices that were an anathema to either side.[40] What is more, the complete privatization of national mining or oil companies would likely result in a populist political backlash – these resources can be rightfully seen as a collectively held asset, and the normative drive for some public ownership or strong accountability for collectively owned assets should be strong. Nonetheless, governments have been demanding between a 15% and 35% share of companies, which could become the new normal.

As a result, IFIs and others interested in helping mineral or oil rich emerging nations grow and develop should be guided by empirical evidence and not push immediate and total privatization of such resources. Having the government share reduced to 50% or below should shift incentives enough to have these companies begin to maximize the long-term profits and efficiency of the sector, and not just be a petty cash fund for short-term political purposes. Even if important societal needs had been pursued by politicians who extracted resources from the sector, monies for these purposes can still come from ownership rights combined with taxation. This would keep the political insulation between economic and political spheres intact and strong. And without such insulation, even more perniciously, elites can more easily raid the coffers off the books and spirit these funds out of country – undermining any potential developmental outcomes that might have resulted from these prior profits.[41] Capital flight is not usually developmental for the home country.

Moreover, opposition politicians (without the ability to command distribution of patronage or capture of rents) ought to campaign to have state ownership minimized or have these firms professionalized, (or both) in order to depoliticize investment and hiring.[42] This could lead to the professionalization of the bureaucracy of the sector as the winners of election would no longer have carte blanche on filling the most important staffing positions without input (or without being able to outvote) the other stock holders. This ethos could spread to government more generally.[43]

Also, international actors, as well as domestic actors can try to strengthen institutions of political or economic accountability to better serve their citizens. Institutions which are charged with managing these resources should be quasi-independent with the state ensuring that regulatory requirements are met. International actors can follow the norms of EITI to help increase this source of international constraint, helping to limit the corruption so often associated with these sectors. MNCs should publish what they pay, and more openness in contracts should follow. Citizens of these countries should be able to access these records as well, else publishing does little good. Also, the opening of African markets to foreign direct investment and more open trading regimes may also deepen the markets for countries in the region, though this too can be a two-edged sword.

Finally, should more countries in sub-Saharan Africa have less than MSO of their oil or mining sectors, this would not work as some magical panacea in the face of the many developmental challenges that would remain.[44] These non-MSO countries in sub-Saharan African had a *much* lower benchmark for growth than the newly industrializing countries (NICs), for example, on average. Nonetheless, if the overall averages on the non-MSO countries in this sample had been applied to the MSO countries, then a swing of 3.2% growth per year for 35 years would have emerged: instead of having –1.8% growth per year, the MSO countries in the sample would have experienced an average annual 1.4% growth instead! For oil exporters, the average growth level for oil exporters was –0.14%, and non-MSO countries grew at about 1.4% per year – this could have been a swing of 1.54% growth per year for 35 years. These changes would not have removed their other developmental challenges or placed them in NICs territory, but actual (positive) growth (however small) would have been a nice start for the political economy of development.

Some scholars have suggested that countries with strong institutions can prosper with MSO, but this would not have applied well to sub-Saharan Africa during the Cold War, where most of the institutions were quite weak.[45] Moreover, this suggestion rests on the assumption that existing strong institutions would not be intentionally undermined by rent-seeking elites who have come to own and control of the natural resource sector.[46] Countries in sub-Saharan Africa have routinely seen the power elite undermine the strength and independence of their institutions.[47] However, increasing political and economic accountability could limit this tendency somewhat. Nonetheless, with less than MSO of oil or mining sectors, the resource curse may become just the resource challenge.

Notes

1 Please see Chapter 1 for relevant citations.
2 For earlier version of this argument, see Quinn (2016, 2004, 2002, 1999). For arguments of managing economic sectors for political outcomes, see Bates (1981), Clapham (1996), and van de Walle, Nicolas (2001).
3 For extractive vs. inclusive economic institution, see Acemoglu and Robinson (2012). For predatory institutions in Africa, see Clapham (1996), Fatton (1992), and Goldsmith (2004).
4 See Quinn (2002, 2008, 2016) for arguments of how the incentives facing the political elite under ownership change and would often lead them to undermine their own domestic institutions, making them more predatory or extractive.
5 For a similar argument about inward-oriented policies being in the interest of a political elite, see Bates (1981).
6 This is like running an ANOVA with the dependent variable interval levels, and the independent variable dichotomous or nominal, but with only two scores comprising the independent variable as opposed to several, which is usually the case for ANOVA.
7 Remember that higher numbers represent fewer freedoms.
8 Ross (2001a).
9 Quinn (2016, chapter 8).
10 MSO-2 countries were not included in the case studies, though many MSO-1 countries also featured MSO of capital-intensive industries as well. This keeps the question more tightly focused just on MSO of the mining or oil sector and not most industries.
11 Ross (2012), van der Ploeg (2011).
12 Quinn (2002, 39).
13 Volume allows comparison of outputs, while value might reflect price changes more than any inherent productive change in the country.
14 For background arguments about this (from different perspectives), see Krasner (1985); for development economists' arguments at the time, see especially Little (1982), Killick (1978, esp. chapter 2), Arndt (1987), Fieldhouse (1986, esp. 85–90), Meier and Seers (1984), Lofchie (1994), Hirschman (1981), Lal (1985).
15 Here we examine correlation and not direct causation.
16 For politics in DRC at that time, see Young (1965).
17 See, for example, Davis (1995), Lederman and Maloney (2007). For an overview of positive, negative, and mixed findings linking mining with growth, see World Bank (2002, appendix E). See also Stevens and Dietsche (2008), also Rosser (2006). For an argument of how to militate against these outcomes with policy, see Humphreys, Sachs, and Stiglitz (2007).
18 In fact, Ross (2012) did not measure oil as a percentage of exports, but as per capita income from oil. However, Ross' (2001a) article looks at oil dependence as fuel exports as a percentage of GDP (he did not include minerals in his analysis).
19 See, for example, Neary and van Wijnbergen (1986, esp. 10–11), also Humphreys, Sachs, and Stiglitz (2007).
20 That is, countries with a large part of their exports comprising of mining or oil may be more likely to have nationalized these resources.
21 Quinn (2002).
22 Deacon and Rode (2015).
23 Shafer (1983).

24 When I was at Peace Corps in Zaire in 1985 or 1986, I went to Air Zaire to book a flight to go from Kisangani to the capital Kinshasa. I asked the clerk when the next flight would be, and she told me that she did not know. I was puzzled and intrigued, so I kept asking questions. She seemed quite nervous in the face of my questions. First, she said that the plane was lost. Then I asked how they could lose a plane (a 737). Finally, after several questions, she explained that President Mobutu had just showed up unannounced and taken the plane on a flight to Belgium for a shopping trip for his family and that they did not know when it would be next available. This would have been unthinkable on a non–state-owned company. (And it should have been unthinkable even in a state-owned company, but it did happen sometime in 1986.) Author's memory.
25 Ross (2001b).
26 Quinn (2008).
27 Data from Mauro (1995).
28 Ross (2012).
29 Krasner (1985), Quinn (2016).
30 For a political lending to countries during Cold War and its end soon thereafter, see van de Walle (2001).
31 For fragments of political accountability, see Sklar (1987); for agencies of restraint, see Collier (1999); for economic accountability, see Quinn (2000); also Kennedy (2007) looked at trade policy, state ownership, and level of economic accountability.
32 See, for example, Zahariadis (1997).
33 Gourevitch (1977).
34 van de Walle (2001) for more harmony of economic foreign policy early post–Cold War.
35 For widespread adoption of these in Africa, see Clapham (1996), Easterly (2005). For a decline of inward-oriented policies, see Quinn (2016); for a decline in currency overvaluation, see van de Walle (2001). For early post–Cold War, see Callaghy and Ravenhill (1993), Herbst (2001, 1990).
36 For an overview on African foreign policy, see Quinn (2019); see also Khadiagala and Lyons (2001), Wright (1999).
37 Khanna (2020).
38 Rose-Ackerman (1999), Glynn, Kobrin, and Naim (1997), Sun (1999), He (2000), Hellman and Kaufmann, 2001).
39 Especially as Botswana has 50% and has done well by most natural resource curse criteria. Also for Botswana and ownership levels, see Quinn (2002, 1999).
40 Also most research on SOE put the ownership at greater than 50% to be so categorized. For example, see World Bank (1995), IMF (2020).
41 See, for example, Ndikumana, Boyce, and Ndiaye (2014); also see Boyce and Ndikumana (2001)
42 For a thought exercise model illustration who would push for reforms such as privatization, see Quinn (2002, chapter 7).
43 For cases of where professionalization of bureaucracy emerges, see Geddes (1991).
44 The natural, empirically based, and logical conclusion is that they would more mirror the other African nations without this ownership structure – none of which were devoid of developmental issues, but most of which experienced positive instead of negative growth levels.
45 See, for example, Khanna (2017).
46 In a later work, Khanna (2020) showed that such ownership could weaken institutions, but that might lead to issues of endogeneity trying to test effects of institutions at the same time as state ownership.

47 For elites in Africa undermining its own institutions, see Clapham (1996); also Reno (2000); for DRC, see Callaghy (1984); for Nigeria see Schatz (1984). For a while, Venezuela seemed like a developing country that was prospering with MSO of oil (and could maintain its democracy), though this soon turned around and they were more like a country with a resource curse. Also, corruption was shown to increase with MSO, controlling for wealth and democracy in a cross-regional/cross-national sample. Quinn (2008).

References

Acemoglu, Daron and James Robinson. 2012. *Why Nations Fail: Origins of Power, Poverty and Prosperity*. New York: Currency.

Arndt, Heinz W. 1987. *Economic Development: The History of an Idea*. Chicago: University of Chicago Press.

Bates, Robert H. 1981. *Markets and States in Tropical Africa*. Berkeley: University of California Press.

Boyce, James K. and Léonce Ndikumana. 2001. "Is Africa a Net Creditor? New Estimates of Capital Flight from Severely Indebted Sub-Saharan African Countries, 1970–96." *Journal of Development Studies* 38(2): 27–56.

Callaghy, Thomas M. 1984. *The State-Society Struggle: Zaire in Comparative Perspective*. New York: Columbia University Press.

Callaghy, Thomas M. and John Ravenhill, eds. 1993. *Hemmed In: Responses to Africa's Economic* Decline. New York: Columbia University Press.

Clapham, Christopher. 1996. *African and the International System: The Politics of State Survival*. Cambridge: Cambridge University Press.

Collier, Paul. 1999. "Learning from Failure: The International Financial Institutions as Agencies of Restraint in Africa." In Andreas Schedler et al., eds., *The Self-Restraining State: Power and Accountability in New Democracies*. Boulder: Lynne Rienner, 313–330.

Davis, Graham A., 1995. "Learning to Love the Dutch Disease: Evidence from the Mineral Economies." *World Development* 23(10): 1765–1779.

Deacon, Robert T. and Ashwin Rode. 2015. "Rent Seeking and the Resource Curse." In *Companion to the Political Economy of Rent Seeking*. Northampton, MA: Edward Elgar Publishing, Inc., 227–247.

Easterly, William. 2005. "What Did Structural Adjustment Adjust? The Association of Policies and Growth with Repeated IMF and World Bank Adjustment Loans." *Journal of Development Economics* 76: 1–22.

Fatton Jr., Robert. 1992. *Predatory Rule: State and Civil Society in Africa*. Boulder, CO: Lynne Rienner.

Fieldhouse, D. K. 1986. *Black Africa 1945–1980: Economic Decolonization and Arrested Development*. New York: Routledge.

Geddes, Barbara 1991. "A Game Theoretic Model of Reform in Latin American Democracies." *American Political Science Review* 85(2): 371–392.

Glynn, Patrick, Stephen J. Kobrin, and Moises Naim. 1997. "The Globalization of Corruption." In Kimberly Ann Elliot, ed., *Corruption and the Global Economy*. Washington, DC: Institute for International Economics, 7–27.

Goldsmith, Arthur A. 2004. "Predatory Versus Developmental Rule in Africa." *Democratization* 11(3): 88–110.

Gourevitch, Peter Alexis. 1977. "International Trade, Domestic Coalitions, and Liberty: Comparative Responses to the Crisis of 1873–1896." *Journal of Interdisciplinary History* 3(2): 281–313.
He, Zengke. 2000. "Corruption and Anti-corruption in Reform China." *Communist and Post-Communist Studies* 33: 243–270.
Hellman, Joel and Daniel Kaufmann. 2001. "Confronting the Challenge of State Capture in Transition Economies." *Finance and Development* 38(3): 31–35.
Herbst, Jeffrey. 1990. "Third World Communism in Crisis: The Fall of Afro-Marxism." *Journal of Democracy* 1(3): 92–101.
Herbst, Jeffrey. 2001. "Political Liberalization in Africa after Ten Years." *Comparative Politics* 33: 357–375.
Hirschman, Albert O. 1981. *Essays in Trespassing: Economics to Politics and Beyond.* Cambridge: Cambridge University Press.
Humphreys, Macartan, Jeffrey Sachs, and Joseph E. Stiglitz, eds. 2007. *Escaping the Resource Curse.* New York: Columbia University Press.
International Monetary Fund. 2020. "State-Owned Enterprises: The Other Government." In *Fiscal Monitor.* Washington, DC: IMF, 47–74.
Kennedy, Ryan. 2007. "Fragments of Economic Accountability and Trade Policy." *Foreign Policy Analysis* 3(2): 145–169.
Khadiagala, Gilbert M. and Terrence Lyons. 2001. *African Foreign Policies: Power and Process.* Boulder: Lynne Rienner.
Khanna, Arpita Asha. 2017. "Revisiting the Oil Curse: Does Ownership Matter?" *World Development* 99: 214–229.
Khanna, Arpita Asha. 2020. "Does Oil Ownership Affect Institutions?" *International Economic Journal* 34(3): 426–447.
Killick, Tony. 1978. *Development Economics in Actions: A Study of Economic Policies in Ghana.* London: Heinemann.
Krasner, Stephen D. 1985. *Structural Conflict: The Third World against Global Liberalism.* Berkeley: University of California Press.
Lal, Deepak. 1985. *The Poverty of Development Economics.* Cambridge, MA: Harvard University Press.
Lederman, Daniel and William F. Maloney. 2007. "Introduction to Natural Resources and Development." In *Natural Resources: Neither Curse Nor Destiny*, ed., Daniel Lederman and William F Maloney, Washington, DC: Stanford University Press and World Bank, .1–14.
Little, I. M. D. 1982. *Economic Development: Theory Policy and International Relations.* New York: Basic Books.
Lofchie, Michael F. 1994. "The New Political Economy in Africa." In David E. Apter and Carl G. Rosberg, eds., *Political Development and the New Realism in Sub-Saharan Africa.* Charlottesville: University of Virginia Press, 145–183.
Mauro, Paolo. 1995. "Corruption and Growth." *Quarterly Journal of Economics* (August): 681–712.
Meier, Gerald M. and Dudley Seers, eds. 1984. *Pioneers in Development.* Washington, DC: Oxford University Press for World Bank.
Ndikumana, Léonce, James K. Boyce, and Ameth Saloum Ndiaye. 2014. "Capital Flight: Measurement and Drivers." In S. I. Ajayi and L. Ndikumana, eds., *Capital Flight from Africa: Causes, Effects and Policy Issues.* Oxford: Oxford University Press, 15–54.
Neary, J. Peter and Sweder van Wijnbergen, eds. 1986. *Natural Resources and the Macroeconomy.* Oxford: Basil Blackwell.

Quinn, John J. 1999. "The Managerial Bourgeoisie: Capital Accumulation, Development and Democracy." In David G. Becker and Richard L. Sklar, eds., *Postimperialism and World Politics*. Westport: Praeger, 219–252.

Quinn, John J. 2000. "Economic Accountability: Are Constraints on Economic Decision Making a Blessing or a Curse?" *Scandinavian Journal of Development Alternatives and Area Studies* 19(4): 131–169.

Quinn, John James. 2002. *The Road Oft Traveled: Development Policies and Majority State Ownership of Industry in Africa.* Westport: Praeger.

Quinn, John James. 2004. "The Effects of Majority State Ownership of Industry or Mining on Corruption: A Cross-Regional Comparison." *Growth,* Poverty Reduction *and* Human Development *in Africa Conference*. St. Catherine's College, Oxford, March 20–21.

Quinn, John James. 2008. "The Effects of Majority State Ownership of Significant Economic Sectors on Corruption: A Cross-Regional Comparison." *International Interactions* 34(1): 81–128.

Quinn, John James. 2016. *Global Geopolitical Power and African Political and Economic Institutions: When Elephants Fight*. Lanham: Lexington Books.

Quinn, John James. 2019. "African Foreign Policies." In *Oxford Research Encyclopedia of International Studies*. Oxford: Oxford University Press. https://doi.org/10.1093/acrefore/9780190846626.013.117.

Reno, William. 2000. "Africa's Weak States, Nonstate Actors, and the Privatization of Interstate Relations." In John Harbeson and Donald Rothschild, eds., *Africa in World Politics: The African State System in* Flux. Boulder: West View Press, 286–307.

Rose-Ackerman, Susan. 1999. *Corruption and Government: Causes, Consequences, and Reform*. Cambridge: Cambridge University Press.

Ross, Michael. 2001a. "Does Oil Hinder Democracy?" *World Politics* 53(3): 325–361.

Ross, Michael. 2001b. *Timber Booms and Institutional Breakdown in Southeast Asia*. Cambridge: Cambridge University Press.

Ross, Michael. 2012. *The Oil Curse: How Petroleum Wealth Shapes the Development of Nations*. Princeton, NJ: Princeton University Press.

Rosser, Andrew. 2006. "The Political Economy of the Resource Curse: A Literature Survey." Working Paper 268, Institute of Development Studies.

Schatz, Sayre P. 1984. "Pirate Capitalism and the Inert Economy of Nigeria." *Journal of Modern African Studies* 22(1): 45–57.

Shafer, Michael D. 1983. "Capturing the Mineral Multinationals: Advantage or Disadvantage." *International Organization* 37(1): 93–119.

Sklar, Richard L. 1987. "Developmental Democracy." *Comparative Studies in Society and History* 29(4): 686–714.

Stevens, Paul and Evelyn Dietsche. 2008. "Resource Curse: An Analysis of Causes, Experiences, and Possible Ways Forward." *Energy Policy* 36: 56–65.

Sun, Yan. 1999. "Reform, State, and Corruption: Is Corruption Less Destructive in China than Russia?" *Comparative Politics* 32(1): 1–20.

van de Walle, Nicolas. 2001. *African Economies and the Politics of Permanent Crisis: 1979–1999*. Cambridge: Cambridge University Press.

van der Ploeg, Frederick. 2011. "Natural Resources: Curse or Blessing?" *Journal of Economic Literature* 49(2): 366–420. www.jstor.org/stable/23071620.

World Bank. 1995. *Bureaucrats in Business: The Economics and Politics of Government Ownership*. New York: Oxford University Press.

World Bank. 2002. *Treasure or Trouble? Mining in Developing Countries*. Washington, DC: World Bank and International Financial Corporation. https://siteresources.worldbank.org/INTOGMC/Resources/treasureortrouble.pdf

Wright, Steven, ed. 1999. *African Foreign Policies*. Boulder: Westview.

Young, Crawford. 1965. *Politics in Congo: Decolonization and Independence*. Princeton: Princeton University Press.

Zahariadis, Nikolaos. 1997. *Theory, Case, and Method in Comparative Politics*. Fort Worth: Harcourt Brace.

Appendix

Countries (and their main natural resource export) included for study: Angola (oil), Botswana (diamonds), Cameroon (oil), Democratic Republic of the Congo (DCR) (copper), Gabon (oil), Guinea (bauxite), Lesotho (diamonds), Liberia (iron ore, diamonds), Mauritania (iron ore), Niger (Uranium), Nigeria (oil), Republic of the Congo (oil), Rwanda (tin), Sierra Leone (diamonds), Togo (phosphates), Zambia (copper).

If a country had less than 30% for a period of three years of more, those subsequent country/year data points were dropped.

Countries with majority state ownership of oil or mining for most of the period (MSO-1): Angola, Congo, DRC, Mauritania, Nigeria, Sierra Leone, Togo, and Zambia.

Countries without majority state ownership of oil or mining for most of the period (non-MSO-1): Botswana, Cameroon, Gabon, Guinea, Lesotho, Liberia, Niger, Republic of the Congo, and Rwanda.

Countries with MSO of industries, with significant mineral or oil exports, but with minority state ownership in oil or mining (MSO-2): Republic of Congo and Guinea.

MSO-2 countries. All MSO-1 countries plus Republic of Congo and Guinea.

Non-MSO-2 countries: Botswana, Cameroon, Gabon, Lesotho, Liberia, Niger, and Rwanda.

Index

Note: Page numbers in **bold** refers to Tables.